Contacting the Autistic Chi

Amid long-standing controversy on their causes, which most regard as neurological, and despite their increasing social impact, there has been scant progress in the therapy of the autistic spectrum disorders. Currently fashionable attempts at treatment through behavioural-cognitive focal approaches do not seek resolution, only re-education and rehabilitation. *Contacting the Autistic Child* explores the clinical process in the early psychoanalytic treatment of autistic children. Organised around five detailed clinical case studies, and drawing on the ideas of major clinicians in child analysis such as Tustin, Winnicott and Alvarez, this book sets out a clear programme for working with and understanding autistic children in a psychoanalytic setting, with a particular focus on issues of clinical technique but also conceptual matters.

Working on the notion that autistic disorders come to be – as Winnicott and Tustin saw it – from an early rupture of the affective communication between baby and mother, this book aims at reinstating such communication in the child–analyst interaction. By way of detailed description of what goes on in the analytic link, the authors strive to make the reader share in what goes on in the clinical setting, evincing how, though at times excruciatingly hard on the therapist, resolution is attainable. Once the "primal dialogue" – to use René Spitz's terms – is reinstated in a stable way in session, it flows by itself into the family ambience. The clinical accounts of this book make the argument that psychoanalysis, carried along Tustin's technical lines, and subject to the proviso that treatment starts early, preferably in the first three years of life, is the treatment of choice for autistic spectrum disorders. The strong methodological narrative is important and notable in light of the doubts, criticism and uncertainty that have surrounded the psychoanalytic treatment of autism.

This novel, highly detailed narrative of five successful early treatments aims to help dispel the pessimism pervading the field and help to redress the lives of many more children. *Contacting the Autistic Child* will appeal to psychoanalysts and psychoanalytic psychotherapists endeavouring to obtain results in a major area lacking resolutive approaches.

Luisa C. Busch de Ahumada is a full member of the Buenos Aires Psychoanalytic Association and an IPA-certified child psychoanalyst.

Jorge L. Ahumada is a training analyst at the Argentine Psychoanalytic Association and a Distinguished Fellow of the British Psychoanalytical Society. He was editor for Latin America of the *International Journal of Psychoanalysis* from 1993 to 1998, and received the Mary S. Sigourney Award in New York in 1996. He was "Meet the Analyst" Speaker at the International Psychoanalytic Association Prague Congress, 2013.

Contacting the Autistic Child

Five Successful Early Psychoanalytic Interventions

Luisa C. Busch de Ahumada
and Jorge L. Ahumada

LONDON AND NEW YORK

First published 2017
by Routledge
2 Park Square, Milton Park, Abingdon, Oxon OX14 4RN

and by Routledge
711 Third Avenue, New York, NY 10017

Routledge is an imprint of the Taylor & Francis Group, an informa business

© 2017 Luisa C. Busch de Ahumada and Jorge L. Ahumada

The right of Luisa C. Busch de Ahumada and Jorge L. Ahumada to be identified as authors of this work has been asserted by them in accordance with sections 77 and 78 of the Copyright, Designs and Patents Act 1988.

All rights reserved. No part of this book may be reprinted or reproduced or utilised in any form or by any electronic, mechanical, or other means, now known or hereafter invented, including photocopying and recording, or in any information storage or retrieval system, without permission in writing from the publishers.

Trademark notice: Product or corporate names may be trademarks or registered trademarks, and are used only for identification and explanation without intent to infringe.

British Library Cataloguing-in-Publication Data
A catalogue record for this book is available from the British Library

Library of Congress Cataloging-in-Publication Data
A catalog record for this title has been requested

ISBN: 978-1-138-21166-7 (hbk)
ISBN: 978-1-138-21167-4 (pbk)
ISBN: 978-1-315-45241-8 (ebk)

Typeset in Times New Roman
by Apex CoVantage, LLC

Contents

Preface		vii
Foreword		ix
Introduction: the expanding frontiers of autistic spectrum disorders		xiii
1	Autism: an historical approach	1
2	Contacting a 19-month-old mute autistic girl: Lila	21
3	Treating encapsulated autism soon after trauma: Axel	41
4	From mimesis to agency: clinical steps in Sophia's work of psychic two-ness	47
5	Autistic mimesis in the Age of Media: Juan, a screen-bred animal-child	63
6	Clinical notes on a case of transvestism in an autistic child: Jaime	87
7	Conceptual remarks on early mind	117
8	A roaming view of the Autistoid Age	129
	Addendum 1 Bion's theory of thinking and autistic-mimetic dynamics: a dialogue with Antonino Ferro	139
	Addendum 2 On Tustin's revised edition, a response to Angela Joyce, and an excursus on Ogden's autistic-contiguous position	147
	References	169
	Index	179

Preface

It is a privilege to introduce this book by Luisa C. Busch de Ahumada and Jorge L. Ahumada. Jorge Ahumada is an intellectual leader of Latin American psychoanalysis: each book and each paper he publishes becomes an event all over Latin America.

Presently, this is a joint book with the talented and highly sensitive child analyst Luisa Busch de Ahumada, built upon an absolutely original clinical material. Never, that we know of, have been published five detailed cases of autism leading to full resolution. We are thus reminded of the impact of Richard's case, published by Melanie Klein.

A specialist in psychoanalytic epistemology, Jorge Ahumada has published many papers on it and also a book: *Insight. Essays on Psychoanalytic Knowing* (2011). Why mention this? As the detailed course of the successful psychoanalyses of five autistic children is here presented, we must stress the deep knowledge of psychoanalytic epistemology that, weaving every line, binds the descriptions of the ongoing psychoanalytic processes into methodologically solid narratives. Given the polemics around the psychoanalytic treatment of autism, such methodological outlook is highly relevant because of the doubts, criticism and uncertainty this approach must deal with.

Psychoanalysis, as a theoretic-practical construct, is based on the idea that there are structures (conceived as generating, by Bhaskar 1978) underlying consciousness, dynamically "hidden" (existing in the form of states of mind expressing object relations), from the latter, which generate effects on the way of perceiving and feeling in our patients' world of relations. These structures produce effects in the form of feelings, perceptions and modes of thinking. Without this conception of the existence of *hidden structures*, we would have little to offer our patients besides sympathy and comments based on common sense.

Detailed description of the children treated by Luisa Busch de Ahumada and, accompanying the narratives, reflection on these processes, permits us to identify such hidden structures, comparing them with the potential effects grasped on reading each step of the clinical material. The reader is thereby invited to join the treatment process.

As highlighted by André Green (1992), the analyst-writer confronts a paradox in attempting to communicate and to convince, to reflect and to be on the right. Analysts, especially when taking support in clinical experiences as here happens, face complex issues on confronting such paradox: how can one transmit the observations and the eminently emotional personal experiences transcurring at the office between analyst and patient, thereby allowing the reader to share such interaction and accompany the reflections, while avoiding imposing his views?

The issue, then, is how to write our observations so that they communicate our experience while keeping open a space for the reader's projection, to allow him to exert his critical sense and to build his own opinion. This method is counterpoised to a way of writing tinged by a veiled authoritarianism which leads the reader to identify with us and what we strive to convey.

Nowhere we find here such veiled authoritarianism: the authors are always concerned to place us *there* where the experience happens; such co-presence allows us to share the analyst's interpretative hypotheses while attaining a space of reflection to unfold one's own ideas, dialoguing with the authors of this seminal book. The method Bhaskar proposed to share in the clinical experiences helps us once and again to build our own hypotheses, be they concordant or alternative. From its start on, the book invites us to a clinical dialogue.

We also underline the interest of the authors' revision of the history of psychoanalytic work with autistic children along the last 50 years: rarely do we find such complete coverage of this theme. They carefully raise their agreements and discrepancies, which are especially evident in their approach to the work of Donald Meltzer, stressing the difficulties in dealing with the initial transference in the work with autistic children.

Whether one agrees or not, the dialogue with Antonino Ferro, currently a highly influential author, is most fruitful. Such dialogue may serve as a model for our often difficult, and at times impossible, psychoanalytic dialogues. The same is valid of their critical appreciation, in the positive sense in which a critique must be processed, of the hypothesis of an autistic-contiguous position proposed by another great author of psychoanalysis, Thomas Ogden.

Finally, we want to express our admiration at the erudition provided by the 10 pages of references. This should serve the new generation of analysts as an example of the richness and complexity that psychoanalytic production requires. Reading this book purveys some of the richest and most vivid dialogues in contemporary psychoanalysis.

Elizabeth L. da Rocha Barros and Elias M. da Rocha Barros

Foreword

To present the clinical narratives of five early treatments of children in the autistic spectrum seems opportune, given a paucity of detailed presentations describing successful resolution of child psychoanalytic treatments of autism. These clinical accounts back our conviction that, subject to the proviso that treatment starts quite early, much preferably in the first three years of life, which in severe cases are our prime 'window of opportunity', psychoanalysis carried along Tustin's technical lines is the treatment of choice for autistic spectrum disorders. Our bet is that readers will be able to make clinical use of the detail provided.

After a historical introduction on the issues of autism (Ch.1) focused in the controversies on technique, the clinical chapters unfold our cases. Chapter 2 describes the first two years of treatment of our severest clinical case, Lila, a shell-type mute girl starting treatment at age 19 months, who as far as we are aware is the youngest treatment described in the psychoanalytic literature: she fully came out of the autistic state if we trust her kindergarten teachers' opinion that she is not a problem child, as well as her later evolution. Axel (Ch. 3), starting at age 2 years 9 months, also an out-and-out shell-type child, was treated twice weekly for less than a year; rather suddenly and unexpectedly, he came out of his autistic disconnection and has sustained such gain in follow-up. Sophia (Ch. 4), brought to treatment aged 3 years 10 months on being deemed a 'dummy', illustrates mimetic-type autism; treatment in a restricted, twice and then thrice weekly setting took five years, leading to complete resolution. Chapter 5 depicts the treatment process of Juan, a boy who was media-bred from age 6 months to age 18 months; he started treatment at age 3 years 10 months, and against all odds he too fully benefited from his five years of treatment. Chapter 6 unfolds the case of a boy starting therapy later on, at age 5 years 10 months, upon a symptom of transvestism: Jaime illustrates transvestism as restitutional for primal depression and an ensuing autistic state, which was still quite symptomatic at the time therapy started, though we did not fully realise this initially. His case links autistic dynamics and sexual perversion: he arrived at full evolution of his retraction as well as of his sexual identity in a five-year-long, twice weekly treatment.

Our eminently practical clinical goal does not exempt us from conceptual work, which finds a place in Chapter 7, "Conceptual remarks on early mind". Chapter 8, "A roaming view of the Autistoid Age", introduces the changes in adolescent and adult psychopathologies in the Age of Media, which increasingly merits being called the Autistoid Age: while it goes beyond our focus on child autism, it seemed too relevant to be evaded. Addenda 1 and 2 discuss in more depth the conceptual issues involved as we respond, respectively, to Antonino Ferro's Bionian comments and Angela Joyce's Winnicottian ones, concerning the case of Sophia.

Chapter 1 and Chapter 2 draw on, and amplify, Busch de Ahumada L.C. and Ahumada J.L., "Contacting a 19-month-old mute autistic girl: a clinical narrative", published in the *International Journal of Psychoanalysis* 96: 11–38, 2015. Copyright 2015 Institute of Psychoanalysis. Our thanks to Wiley for their kind permission of copyright.

Ch. 3 was published in German by Busch de Ahumada L.C. and Ahumada J.L. as "Formen autistische und autistoid Dynamic: Das Zeitfenster für eine günstige Wendung (window of opportunity)", in *Spaltung. Entwicklung und Stillstand* (pp. 342–356). U. Reiser-Mumme et al. (Eds.). Deutsche Psychoanalytische Vereinigung Tagungband 2012. Copyright 2012 Deutsche Psychoanalytische Vereinigung. It was republished in an expanded version in *Jahrbuch der Psychoanalyse Bund* 68, 193–216 (2014), with the summary of the case of a post-adolescent girl, Florence, here included in Chapter 7.

Ch. 4 was published as Busch de Ahumada L.C. and Ahumada J.L., "From mimesis to agency: clinical steps in the work of psychic two-ness", in the *International Journal of Psychoanalysis* 86: 721–736, 2005. Copyright 2005 Institute of Psychoanalysis. It was republished in French in *L'anné psychanalytique international*, in Italian in *L'annata psicoanalitica international*, in German in *Verkerte Liebe. Ausgewählte Beiträge von aus dem International Journal of Psychoanalysis* and in Spanish in *Revista de Psicoanálisis*. We are thankful to Wiley for their kind permission of copyright.

Ch. 5 was published in German in a slightly shorter and different version as Busch de Ahumada L.C. and Ahumada J.L., "Autische Mimesis im Medienzeitalter: Eine Fallgeschichte", edited by Bernd Nissen. *Die Entstehung des Seelischen. Psychoanalytischer Perspective* (pp. 141–163). Giessen, Psychosozial-Verlag, 2009. Copyright 2009 Psychosozial-Verlag. A later version in German and English was circulated by invitation at the Tustin Memorial Meeting in Berlin in May 2010 and published in Italian in *Richard e Piggle*, Rome, in 2013. Copyright 2013 Richard e Piggle. The present draft draws from both versions. Thanks are due to Psychosozial-Verlag and to Richard e Piggle for their kind permissions of copyright.

Ch. 6 was authored by Busch de Ahumada L.C. as "Clinical notes on a case of transvestism in a child", in the *International Journal of Psychoanalysis* 84: 291–313 (2003). Copyright 2003 Institute of Psychoanalysis. Our thanks to Wiley for their kind permission to republish.

Chapter 8, "A roaming view of the Autistoid Age", includes accounts of the cases of Tom, a 15-year-old post-autistic boy, originally published by Ahumada J.L. in "Counterinduction in psychoanalytic practice: epistemic and technical aspects" in Ahumada J.L., Olagaray J., Richards A.K., and Richards A.D. (Eds.), *The perverse transference and other matters: essays in honor of R. Horacio Etchegoyen* (pp. 181–202), 1997 (Copyright 1997 Jason Aronson), and of Florence, a post-adolescent in the Autistoid Age, published in Spanish in *Revista de Psicoanálisis* (Ahumada 2010) (Copyright 2010 Revista de Psicoanálisis). Thanks are due to Rowman and Littlefield and to Revista de Psicoanálisis for their kind permission to republish.

Addendum 1 is based on "Further comments on Sofia's mimetic autism with special reference to Bion's theory of thinking", published in *Early development and its disturbances* (pp. 153–173) edited by Marianne Leuzinger-Bohleber, Jorge Canestri and Mary Target (London, Karnac, 2010). Copyright 2010 Karnac. Thanks are due to Karnac for their kind permission of copyright.

Addendum 2, "On Tustin's Revised Edition", a response to Angela Joyce's Winnicottian critique and an excursus on Ogden's autistic-contiguous position, responds to a comment on Sophia's case by Angela Joyce, published in *Early development and its disturbances*, edited by Marianne Leuzinger-Bohleber, Jorge Canestri and Mary Target (London, Karnac, 2010). Copyright Karnac 2010. Thanks are due to Karnac for their kind permission of copyright.

Introduction
The expanding frontiers of autistic spectrum disorders

In the decades elapsed since Leo Kanner first described early infantile autism in his paper "Autistic disturbances of affective contact" (1943), the field became a diverse realm which included early infantile autism, Asperger's syndrome, attention-deficit/hyperactivity disorder (ADHD) – the most common variant – and attention-deficit disorder (ADD). Deficit or disturbance of attention – at its core, of emotional and social attention – is the unifying trait. Recently, these diagnostic categories collapsed in the *Diagnostic and Statistical Manual of Mental Disorders* (DSM-5) into a single taxonomic entity, autistic spectrum disorders (ASD).

Its visibility has made it commonplace to speak of an "epidemic of autism", which gained widespread news press coverage as it became a major public health issue. Kanner considered it an organic disease, estimating its rate at 1: 10.000, and the psychiatric establishment has long clung to a conviction that the manifold field of autism responded to a yet-to-be-discovered organic causation, that is, to a genetic brain disorder; alternatively, the general public often attributes it to alimentary, toxic or vaccinal etiologies. Despite the fact that the hard-and-fast causation sought for decades in genetics has led nowhere, the officially promoted therapeutic strategy continued to be medication: according to Leuzinger-Bohleber et al. (2010), 10 million children worldwide are currently medicated, while in the US two-thirds of children diagnosed received stimulant medication, be it methylphenidate or amphetamines.

To everybody's surprise and dismay, the prevalence of child autistic spectrum disorders went up and up along the years, to the point that currently the official US statistics agency, the Centers for Disease Control and Prevention (CDC), estimate it at 1 in every 10 schoolboys, and acknowledges that "there are no medications that can cure ASD or even treat the main symptoms" (CDC 2013). The slack between the ever-increasing 'epidemic of autism' and the paucity of effective medical responses was taken up mostly by cognitive-behavioural therapies seeking to focally promote wanted behaviours and extinguish unwanted ones (Toth and King 2008). Cognitivism privileges the 'training' of focal skills. This is not a question of cost-effectiveness: much to the contrary, according to a medical supporter, the American Academy of Pediatrics, cognitive interventions, namely applied behaviour analysis (ABA), must be massively intensive, at least 25 hours weekly 12 months a year. Along akin lines a main psychiatric authority, the US National Institutes of Mental Health, which long advocated genetics as the final, yet-to-be-disclosed causal basis of autism, upholds operant conditioning as the single scientifically validated treatment. Only lately did the emotions gain a foothold in the neurosciences and the psychiatric establishment, in the attempt to develop an 'affective neuroscience': a pioneer of such emerging discipline, Jaak Panksepp, concedes though that in the case of the treatment of autism, its practical results will likely be rather little for the foreseeable future (1999, p. 15).

The overall, worldwide impact of autistic spectrum disorders is likely best reflected in that the Secretary General of the United Nations, Ban Ki-moon, dedicates an annual message to the issue of autism, and the General Assembly of the United Nations unanimously declared April 2 as World Autism Awareness Day. However, inasmuch as it is firmly committed to a vision of autism as a neurological condition, their efforts are addressed to obtain a more receptive public attitude in order to ameliorate their plight.

In our own field, psychoanalysis, attention to autism was for a long time scant, coming mainly from child analysts. Lack of interest was in part due to the fact that the founders of child analysis, Anna Freud and Melanie Klein, did not refer to autism nor made place for it in their conceptions of early mind, while that other giant of child analysis, Donald Winnicott, considered it a variant of infantile schizophrenia and was sceptical on its treatability. Furthermore, as was hinted by Gilmore (2000) in the case of ADHD, psychoanalysts likely have shunned involvement with a disturbance widely assumed to have an organic basis. And, last but not least, as Frances Tustin (1988b) recalled, in the 1950s psychoanalysts working with the classical technique devised for the neuroses raised hopes that went unfulfilled, which much hindered development in the field.

This being a clinical book, we will not review at length the ongoing 'Brain vs Psyche' discussion on the etiology of autism. Suffice it to state our stance that, methodologically, inference from the treatment to the cause is common practice in medicine – the 'therapeutic test' – especially when, as often happens, etiological diagnosis (causation) cannot be forthrightly reached by other means. As is well known, from early on Freud supported the legitimacy of inferencing from psychotherapeutic result to psychogenic etiology, and he brilliantly used it to establish the autonomy of hysterical (psychogenic) from organic paralyses: the first responded to psychic abreaction under hypnosis while the second did not; as he succinctly put it, *"Cessante causa cessat effectus"* (Freud 1893, p. 35). An akin inferential line seems valid for autistic disorders; we are aware though that no amount of clinical evidence will convince those that, as happens for Grotstein (1997), deem evidences coming from the neurosciences to be supraordinated to clinical ones. However, as a Tustin associate, Charlotte Riley (1997, p. 69) reminds us, that a sense of total emotional unrelatedness led Spitz's babies to die from it, should be evidence enough of the potentially lethal consequences of emotional disconnection.

Chapter 1

Autism

An historical approach

Leo Kanner was a child psychiatrist, not a psychoanalyst, but the title of his landmark 1943 paper, "Autistic disturbances of affective contact" continues to define the field. He described a unique syndrome starting before age 2, of which the outstanding disorder is

> the children's *inability to relate themselves* in the ordinary way to people and situations from the beginning of life. Their parents referred to them as having always being "self-sufficient", "like in a shell", "happiest when left alone", "acting as if people weren't there", "perfectly oblivious of anything about him".... There is from the start an *extreme autistic aloneness* that, whenever possible, disregards, ignores, shuts out anything that comes to the child from the outside.
>
> (Kanner 1943, p. 242)

Of his initial 11 patients three were mute, the others used language peculiarly, mostly as parrot-like repetitions of heard word combinations, unhooked from purposes of personal communication: affirmation, Kanner says, was indicated by the literal repetition of a question. Their performances were as monotonously repetitive as their verbal utterances, and they became greatly disturbed upon the sight of anything broken or incomplete; dealing repetitively with objects – typically, by spinning – provided them a gratifying sense of undisputed power and control. They never looked at anyone's face. Some had phenomenal memory capacities.

Among Kanner's many astute observations stands his noting in 1951, having examined 100 cases at Johns Hopkins Hospital, that the autistic child does not differentiate between himself and others or between an "I" and a "you", and that there is no sympathy, *treating the animate, mother included, as inanimate*: as is often mentioned they look through you, not at you. Such children, he highlighted, strenuously resist education, which is lived as a dire intrusion.

To Kanner, differing from later authors, in all cases the disturbance was there from birth on. Initially, he said, parents going to the crib to pick up the child notice that there is no anticipatory reaction; later the child does not run to the parent when he comes home and does not respond to verbal address. Soon after, he was able to boast at a panel in the American Academy of Pediatrics that "Certain features are so typical that, when a 4 year old autistic child is brought to the clinic for the first time, my secretary comes in and tells me that there is an autistic child in the waiting room, and she is usually right" (1953, p. 403).

Kanner kept infantile autism conceptually apart from child schizophrenia, though he granted that some children later fell into it; others emerged by themselves from the autistic disconnection, while still others remained in extreme withdrawal. Adults starting as autistic children were, he said, peculiar and withdrawn, but they never had delusions or hallucinations. In the assumption that "these children have come into the world with innate inability to form the usual, biologically provided affective contact with people" (1943, p. 250), just as other children come into it with innate physical or intellectual handicaps such as dyslexia, Kanner held that infantile autism was not influenced by any form of therapy. Independently, Hans Asperger in 1944 had described an akin syndrome, which differed in that language was preserved and children with the syndrome often showed surprising abilities. Coincidentally with Kanner, Asperger considered that the syndrome he described "was of constitutional origin and genetically transmitted" (Firth 1991, p. 13).

For Kanner autism was a varied lot, encompassing typical childhood cases as well as withdrawn but seemingly functioning adults (usually described as schizoid). Such wide panoply in the severity of autism was, however, mostly lost to the public, likely because Margaret Mahler and Bruno Bettelheim, who brought child autism into the psychoanalytic fold, considered autism to be the severest of child psychoses. Bettelheim (1967), in his widely influential book *The Empty Fortress*, put the clinical lens on the sickest cases, interned for treatment at late age, years after illness started. Indeed, the three patients he detailed – Laurie, Marcia and Joey – were long-standing cases who presented elaborate delusional systems, blurring the limits with childhood schizophrenia. His work took place in an in-patient setting; he privileged residential treatment under psychoanalytic guidance, holding that outpatient treatment works only when the disturbance is relatively mild and the child is still very young (p. 407). Fortunately, by the standards of his three detailed cases, most autistic disturbances, when seen early enough, can aptly be considered "relatively mild": it is precisely the children being "very young" and their being treated as soon as feasible after going into autistic retraction that brings fully into play psychoanalysis's therapeutic "window of opportunity".

Among Bettelheim's perceptive clinical observations we single out, firstly, that these children have, and impose, an out-of-this-world, *mechanical* view of their universe; secondly and notably, on the "I": when asked "do you want milk?" the autistic child replies "you want milk" (meaning "yes, I want milk"). This echolalia serves defensive purposes; in creating a language that fits his emotional experience, the autistic child evades using personal pronouns the more so these refer to himself, avoiding the term "yes" as much as the word "I". As he magisterially puts it, such language derives from the child's *anxiety about being himself*; his depleted selfhood can assert itself only in negation (pp. 424–428). The survival value of such posture, he masterly adds, is that "if 'I' do not really exist, then neither can 'I' really be destroyed" (p. 429).

As previously said, Kanner was sceptical about treatability. Bettelheim, though, stressed having been able in long-term residential psychotherapeutic treatment at the Orthogenic School in Chicago to reverse autism's course. Prognosis was better for speaking children than for mute ones: out of his 26 speaking autistic children, improvement in 17 he deemed "good", being for all purposes "cured" and functioning well in society despite residual quirks (1967, p. 417); several of his inmates went on to complete university studies. He compared his results with those of operant conditioning, which forsakes the child's need for spontaneity: whereby, he bluntly argued, autistic children "are reduced to the level of Pavlovian dogs" (p. 410). Such polemic, initially raised half a century ago, is alive and well today.

The first autistic child to be psychoanalyzed was Melanie Klein's patient Dick, in her classic paper "The importance of symbol formation in the development of the ego" (1930), but at that time he was not recognised as autistic. Revisiting Dick's case, Frances Tustin pointed out that Klein registered substantial differences between her patient Dick and the schizophrenic children she had analysed, noting that such cases are often classified as mental deficiency, that Dick was largely devoid of affects and rarely displayed anxiety and then only in an abnormally small degree, and that "against the diagnosis of dementia praecox is the fact that the essential feature of Dick's case was an *inhibition* in development and not a *regression*" (quoted by Tustin 1986, p. 50, italics in original). She also noted substantial differences from Klein's usual technique: Klein acknowledged that she did not interpret the material until it has found expression in various representations, but in this case, where the capacity to represent was almost entirely lacking, she was obliged to interpret on the basis of her general knowledge (Tustin 1986, pp. 52–53).

Margaret Mahler (1952, 1958, 1968) pioneered, from the 1950s on, the study and conceptualization of an 'infantile symbiotic psychosis' as part of the childhood psychoses, side-by-side with Kanner's early infantile autism. She considered infantile autism and the "symbiotic infantile psychosis" as two variants of childhood schizophrenia. Mahler drew on Ferenczi (1913) for a notion of a "primary mother-infant symbiotic unit" (1952, p. 288); however, keeping faithful to Freud's and Hartmann's conceptions of the initial stages of mind, Mahler postulated a pre-symbiotic, normal autistic phase in the first month of extrauterine life, sustaining that "in the normal autistic phase, the infant is not yet aware of anything beyond his own body, whereas in the symbiotic phase he seems to have become vaguely aware that need satisfaction comes from the outside" (1968, p. 165). The normal autistic phase took place from two or three months on to a symbiotic phase in which the infant behaves and functions as though he and his mother were an omnipotent system, a dual unity (1958, p. 77). To Mahler, as used in this context, the term "symbiosis" is a metaphor not having the connotations of the biological term, which implies a mutually beneficial relationship: as found in the symbiotic child psychoses, it can be described as a "parasitic symbiotic" union (1968, p. 55). The term was chosen to describe the state of indifferentiation, of fusion with the mother, in which the "I" is not yet differentiated from the "not-I", and in which inside and outside are only gradually coming to be sensed as different; unpleasurable perceptions, external or internal, are projected beyond the common boundary of the symbiotic *milieu intérieur*, which includes the mothering partner: in this, she says, symbiosis resembles the Freudian notion of the purified pleasure ego (1968, p. 9). Mutual cuing signs the symbiotic phase:

> the mother conveys – in innumerable ways – a kind of "mirroring frame of reference" to which the primitive self of the infant automatically adjusts. If the mother's "primary preoccupation" with her infant – *her* mirroring function during early infancy – is unpredictable, unstable, anxiety-ridden, or hostile; if her confidence in herself as a mother is shaky, then the individuating child has to do without a reliable frame of reference for checking back, perceptually and emotionally, to the symbiotic partner. . . . The result will then be a disturbance in the primitive "self feeling" which would derive or originate from a pleasurable and safe state of symbiosis, from which he did not have to hatch prematurely and abruptly. The primary method for identity formation consists of mutual reflection during the symbiotic phase.
>
> (1968, p. 19)

Patients who do not achieve true identificatory and internalization processes fall back to the primary mode, the "mirroring kind of maintenance of identity" (1968, p. 31).

Omnipotent symbiotic dual unity eventually leads to a separation–individuation phase with the advent of autonomous ego functions such as locomotion and the beginnings of language: the peak of the symbiotic phase, the third quarter of the first year, coincides, says Mahler, with the beginning of differentiation of the self from the symbiotic object, and thus marks the onset of the separation–individuation phase (1968, p. 220). The intrapsychic separation–individuation process – the child's achievement of separate functioning in the presence and emotional availability of the mother – continually confronts the baby with minimal threats of object loss; however, pleasure in separate functioning enables the infant to overcome such separation anxiety, as is entailed by each new step of separate functioning. The negativistic behaviour of the anal phase, in the frame of the toddler's spurt for individual autonomy, is important for intrapsychic separation and self-boundary formation. This, what Mahler calls the practicing period, culminates around the middle of the second year with the freely walking toddler at the height of his mood of elation, at the peak point of his belief in his own magic omnipotence, in good measure derived from his sense of sharing in his mother's magical powers (1968, p. 20). Attainment of libidinal object constancy (in Hartmann's sense) is much more gradual than the achievement of object permanency (in Piaget's sense). During the second half of the second year of life, says Mahler, the child has become more and more aware of his physical separateness and, along with this awareness, the relative obliviousness to his mother's presence signing the practicing period wanes, which brings in the *rapprochement* phase with an increased need, and a wish, for his mother to share with him new acquisitions of skill and experience (1968, pp. 24–25).

As Mahler initially put it, infantile autism regresses to primary narcissism: there seems to be, she said, a primary lack, or a loss, of that primordial differentiation between living and lifeless matter that von Monakow called *protodiakrisis*, and thus the child's self, even his bodily self, seems not to be distinguished from the inanimate objects of the environment (1968, p. 79). Symbiotic psychosis implied fixation or regression to a delusional omnipotent symbiotic fusion with the need-satisfying object: such fusion evolved through crises of catastrophic panic reactions, inasmuch as inner and outer reality are fused (1958, p. 78). These symbiotic children rarely show conspicuous disturbance in the first year of life except perhaps disturbances of sleep, and tend to be described by their mothers as crybabies or oversensitive; as soon as ego differentiation and psychosexual development challenge the child with a measure of separation from the mother, which usually happens in the third or fourth year of life or with the advent of the Oedipus complex, the illusion of symbiotic omnipotence is threatened and severe panic reactions occur (1952, p. 292). In the idea that the "phantasy of oneness with the omnipotent mother . . . coercing her into functioning as an extension of the self" (1958, p. 79) is psychotic despite being part of the healthy baby's early mindset, she fitted autism proper and symbiotic disturbances into the child psychoses, deeming pathological, overly fusional symbiotic states between baby and mother as the risk factor for symbiotic psychosis.

At first Mahler made a sharp distinction between autistic and symbiotic psychosis syndromes, but years later, after treating nearly 40 cases, she concluded that "there is a broad spectrum of combinations of autistic and symbiotic features within the infantile psychosis syndrome" (1968, p. 77): placing each case within this spectrum rests on whether the autistic or the symbiotic defences are paramount. She also came to avow that the intrapsychic situation in the psychotic child "does not involve a regression to any known phase of development" (1968, p. 55). The autistic child's most conspicuous symptom is that "The mother as representative of the outside world does not seem to be perceived *at all* by the child" (p. 64). She added that the autistic defense is "primarily a response to the fear of human contact, an armor plating against such contact", which results in a shutting out of the actual human object in order to effect a delusional denial of the existence of the human object world and therefore of the danger of annihilation while the self becomes deanimated ("devitalised"), a psychotic mechanism that has no parallel in any phase of normal development (1968, p. 79). The symbiotic defensive organization is conceived of as primarily a response to separation panic, that she calls "panic" advisedly because the extent of traumatic anxiety, which includes a fear of re-engulfment by the symbiotic object, cannot be considered a part of the ordinary experience of normal infancy. Fear of re-engulfment is conceived as a dread of dissolution of the self (loss of boundaries) into an aggressively invested dual unity that the child cannot magically control (p. 80–81). But, while time and again she described autistic dynamics as psychotic, in a late statement she opened the way to a wider picture: "Milder than psychotic disturbances, I believe, occur in children who, though they have passed through a separation–individuation process, have shown ominous deviations from the orderly progression of the subphases" (1974, p. 102). In such manner, going beyond her initial notion that infantile autism and symbiotic disturbances were variants of childhood schizophrenia, she joins Kanner's idea of a panoply in the severity of autistic dynamics. On all these points we coincide.

Mahler's psychoanalytically inspired treatment scheme was built on a "tripartite therapeutic design" (1961, p. 348), which included baby, mother and therapist, a set-up where the therapist served as the catalyst, the transfer agent and the buffer between the child and mother; she thus pioneered parent–child therapies. Her aim was to reestablish a "corrective symbiotic experience" between the baby and the mother as primal object. She was not so optimistic about results, avowing that treatment must extend over many years of the child's life and that "even with cautious, prolonged, and consistent therapy the prognosis for arresting the psychotic process and consolidating the ego is only moderately favorable" (1968, p. 169).

As his scant references to it, late in his work, are fully set in the context of the child psychoses (1965, p. 153, 1967b, p. 221, 1968, p. 198, 1974, p. 90), it might be thought that Donald Winnicott is not part of the history of autism, but despite his lack of acknowledgment of autism as a nosological entity distinct from infantile schizophrenia, his conceptual contribution is crucial. His statement that

> The autistic child who has traveled almost all the way to mental defect is not suffering any longer; invulnerability has almost been reached. Suffering belongs to the parents. The organization towards invulnerability has been successful, and it is this that shows clinically along with regressive features that are not in fact essential to the picture.
>
> (1968, p. 198)

concerns a limit-case, ironclad isolation in shell-type encapsulated autism. Based on this fissure-less idea of autistic invulnerability, he was unremittingly pessimistic about treatment: "therapeutic work with autistic children is maximally exacting, and constantly makes the worker feel: is this worthwhile? There is but slight possibility of a 'cure' – only amelioration of the condition and a great increase in the child's personal experience of suffering" (1967b, p. 221). Thereupon autism was not a focus for Winnicott, but his notion of psychotic depression was a main stepping stone for Tustin's developments, as was his model of primal mind – a model fusional to a much greater extent than is usually acknowledged – that Tustin in good measure owes to him. Winnicott's overall concepts of going-on-being, mirroring, transitionality, impingement and play-as-such (distinctly from Klein's masterly technical use of play technique in session), topics on which little can be found in Klein's work, find ready place in describing how healthy development proceeds and how the autistic disconnection is overcome. We agree with Winnicott in that therapeutic work with autistic children is maximally exacting, but we trust that the clinical material here presented backs the idea that half a century later we need not subscribe to his therapeutic pessimism.

Let us now address the Kleinian approach furthered by Rodrigué, Bick and Meltzer. Despite titling his paper "The analysis of a three-year-old mute schizophrenic", Emilio Rodrigué in 1955 held that his quite detailed, if interrupted, case, treated for seven months along Kleinian technical lines with much though partial progress, fitted Kanner's early infantile autism. The child's visual hallucinations in the analytic process raise a question about this being a 'mixed' case: as happened with Bettelheim's patients Laurie, Marcia and Joey, with their elaborate delusional systems, the finding of visual hallucinations can be thought to blur the limits with childhood schizophrenia. It merits mention though that despite Kanner's claim that autistic children do not hallucinate, Tustin's (1972) key child patient John also presented fleeting hallucinations during treatment: Rodrigué and Tustin coincide in that this meant a step forward in the clinical process (as far as can be gathered, none of our patients presented hallucinations before or during treatment). Along Kleinian lines, he conjectured that his child patient felt he was in possession of an extremely idealised internal object.

Given that it set the mainstream paradigm for the psychoanalytic treatment of child autism in the British Isles, in continental Europe and in South America, the work of Donald Meltzer needs to be examined. After training in psychiatry in the US, Meltzer went to London in 1954 to be analysed by Melanie Klein. At the time another Kleinian psychoanalyst, Esther Bick, was head therapist at the Tavistock Clinic, where she brilliantly developed infant observation technique (1966) and later published her brief but influential paper "The experience of the skin in early object-relations" (1968). She there set the basis for her (and Meltzer's) concept of "adhesive identification", holding that through imitation the patient seeks to adhere to the surface of the therapist's body standing for the mother's body; as she understood it, adhesive relations deploy themselves mimetically on the surface of the object in a bi-dimensional space and are to be contrasted with projective identifications, which presuppose an internal space. To Bick the baby's foremost issue was the spilling out of the parts of an initial ego, and the issue of bi-dimensionality emerged from the need to hold them by means of a bodily/psychic skin-container.

For his part, having successfully treated for two years an autistic boy while still in the US, Meltzer (1960) started supervising autistic children at the Tavistock Clinic, where he started a research group, which met from 1965 to 1974, leading to the publication of a joint book, *Explorations in Autism* (Meltzer et al. 1975). Although he asserted that his book could not make therapeutic claims and that he was in the business of locating problems rather than solving them (pp. 4–5), Meltzer nonetheless took as his task to put up "a definitive view of autism . . . which differed greatly from anything previously suggested" (p. 3); disregarding the work of the early pioneers Kanner, Bettelheim and Mahler, he thought out autism within the conceptual framework of Kleinian theory. While he incorporates Bick's adhesive identification as being chronologically earlier than the splitting-and-idealization signing the paranoid-schizoid position, he keeps in the main to Klein's overall assumption that the baby from the start has a self that is already differentiated from the object. Despite finding in the child patients he supervised neither the spilling-out of parts of the self nor the secondary skin function described by Bick (Meltzer et al. 1975, p. 19), he takes key support in the concepts of adhesive identification and the container-skin. While positing that his technique for treating autistic children follows closely upon Klein's approach to neurotic or psychotic children, he went on to introduce a new conceptual set reaching quite beyond Klein: primitive obsessional mechanisms, dismantling of the senses and one-, two-, three- and four-dimensionality. *Obsessionality* is accorded priority as a general term for omnipotent control of the objects, relying on attacks on linking to separate the objects in order to better control them. Autistic mindlessness is obtained by way of *dismantling* the child's sensory equipment from a united or consensual mode of functioning, each individual sense then seeking out by itself items in the environment: amid such suspension of attention, events cannot be considered as mental acts and cannot be experienced in ways allowing for integration. By suspending attention in a passive, falling-to-bits way, the child withdraws from the world, evading persecutory anxiety and despair, since violence to neither self nor object is involved. This differentiates dismantling from splitting processes employing destructive impulses to make attacks on linking, which results – secondarily – into splitting of the self. Adhesive identification – which he sees as mimetic and in the main tactile – sets the ground for a conception of *dimensionality* embracing one-dimensionality (autism), bi-dimensionality (adhesive identification), tri-dimensionality of the self, allowing for projective identification amid a circular conception of time, and four-dimensionality, which includes time and alone admits development as a possibility. Then he introduced a novel classification of infantile psychotic disturbances: (a) autism proper and post-autistic states, (b) geographical confusional psychoses, (c) primary failures of mental development and (d) failures of post-natal mental development (1986, p. 123), these last three being deemed not autistic.

The notion of aesthetic conflict as the core developmental conflict from birth onward obtained pride of place in Meltzer's later views. The Introduction of his book, *The Apprehension of Beauty*, co-authored with Meg Harris Williams, voiced the intention to deal with psychoanalysis as an art form interdigitating clinical psychoanalysis and literary criticism (1988, p. xii): such literary interdigitation permits that the event of a child entering his first therapy session with a beautiful new female therapist, who murmured in astonishment, "Are you a woman – or a flower?", be bewilderingly accorded the highest status, as "a glimpse of the reaction of the newborn at the first sight of its mother and of her breast" (Meltzer and Harris Williams 1988, p. xvi). As he puts it, newborn children are "overwhelmed by the aesthetic impact of the outside world and the prime object that represents it both concretely and symbolically: the mother, her breasts and nipples, and her eyes and mind" (Meltzer 1987, p. 3). It is "her mother-liness, the manifestation of her interior qualities, that delivers the blow of awe and wonder", while correlatively "the baby's interior qualities, in which it excels all other creatures, deliver a corresponding blow to the parents". The baby's qualities are evoked in untrammeled imaginative terms:

> What it possesses that is the essence of its baby-ishness is the potentiality to become a Darwin, a George Eliot, a Rembrandt, a Mme. Curie, a human being. Its baby-ishness impinges directly on the imagination and sets us peering into its future. This ravishment, the love-at-first-sight that it can evoke is, I contend, the sine qua non of the baby's tolerance to the aesthetic blow it receives from the mother.
> (Meltzer 1987, p. 13)

Though the aesthetic conflict is posited in Kleinian nipple-breast organ terms, his conception of the aesthetic conflict reverses the Kleinian chronological precedence of the paranoid-schizoid as regards the depressive position (Meltzer and Harris Williams 1988, p. 26), displacing the role hitherto assigned to the separation anxieties as follows: "separation difficulties are of a pregenital part-object nature, centering on the breast and nipple as the overpowering combined aesthetic object" (Meltzer 1986, p. 215).

As concerns technique, besides upholding systematic initial investigation of the transference, Meltzer asks that the analyst quite actively strive to constantly retain the child's attention: to this end, continual interpretation is required of the transference-state-ante preceding the lapse into autism. This happens amid overriding permissiveness as regards physical contact with the analyst in touching, looking, smelling and tasting (Meltzer et al. 1975, p. 15).

Importantly, Timmy, the child who provided the foundation of Meltzer's concept of Autism Proper (Meltzer et al. 1975, p. 35), starting treatment quite late by our standards, at age 6 years and 9 months, was *not* an out-and-out shell-type autistic child: though severely autistic, Timmy had, by the time treatment started, developed marked entangled (schizophrenic-like) dynamics, as happens with shell-type children as years go by, and was in his highly bizarre way well aware of the therapist's presence. Timmy's autistic retraction had begun long before, at age 2 years, after an operation for umbilical hernia and the birth of his brother Bobby; he was seen five times per week for some four years with significant, but on the whole disappointing, results. Let us quote how the notion of Autism Proper was reached based on Timmy's case:

> Over a period of months it became clear that certain forms of behavior which appeared in great abundance constituted Timmy's autistic phenomena; and by culling out of the record those items which seemed clearly outside this category, and linking them together like pearls on a thread,

we were able to construct sequences (sometimes covering several sessions) which could then be interpreted as if they had been indeed quite consecutive.

(Meltzer et al. 1975, p. 6)

Thus he delimited two categories of phenomena, in which the autistic disruption seemed "like the intrusion of a petit mal attack into the conversation", a suspended mental functioning bringing in a "suspension of the transactions in the transference" (Meltzer et al. 1975, p. 7), which he deems the central problem in autism. The therapist's interpretations of the Autistic Phenomena Proper, he avows, could hardly be called psychoanalytic in that they undertake to bring together the fragments of dismantled experience – this, in a two-dimensional world where surfaces seemed fairly crawling with minute rivals elicited by the dots on the lino (flooring) and the birds in the garden, representing rival babies in a climate of impotent rage (pp. 40–41). Only after the third year of therapy, a more linked transference process centreing on a particular object, "the therapist's head, perhaps even his mind" (p. 42), emerged from the welter of autistic debris (which to us are schizophrenic-like restitutional entanglements). To Meltzer transference processes could be seen to be embedded in a matrix of autistic items; to us this does not take into account that in out-and-out shell-type children the analyst is not *felt* as a human object, diverse from an inanimate one, as happened to our child patient Lila during most of the treatment. That out-and-out autistic dynamics feel and treat the animate as inanimate (the mother and also the analyst) guided the work of the pioneers Kanner, Bettelheim, Mahler and Tustin. In this same line of thinking fits the fact that Timmy's analyst John Brenmer did not feel ignored, he felt non-existent (Meltzer et al. 1975, p. 38).

In *Explorations in Autism*, Meltzer et al. (1975) presented four extended clinical treatments by different therapists under his supervision, their sequential overlap illustrating four decreasing degrees of severity of the disorder; however, as no child attained psychic health, no clear path to resolution is traced. *Explorations in Autism* has been widely influential though, as we soon shall explain, Meltzer in the following decades revised his posture on the pertinence of early interpretation. His later clinical depictions of child autism are sparse, all of them derived from supervisions (Meltzer 1983, p. 30, p. 75, p. 79, 1986, p. 128, 1995, p. 45; Meltzer and Harris Williams 1988, p. xiii, p. 42), with few hints given about the children's evolution and later course.

Following Klein's (and Bion's) notions on the paranoid-schizoid position, assuming as *ab initio* psychically distinct these two entities, the baby and the mother-as-object who will thereafter connect by way of projective and introjective identifications, Meltzer's stance makes no conceptual place for the states of merging and the ensuing dread nor for the anxieties of rupture and loss-of-self. Centrality accorded to the aesthetic object and the aesthetic conflict place his views fully within what Michael Rustin (1991) considered the Romantic turn in post-Kleinian psychoanalysis. Our clinical work has found no use for Meltzer's concepts of primitive obsessionality, dismantling of the senses, bi-dimensionality or to the priority accorded to the aesthetic conflict, nor for his admonishment for an initial uncompromising investigation of the transference. We willingly concede that an aesthetic dimension plays a role in development, especially in moments of ecstasy and glee, but not in that it purveys the core developmental conflict, in which case the aesthetic conflict would supersede affective, erotic and aggressive conflict. From our standpoint on autistic states, which centres on the baby's contact with mother's emotions, no clinical purpose is served by imaginative hyperbole in terms of organ language or psychic dimensionality in approaching the earliest stages of mind. To us, as happened for Mahler, Winnicott, Tustin and Eugenio Gaddini (1969), the search for continuity and the ensuing struggles against and for separateness and differentiation are at the centre of the earliest defences.

Before considering Tustin's work, let us explain that, coming from a Kleinian-Bionian-Meltzerian training, we came into contact with it in the 1980s on confronting what we thought was an autistic level in the study of a narcissistic personality, in which transference processes did not operate (Ahumada 1984). So we were not raised in Tustin's work, nor do we have any partisan interest in upholding it: we came to it, so to say, in a similar clinical-technical trajectory two decades after she arrived at similar conclusions, which were later expanded in working with autistic children.

Frances Tustin trained in the Tavistock Clinic as Kleinian at the time that Esther Bick was director of training; she there attended seminars and supervised with Sydney Klein and Donald Meltzer. Midway in her training she spent a year in Boston, where she contacted Margaret Mahler and visited autistic children and their families. She was long in analysis with Wilfred Bion, but the technical and conceptual schemes developed in her work with autistic children differed from those coming out of Bion's work with adult schizophrenic patients; much to Bion's credit, he fostered her emergent ideas even as these differed from his own. She also kept her conceptual autonomy from the Bick-Meltzer autism team at the Tavistock Clinic and was not a co-author of *Explorations in Autism* (Meltzer et al. 1975). It came as a shock for her to realise on treating her first autistic child, John, that "Melanie Klein's insights did not seem to apply to the early stages of work with autistic children" (Tustin 1986, p. 39). Contact with Winnicott's work came in the late 1960s: it was on presenting her first paper on autism that her attention was called to Winnicott's ideas, which played a major role in the build-up of her own. This is how she started her clinical comment in her first book, *Autism and Childhood Psychosis* (1972), initiating a line of thinking that she kept to throughout her work:

> Of *psychotic depression*, Winnicott . . . writes: "For example, the loss might be that of *certain aspects of the mouth* which disappear from the infant's point of view along with the mother and the breast when there is a separation at a date earlier than that at which the infant had reached a stage of emotional development which could provide the equipment for dealing with loss. The same loss of the mother a few months later would be a loss of object without this added element of *loss of part of the subject*".
> (Tustin 1972, p. 4; emphasis added)

She went on to add that psychotic depression has also been termed "primal depression" and was found by others to be the turning point for the arrest of emotional development in abnormal (psychotic) children. Such was to her, upon her findings in her key patient John, also the starting point for autistic disorders:

> A precipitating factor for all types of pathological autism seems to be the mouth-experienced "hole" type of depression associated with feelings of terror, helplessness and defectiveness. This has been termed psychotic depression.
> (1972, p. 69)

Thus, following upon Winnicott's notion of psychotic depression, to Tustin autism resulted from the shock of unbuffered awareness of bodily separateness from the mother, shoving the child into primal depression: this turned out later, as the treatment process evolved, into the image of the 'black hole'. Coincidentally with Bettelheim, she avowed that despite the child *not having a sense of self*, the greatest dread is losing his sense of existence; as she later put it:

> the shock of sudden awareness of bodily separateness has left them in the grip of elemental terrors, of which losing the sense of existence – their "going-on-being" (Winnicott) – is the most outstanding.
> (1988a, p. 45)

Fear of loss of a sense of existence leads to engendering a protective covering of auto-sensuous, predominantly tactile "me" sensations in order to keep the dreaded "not-me" at bay. In such "encapsulated" or "shell-type" autistic children, pathological self-sufficiency comes about based on fear: while this will not show up at the start of treatment, they are terrified of the "black hole" or the "blacked-out" mother; as treatment proceeds, their fears of being "blacked-out" are revealed. Though some look angelic, they are at the mercy of untransformed dark internal forces, the omnipotent violence of which may make them into "little Hitlers" (1994a, p. 106). Numbing and deadening insulation is generated by both the "hard" autistic objects they clutch to and by autistic "shapes", soft endogenous whirls of sensation produced by bodily fluids and movements, which are not the same as masturbation in that they do not involve people. The autistic child, says Tustin, seeks sensations rather than objects as such: he feels continuous with the outside world in a state of imitative "identicality", an "imitative fusion" (E. Gaddini 1969), as is evinced by the normal young baby putting out his tongue in response to his mother doing the same.

Tustin highlighted that in the schizophrenic child the processes of projective identification are quite active, and we find a contact with the awareness of an inside and an outside, jointly with an acknowledgment of objects distinct from himself, whereas the autistic child connects with sensations rather than with objects as such, feeling continuous with the world rather than separate from it. Living as he does in a state of imitative fusion with objects in the outside world, she insists that a primal sense of "me-ness" has to be well established before long-standing awareness of the "not-me" can be tolerated (Tustin 1986, p. 55). The result is an extreme vulnerability, where behind the apparent imperviousness the child's energies focus on generating a protective cover of "me" sensations in order to keep off the threatening "not-me".

On types of autism

For Tustin the model for autistic disconnection was provided by *encapsulated "shell-type"* children, which she deemed *asymbolic*: in holding that the children experience the mother (and the analyst!) as inanimate extensions of their own bodies, she pursues Kanner's (1951) prescient observation that autistic children treat the animate, mother included, as inanimate. At such levels, she holds, it is improper to speak of transference dynamics, and attempts at transference interpretation will be felt by the child as intrusions to be strenuously resisted. Besides such "shell-type" autism, she acknowledges an *"entangled" or "confusional"*, *schizophrenic-like* autism that Mahler called "symbiotic psychosis"; such children have a confused awareness of bodily separateness as well as of insides and outsides: here projective identification as described by Klein is active and obvious (Tustin 1986, p. 53). These are the two main types, to which she added a third type, the jelly-like, soft, *ameboid* child that she illustrated decades later by Anne Alvarez's (1992) patient Robbie, which she deems the sickest type of case (Tustin 1993, p. 125). In *Autistic States in Children* (1981), Tustin incorporated, after Meltzer et al. (1975), another type: the *segmented* children (secondary encapsulation), in which segments of functioning such as the child's own perceptions are encapsulated; she mentions that as a rule these children are not mute, but they are often echolalic and are more difficult to treat than shell-type children.

Both the ameboid and the segmented children should, in our opinion, be considered as varieties of entangled autism. On our side we described a *mimetic-type* child autism (Busch de Ahumada and Ahumada 2010) (Ch. 4), which is well outside the realm of child psychoses, whose dynamics provide a clinical and conceptual bridge to adolescent and adult autistoid cases; though their mimetic entanglement may resemble confusional childhood psychoses, they are in no way psychotic in the proper, restricted sense of the term. This is valid for Sofia's case (Ch. 4), where mimetic entanglement corresponded to the healthier part of her psyche and led the way in her therapy to emotional contact with the analyst and in due time to resolution, and also, more controversially, for Juan and Jaime. While especially in Juan's case, mimetic entanglement might hardly be set apart from psychotic dynamics, overall he kept partly outside of such dynamics, which would not happen for a genuinely psychotic child.

Tustin's ideas on child autism derived from ten patients she treated, claiming that her four out-and-out encapsulated cases recovered fully; six other patients "used marked autistic modes of protection but . . . used symbiotic ones as well" (1990, p. 28): these entangled patients are – she holds and we agree – even more difficult to treat (as said, admixtures of autistic and mimetic-symbiotic dynamics happened with three of our child patients: Sophia, Juan and Jaime). Her key patient, John (1972, p. 5ff, 1986, p. 68ff), whose treatment set the main bearings for her outlook, started at age 3 years 7 months, achieving resolution of his autistic disconnection within a three-year time period. The evolution of her other key patient, David, who started treatment much later, aged 10 years 10 months, being treated four times weekly for six years, was a different matter: despite much progress, he was rehabilitated rather than recovered (1990, p. 70).

Later on, in 1981, she detailed a third patient, Sam (treated by Sandra Stone), a segmented encapsulated child starting thrice-weekly treatment a month before his sixth birthday, who after three years and nine months of treatment she deemed had become a relatively normal little boy. Also in 1981 she described Peter, a nearly mute encapsulated child who had become segmented, so autistic as to appear brain-damaged, who started treatment at age 6 and after some four years of therapy turned into a charming, original and intelligent boy. With those exceptions, she relied on short vignettes rather than on detailed description of evolving treatments. Choice of the severest case is valid for Anne Alvarez's (1992) patient Robbie, who started five-times-weekly psychoanalytic therapy quite late, at age 13: though he progressed much in his decades-long therapy, he was rehabilitated, not recovered.

One might expect that four decades after Tustin's (1972) seminal book, *Autism and Childhood Psychoses*, publications of successful resolution into health of early treatments of child cases in the autistic spectrum would, in the frame of the current epidemic of autism, have become commonplace, but this is far from being so. Child cases depicting evolving therapeutic processes were published, among others, by Alvarez (1992, 2010, 2012), Bisagni (2012), Cecchi (1990), Dale (1997), Haag (1993, 1997), Houzel (1999, 2004), Korbivscher (2013), Lechevalier (1997), Maiello (1997), Rhode (1997, 2004, 2005, 2008, 2012) and Rodrigué (1955). However, most clinical narratives did not proceed to termination, nor was the end result clearly stated. The conclusion of a review of Kate Barrows' (2008) "Autism in childhood and autistic features in adults" in the *International Journal of Psychoanalysis* is witness to a wide-ranging pessimism: "After all, at the coal-face, we do need reminding of how little we can do, how important it is to try our best" (Truckle 2010, p. 1545).

In our experience early start of treatment is crucial for the attainment of a resolutive outcome: the younger the child, and the sooner after autistic retraction began, the better is the prognosis. Also, we have been fortunate in that the children treated lived at intact homes with both parents, in that none of the parents exhibited gross psychopathology, and in that they were much concerned and interested in their children's progress and willingly collaborated. The cases of Daniel and Lina, presented by a long-standing, talented contributor to the field, Maria Rhode (2012), exemplify an altogether different panorama. Daniel, starting treatment at age 9 in a one- and then two-sessions-a-week basis for seven years, had been sent from a National Health Service (NHS) residential unit as uneducable, and was a deprived child besides being autistic. Lina, an immigrant child with disturbed language, was seen in once- and later twice-weekly sessions for five years from age 6 ½ on, long after her autistic retraction started. Such cases attain, after painstaking work, rehabilitation rather than resolution. It is crucial, though, that the sorry picture of such deprived children not be taken as representative of the potential for very early treatment in the wider group of autistic spectrum disorders.

Contributions on autistic 'barriers', 'nuclei' or 'enclaves' in adolescent and adult patients, in the wake of Sydney Klein (1980) and Tustin (1981), have taken the slack for the dearth of detailed early child analyses: thus a recent book by a well-known contributor, Judith Mitrani's (2001) *Ordinary People and Extraordinary Protections: A Post-Kleinian Approach to the Treatment of Primitive Mental States*, presents detailed material and thoughtful technical suggestions on the handling of autistic enclaves in adult patients who are commonly deemed neurotic. Anne Alvarez's book, *The Thinking Heart: Three Levels of Psychoanalytic Therapy with Disturbed Children* (2012), presents a wealth of child and adolescent clinical sketches as well as valuable technical suggestions, but does not single out autistic cases from other highly disturbed children such as psychopathic or deprived ones: only Samuel's case, starting treatment at age 4, and those of Joseph and Jessie, both starting at age 8, stand as clear-cut autistic cases; but these are presented as vignettes to illustrate clinical and technical points rather than as detailed clinical cases, and it is not manifested whether treatment led to resolution.

We shall keep our discussion to the psychoanalytic contributions on psychogenic aetiology. In all her cases, Tustin found that the mother had been severely depressed, usually before the birth and always immediately after it; also that, in many cases, for various reasons the mother had not been adequately supported by the father and had been in a lonely state, in some cases being out of their country of origin (1986, p. 36). As stated, in her final stance, Tustin adroitly held trauma in the nursing situation to be at the fore, sustaining that for autistic children

> the traumatic situation has been the sudden loss of control over what had been felt to be a vital sensuous part of their tongues which fared them a sense of "being" when the nipple part of the tongue was no longer there when it was needed, their sense of "being" seemed to be under threat. The black hole of "not-being" loomed.
>
> (1990, p. 38)

In "The perpetuation of an error" (1994b), she added that (as Mahler had already advanced) an excessive abnormally perpetuated state of unity with the mother seems to be a first step previous to the trauma of rupture.

Our clinical findings coincide on that autism is a protective reaction specific to psychic trauma. On the how and when of traumata, however, we meet relevant differences: in our five child cases, we encounter diverse sorts of traumatic impacts impinging during the first three years of life, a span coincidental with what Mahler described for symbiotic psychoses. Except for Sophia (Ch. 4), whose mother's mind-blindness was present from her birth on, in none of our cases does trauma appear to have mainly impinged at birth nor during nursing; also, we do not find the history of early feeding difficulties that Tustin emphasises. Other relevant differences are that mothers were not depressed before or immediately after their birth, though this did often happen later, and in no case we found evidence of gross adhesiveness in the baby-mother link.

Given that, in all our children, outset of the autistic withdrawal came later than the nursing situation proper, we find that the traumatic situation cannot be described primarily in terms of organ language, as does Tustin with the notion of the pathogenic primacy of tongue-nipple rupture. While the occurrence of hidden traumata in the nursing situation proper cannot be ruled out, our children's history and clinical course provide no evidence for such happenstance. Outset of autism as resulting from a felt sudden bodily rupture should not be taken for granted: in several of our cases, a deadening of the primal dialogue, leading to its interruption, is as likely a description. Also, in most cases the "black hole" did not make a distinct appearance as it did in Tustin's key patient John: only in Jaime's treatment (Ch. 6), the idea of a "black hole" eventually came to be manifest, transposed to the phallic-genital level as the "vagina with teeth".

Our cases evince maternal depression coming about later on (Axel, Jaime), maternal mind-blindness from birth onwards (Sophia), maternal abandonment (Lila, Juan, Jaime) and the occurrence of mother's pregnancies (Axel, Jaime); in two of our child patients, the traumatic impact came upon long-drawn maternal displacement by visual media cast in the role of spurious mother substitutes (Lila, Juan). One of these media-bred children, Juan, is a case of mimetic autism in which overflowing mimetic-parasitic dynamics proceeded via the TV screen; the other child, Lila, became an encapsulated, shell-type autist. Coming about far from the nursing situation, we find it natural to deem them as resulting from either rupture or deadening of the primal dialogue, that is as consequent to a disturbance of contact with the mother at the emotional psychic level. This is to say, differently from a notion of brusque bodily rupture coming about during the nursing situation, with the likely exception of Jaime, our cases remit to a deadening of the emotional ongoings in the primal infant–mother dialogue well after the nursing situation proper. Each of our cases – treated in private practice – evinced traumatic occurrences in the form of early cumulative trauma displacing or distorting the affective "primal dialogue" between infant and mother (Spitz 1964). Based on our five cases, we cannot adhere to the currently rampant therapeutic pessimism, because all of them evolved to resumption of the primal dialogue in session and thereafter to clinical resolution.

So the question is: why is it that results in our short series of cases have been uniformly successful while most cases published struggle along with partial or dubious progress, which has led to pessimism being a mark of the field? To our mind, therapeutic pessimism arises as an offshoot of the technique used. In the current mainstream stance, "the core of the method is systematic and uncompromising investigation of the transference" (Meltzer et al. 1975, p. 4): it happens though that systematic and uncompromising investigation of the transference demands a level of emotional acknowledgment of the presence of the analyst and a level of verbal understanding that, as the case of Lila (Ch. 2) illustrates, encapsulated children do not attain. Premature transference interpretations, Tustin crucially sustained, "can seem to be pressurising and intrusive to children whose pathology has arisen from an inhibitory recoil from the 'not me' mother, who is felt to be full of hardness, roughness, irritation, darkness, blackness and nastiness"(1981, p. 169), and thus these effectively detain therapeutic progress.

As was mentioned before, Meltzer reversed two decades ago in the case of autistic children his previous emphasis on the need and pertinence of systematic transference interpretation from the start of therapy:

> I now consider that interpretation content has very little impact in this phase of analysis and for a very evident reason... the analyst's behaviour, verbal or otherwise, has the impact of actions rather than communications.
> (1992, p. 42)

However, such honest-to-goodness admission, which acknowledges the lack of symbolization in autistic children, has met with little resonance: it happens that, while most relevant authors acknowledge their debt to Tustin, especially upon her findings on autistic objects and autistic shapes, as concerns technique, the field continues to be ruled by the technical guidelines set by Meltzer et al. in *Explorations in Autism* (1975), affirming that technique does not basically differ from that employed by Melanie Klein in the treatment of neurotic or psychotic children.

We maintain, after Tustin, that shell-like encapsulated children being asymbolic, transference interpretation must be withheld until the moment arrives in which the living presence of the analyst starts to be acknowledged and a transference link begins to evolve. This is to us valid also in the case of mimetic and entangled autistic children until transference becomes established in a definite way, as is illustrated in the case of Sophia (Busch de Ahumada and Ahumada 2005, here Ch. 4).

Thus, an all-important technical gap between Meltzer's and Tustin's stances is that while Meltzer (1975, p. 4) fosters "systematic and uncompromising investigation of the transference", our child cases clinically illustrate once and again that systematic and uncompromising interpretation of the transference would demand from these children a level of understanding that initially they simply do not attain. It merits being mentioned on this topic that Meltzer's coauthor, Isca Wittenberg, John's analyst in *Explorations in Autism*, perceptively granted that often she was restricted to a running commentary on his actions, which in the context of these children's high sensitivity to the analyst's states of mind was the psychic equivalent of holding him (Wittenberg 1975, p. 67), a stance we fully endorse. We shall postpone further discussion on technique and on the crucial role of the 'quality of attention' until after presenting our first case, Lila, in order to illustrate clinically the technical handling.

Chapter 2

Contacting a 19-month-old mute autistic girl: Lila

Lila, a nice, smallish, well-proportioned girl with an absent expression, came to consultation (LBA) at 19 months of age, brought upon her mother's worry that she did not speak. Initially, the mother came alone, having sought on the Internet information on pervasive developmental disorder (PDD), autism, etc; only when Lila's father's much-respected boss, after meeting Lila, told the father that "This girl is from another planet" did he accept that something might be wrong. Pediatric and neurological consultations ruled out organic disturbance. Lila was breast-fed for four months; there was no babbling or lalling and no transitional object. Lila did not use a pacifier, but she sucked her fingers; a sibling, Bob, was aged 3.

The mother carried Lila in her arms to the first evaluation interview. Running on tiptoe, Lila swept past me, her gaze pausing nowhere. My greeting, "Hello Lila", brought no reaction. She ran around, went several times to the window touching the glass; the mother told her: "Look, so many things, a stroller like yours", again with no reaction. Lila went to the table: there, given that her brother plays with cars, I had put two cars; she picked one up, biting its tires while continuing her drifting. The mother enticed her to use the stroller, to no avail. Lila took the other car with no sign of recognizing it nor any attempt to make it run, and proceeded to bite its tires and body. Same as at home, said the mother: "She always comes and goes, she moves a lot". When she came close, I made comments, but she ignored me. Her gaze swept by; at times she smiled pointlessly. The mother insisted with the stroller; Lila dragged it with one hand; the mother said "No, with both hands"; finally she did this, rather haphazardly. She kept returning to the window. I drew the curtain showing her the plants, but she kept on running; at a certain moment she moved her hips and bottom, which brought the mother to ask: "Are you dancing? She does that with music", but Lila just kept running. I offered her the doll, but she paid no attention and went on biting the cars. I offered a cart with cubes drawn by a string, and the mother said "she loves those things"; Lila drew up the string, and the cubes fell down; the mother insisted that she pulled it, but she did not respond. She again put her open mouth against the window glass, and the mother told her not to suck it, but to my mind she intended to bite it. I asked her "Where is Dad?" to which no response, the same as when I asked "Where is Bob?". She did a hopping movement, and the mother said "she loves that"; she took Lila hopping on her knees, which she seemed to enjoy but soon got down. Her much distraught mother offered her a cup; Lila let it fall, took some foods, bit them and let them fall. Approaching the chair, she bit its metal armrests. It was already time to end, but my goodbye got no response.

Both parents came to the second interview. Again Lila ran aimlessly, smiling; she seemed happier, and took up a car and bit it. Mom insisted with the stroller, so Lila pushed it a little. She wanted to touch the books: on her mother's imperious "no", she stopped; she only responded to a peremptory "No", at a time verbal and gestural. The father tried talking to her but was ignored. Lila took the other car and bit it; she grabbed the doll and let it fall. She bit hard objects and ignored soft ones. At times she made a screeching sound "*e,e,e,e,e,e*" with slightly varying intensity. Three times she walked strangely, arms and hands extended before her. Both parents made her hop on their knees, which she seemed to enjoy; she also enjoyed her father throwing her up in the air.

Evaluation findings can be summarised thus: no intent to communicate, lack of vocalization, inability to play, lack of curiosity, no pointing by gaze or hand, seeking hard things to bite while ignoring soft objects, permanent ambulation and accessing human contact only through motricity, hopping on her parent's knees or on being thrown up in the air by father. In the final interview, the mother volunteered that during breast feeding Lila and she looked at each other's eyes. Also, and to us crucially, she told us that from early on Lila had looked at TV the whole day, mostly Mickey Mouse that "rejoiced her so much" while her mother took care of her brother and did the household chores. The stark issue is that Mickey Mouse cannot hold up affectionate mirroring and sustain a 'primal dialogue'. Lila's autistic retraction came up long after nursing proper and does not seem to have resulted from "a precocious and abrupt awareness of their separateness from the mother's body" (Tustin 1988a, p. 46) but from a protracted deprivation of affective maternal contact and a withering away of the 'primal dialogue'. (A similar, equally traumatic maternal deprivation happened to our patient Juan (Ch. 4), who was brought up on the *Animal Planet* channel from ages 6 months to 2 years and believed himself to be a not-yet-grown animal rather than a human child.) These last weeks, at the neurologist's prompting, Lila had been kept off TV. She was never taken to the park, only to the grandparents' home close by. I explained her predicament, and her parents agreed to bring her four times weekly, which they have done dutifully.

The clinical process

At the initial evaluation, I advised that eventually Lila was to be left alone with me. Coming to the first session, the mother said "If I leave her with you, she will not notice it"; I told her this was premature, but she anxiously replied that she would stay in the lobby and took off. For some minutes, Lila continued to move about, I talked to her, she did not look at me, and at some point she looked around and was anguished, though she did not cry. I told her that she was seeking Mom and was afraid at not finding her; she went to the door and started knocking on it. I picked Lila up, which she did not resist, and I told her we were going to call Mom; the mother returned, astounded that Lila had felt her absence. She embraced her, saying "I am here" and sat down, while Lila returned to running around, grabbing the cars and biting them. She pushed the stroller on its side with one hand while the other hand held the car she was biting. I commented on what she did, and also asked her "Where is Mom?", to no avail. The mother tried talking to her, and I told her the cars are like her brother's; she seemed not to hear us. The mother strongly demanded that she stopped biting the cars; after four or five times, Lila looked at her but went on biting.

In the second session the mother left, saying that what had happened would not happen again; Lila did not seem to register. Two or three minutes later, though, she went to the door and knocked on it, starting a faint "*e,e,e,e,e,e*" with some anguish. I again talked to her, picked her up, and called her mother by phone. As she came, Lila continued her "*e,e,e,e,e,e*", her face against my neck. Mom told her "How fond you are, I'm here, I won't be going". As she put her on the floor, Lila started running around, biting hard objects in her way. She accidentally discovered that my empty chair gyrated, and she made it turn and turn and then tried to get on it. I put her up on it, had it softly turn, and commented that she liked this quite a lot. She fleetingly looked at me with a bit more intention, and I put myself on my knees in front of her. A car slipped from her hand to the chair and fell to the floor, so I picked it up and put it on the chair, saying "Car, it comes, comes, comes . . . and it falls". She smiled intentionally for the first time. I repeated the game several times and again she smiled; then she resumed roaming around and biting.

In the third session I asked that the mother stayed. Rambling around, Lila stepped by chance upon a light interrupter on the floor: a tall lamp lit up over her head, much to her surprise. I got close, put out the light and put it on again, saying "*luz*" [light], and then put it out saying the light had gone; again I put it on and pointed with my finger, saying "*luz*" as is done to babies; after four or five times she left and resumed her running. From then on, she always went to the light, and I insisted that she put it on with her foot; this she did several times.

The second week of analysis went on similarly: she ran around distractedly, bit cars and blocks, and rejected what is soft. Putting the light on and off made her laugh. Near the end of a session, she picked up the doll she usually let fall, looked at it and briefly held it. When she approached Mom, she soon was told "All right, but now continue playing".

In the third week, Lila checked that the mother stayed. Then she started her sequence: she walked around, took the doll out of the stroller and pushed the stroller. She went to the light: when she put it on with her foot, I applauded: "The light came, applause, applause". She looked at me cheerfully and applauded once and again. She put it out, I did not applaud, and she looked at me, waiting; she put it on, I applauded, she applauded, and this went on several times. Sessions later, she said "*uz*" [light]. Up to then she had only vocalised her "*e,e,e,e,e*" sound; "*uz*" was the first term she uttered. (As already said, Lila did *not* respond to her name even when said loudly, nor to strong noises; she was examined for deafness, but the findings were normal.) She bit cars less; she threw down some folders, and I commented on this. She opened the door of a piece of furniture; I let her do this, opened the other door and commented on it. We closed them, then opened them, she took out some little plastic bags, we closed the doors, she laughed more and more heartily; this went on some 15–20 times, and thereafter she said for the first time: "ta-ta-ta". I should mention that after Lila's sessions I was thoroughly exhausted, quite differently from with other child patients.

After three months we were approaching summer vacation. Sessions were a farrago of repetitiousness, the incidents mentioned being exceptions. In a previous session she had touched my pearl earrings, similar to hers, which I mentioned: this time I had not put on earrings; her visual sweep stopped on my earlobe, and she fleetingly looked at me in the eye perhaps with some interrogation, and then looked at my other earlobe. She repeated this, and I told her that today I have not put on earrings. I included the ceiling light in the "light on, light out" sequence with no manifest response, though I gather she registered that it was also "light".

After the summer vacation, she seemingly recognised the office and the toys. Mom wanted to leave, and Lila emitted a complaining "*e,e,e,e,e,e*" sound; I told the mother to stay because Lila and I had not seen each other for some time. I spoke to Lila: she did not look at me. She went to the table, moved a car to and fro but did not put it in her mouth. She pushed the doll's stroller: the more Mom tried to inject enthusiasm, the less Lila pushed it. I told her: "The light is not on", and she looked at me in a low-intensity way, but at some moment we looked into each other's eyes. She ran around, and the mother said "Well, I'm going, call me later" and left. Lila looked at the door unhappily, touched it with both hands and emitted her "*e,e,e,e,e,e*" sound. I waited, she turned to the table, found the rubber doll, went to the bathroom and grabbed the lavabo (wash basin); I put the light on and told her that she seemed to want to bathe the doll (she emitted a more neutral "*e,e,e,e,e*", neither complaint nor joy). I fetched the small chair, she got up on it, opened the tap and sat the doll on the tap. She played, contented. I commented on what she did and on what happened to the doll. After a few minutes, she stretched her hand toward the light interrupter, and I lifted her up so that she was able to reach it, telling her that the light goes on, the light goes out. She smiled. In front of the mirror where we can see each other, at times our gazes coincided. When she looked at herself I touched the mirror saying: "Here is Lila", and she looked at me in the mirror and then again at herself. This, I felt, had a subtle promise of more solid contact. After some time she wanted to get down, which I helped her do. She rambled around, went up and down my chair; she drew the curtain and looked at the balcony, then moved a car, etc. After some 45 minutes (she had a keen sense of time), she went to the door emitting her discomforted "*e,e,e,e,e*"; I told her that we will call Mom because Lila wants to go.

The next month she uttered glued-up syllables: "*tatatataeeeeeeedadadada*". She put toys in my hands or on my leg; when I sat on the floor, she filled me up with all the toys and then threw herself over me, putting her arms around my neck in a strong embrace. I told her "Lila wants Maity [my nickname] to have all the toys, but also Maity to have Lila and thus have everything together"; she smiled, emitting her happy "*e,e,e,e,e*". At this point, in the fourth month of therapy, Lila received her first transference interpretation at a moment in which she came to fill the analyst with all the toys and then put her arms around her neck in a strong embrace, which indicated she was *using the analyst as a 'container'*, that is, that she had spontaneously contacted – however fleetingly – her analyst's affective humanness.

Up to this time she had run on tiptoe over the scrambled toys, but now she sidestepped the toys instead of stepping on them. The light no longer had primacy in her routines, and often she did not mention it; the sequence she repeated, at midsession, was bathing the dolls.

In an April session she took the puppet by the hand; when I mentioned this, she seemed interested but then rapidly shifted and did not repeat it. She used the cooking pots as a telephone. I made "peek-a-boo" with the towel, and she looked at me but did not respond; however, when by chance she passed behind the curtain she did make a "peek-a-boo" gesture. It is noteworthy that she seemed quite deaf, not responding when she was not in the same tune: she only registered what I said when she was already connected with what I mentioned; when not already connected, my voice was felt as a background noise. She vocalised her "*tatataeeeeeeedadada*", with just brief silences. Now she took me more into account: she gave me the puppets and passed me her foods after biting them; at times she did not involve me but, for example, should I get up while she was putting together her puzzles, she looked at me. When going to play in the bathroom, she carried along her little chair.

By mid-month the mother reported that Lila counted up to three. Though she did not respond when I asked her to put away her toys in the box, when I sang "put away, put away" or just did the tune, she did put her things in the box, and while she did, her "*tatataeeeeeeedadada*" took an intonation of "put away, put away". Also, she allowed a sort of salute on entering: being currently interested in puppets, she entered running as usual, picked up a puppet, gave it to me and I put it on: if I (speaking from the puppet) asked her: "Will you give me your hand?", she gave her hand to the puppet, be it woman, tiger or whatever; should I attempt to do this at other times, she did not respond. A game composed of seven fitting bits of wood depicting dress garments was what she spent more time on, up to five minutes in a row; she usually fetched the correct piece but always inverted. I turned it the right way until they fitted, and I told her "Very well", and sometimes she applauded. She kept more silences where she did not emit sounds and was generally quieter; also, she did not cry out or shriek when going up or down the lift (elevator). Kneeling on a chair, she accessed the table and got interested in the markers and pencils. I put out a sheet for her, and she gave me a marker, saying "*eeeeee*". I took off its cap and gave it back to her, showing her the cap while saying "*tapa*" [cap]. She made some lines while still looking at the cap in my hand, and she took it and tried to put it on while I went on: "*tapa, la tapa*"; attempting to repeat this, she uttered something like "*apapa*", her first meaningful vocalised term since uttering "*uz*" [light] six months before. To her mother's surprise and joy, on coming in she asked for the first time ever that I help her to take off her jacket. She now often played with the '*apas*' (the markers and the Playmobil figures, whose hats she put on and removed) and also the painting tubes; also, she made definite – though barely understandable – attempts at counting.

In the next months she increasingly interacted, giving, pointing or showing me various objects: the initiative, with few exceptions, had to be hers, otherwise there was no response. To give some examples: if, on her approaching the lamp, I asked her: "Where is the light?", she readily pointed or looked at the light, because she was already on that track; when she went behind the curtain and I asked: "Where is Lila?", she came out smiling: she sets the agenda and I must accompany her lead. She took a toy, gave it to me babbling like a 1-year-old, and she pushed a car toward me; also, she took some markers (now saying "*apa*", cap), I took off the cap, and she made some lines with it repeating the sequence several times. She would fetch a book, put it on my lap, and I pointed and mentioned some drawings but she did not respond; she just passed the pages rapidly not detaining on any drawing; then she set that book aside and fetched another. She gave me diverse objects, but only in the case of the markers she responded to my interventions, saying "*apa*". There resulted a curious one-way interaction in which she acknowledged my presence and involved me in what she did, but went her own way taking no account of my response or lack of it.

After the winter vacation, nothing had changed; she might as well have been here the day before. As usual I greeted her to no response; she came in running on tiptoe, gave me her coat, saying something that sounded like "take it", went for the books, took one out and went straight for the little table where we looked at books: I told her the table is not there because it is being repaired, and she looked disconcerted. I sat down on a chair; she put the book on my lap and turned the pages haphazardly, and then she paused on some figures, pointing with her finger and attempted pronouncing syllables, sometimes consistently, sometimes not. She brought another book and I named the objects she pointed to; she often pointed to a hand, so I named it, "Hand", and then added "Lila's hand", pointing to her hand; she emitted some sounds similar to a lalling. She pointed to the table games cage, saying "*apa, apa*", which I took as meaning whatever needs being opened; I gave it to her, she opened the Memotest and looked for two or three pairs, and when she found them she hit them against the floor, happily. I commented on this: actions and intentions must come from her, otherwise she did not respond. It came to my mind to pick up the empty juggle cup and drink from it as if it were a glass, which must have been on her track because she laughed and imitated me. Then she took a puppet and gave it to me, took another one, looked inside it, attempted to put it on and passed it to me.

In October, one year after starting treatment, she still did not respond to my greeting; however, she saluted her Mom with her hand when she left, mumbling "Mama": she stared at the door until I closed it, saying that Mom has left and will come back. She ran to the book closet and fetched the witch book, and I told her she liked it very much; she pointed to the witch, the cat, a hat, etc., and I named them. At an image in which the witch falls down the stairs, where I always said "Ay!, the witch fell down", Lila also said "Ay!". Importantly, *I must just mention objects, I must not unfold a narrative, which means nothing to her*; she repeats "door" while the stairs she calls "*ubir*" (*subir*, to go up). If I asked: "Where is the witch?" (or the witch's nose, or the cat), she nearly always pointed to it. A year into treatment, Lila's capacity for attending to verbal symbolization had evolved but was still extremely limited, as shown by the fact that I had just to nominate the sequence of objects she seemed to be showing some interest in. Were I to ask instead "Where is Lila?", she did not point to herself, nor did she react when I named her. She went on with her sequence, taking the doll to the lavatory, getting up on her chair, bathing the doll, sucking her wet hair, always the same routine which I commented on. Then she put a pot to her ear and said "Hello". When I approached she handed me another pot; I told her she wanted us to talk and said "Hello Lila, how are you?", and she responded "Hello, Hello".

After a three-week interruption she smiled and then entered at a slower pace. When Mom left, she stared at the closed door asking "Mom?". She pointed to the game of the Mother Goose and the Memotest, saying "*apa, apa*" (cap). I opened the game and she paused at the figures longer than usual while striving to repeat the names I mentioned. She approached the markers, saying "*apa, apa*", I gave her a sheet of paper, and she gave me the markers one by one for me to uncap, which I did; she made a small line and then gave me another marker, which repeated several times. Then, putting her little finger on the sheet, she said "Dad"; I asked her whether she wants me to draw her dad, and she insisted "Dad". I drew a male face, saying "This is Dad, with short hair, eyes, nose, mouth and ears", and she repeated "Dad"; she put her finger to the side of the drawing saying "Mom". I drew her mother, saying "Lila wants me to draw Mom, with eyes, nose, mouth and long hair"; Lila said "Mom" and then mentioned her brother, which I also drew, as she uncapped several markers. I then asked "And Lila? Should we draw Lila?", but she did not respond. I repeated my question and she got down from the chair, running with a smile to seek the witch's book saying syllables I did not grasp. I told her "Lila does not want me to draw her, she wants to look at the witch's book which she very much likes"; she opened the book and for several minutes pointed to diverse figures, saying their names, and where the witch falls she said "Uyy!". She fetched a small cup from her box, said "Milk", pretended she drank and then gave it to me. I said "Tasty milk" and in turn drank from it. She took out a plate, a fork and bread, stuck the fork on the bread and ate, then she gave me the fork. Time was up, but to my saying that I shall call Mom, she replied "No" and ran to the couch; the mother took her out under protest. In the next session she went back to the table games, the markers and the sheet with the drawings of Dad, Mom and her brother; when I asked whether I should draw Lila, she got down and went to seek the witch's book. Then she went to her box, saw the doll, and took it saying "Girl" and then asked "Baby?". I found it, she grabbed her little chair and we departed for the bathroom, where she soaked her hands and sucked the doll's wet hair. Suddenly she got down, said "Bread", and I told her she was seeking the bread we played with yesterday – it must be in the box. She fetched it as well as a plate and a fork. When told I'll call Mom, she again said "No", and when the mother came, she had to take Lila up in arms, crying and kicking.

Some sessions later, Lila brought a small doll, then sought the "girl" and the "baby". She took a Memotest figure, searched for its pair, and on finding it she joyously banged them on the table; she searched for other figures, and I followed with my comments. When she took a car, I asked "Where is the other car?". She was more connected: if I stopped commenting on what she was doing, she looked at me and waited for me to go on. A few sessions later, commenting upon the witch's book "where is the hat, the cat, etc.", I added "Where is Lila?, and she momentously touched her cheek with her finger, saying "Here", and asked me to include her in the drawing of the family! In the following sessions, she sometimes pointed to the faces in the family drawing, repeating "Dad", "Mom", and her brother's name, badly mispronounced. I said "Yes, do we draw Lila?"; sometimes she said no, and at other times she simply ignored me. As yet she had never said "Yes" or verbally responded to her name, though by that time she was better connected; this had to happen in line with her vein or endeavour: while seemingly understanding most or all that I said, she continued to be deaf to what she wanted to ignore. We approached the year's end and the summer vacation: she still ran around on tiptoe, rarely walked, and her unintelligible monologue displayed no intention that I should grasp it or respond.

After the second summer vacation, some sixteen months into treatment, Lila began at the kindergarten her brother attended; having accompanied Bob and Mom there since early on, she had always wished to stay. Sphincter control was a condition: the mother tried every way to convince her, but to no avail; shortly before the due date to begin, she stopped the nappies (diapers). After a day messing around, Lila controlled herself. The mother did not inform the staff that the girl was in treatment, letting the kindergarten judge. Lila was happy about it: difficulties, mainly that often she did not respond to orders, were kept within limits; in a meeting about problem children, she was not mentioned to be one of them.

On coming back from vacation, coming up in the lift she called my name: "*..aity, ..aity*" [Maity, Maity]; bringing a baby doll, she entered as though no interruption had existed. She had turned 3 years old the day before, but she did not respond to my greeting nor when I asked about her birthday. At a certain moment, when she turned to the "girl" and the "baby", I said to her "This is the girl, and this is the baby. Where is Lila?" and to my surprise she put both palms to her chest and said "Here Lila, here". Her unending monologue became gradually more intelligible, and I was able to pick up more and more words; I asked her about the kindergarten, but she did not respond. She concentrated on the puzzles, which she put together with increasing dexterity, being keen on those depicting dolphins and sharks. Then she fetched the sea animals book. I named new ones, and she repeated their names and proceeded to name their parts ("*e ojo efin*", the eye of the dolphin). Soon after, while putting together the garments puzzle, she mentioned "*apato*" (*zapato*, shoe), and I happened to ask her "Whose shoe is it?" and for the first time she said "*mío*" (mine) clutching her belly. Then she grabbed the dress puzzle, and again I asked and again she responded "Mine". She played more and more with animals, arranging them in families: mothers, sons, babies; she asked me to name things and named things herself, such as "black hair" or "pink hat". Her interest and enthusiasm led me to ask her about emotions: which animal is angry, or happy, or sad, and she readily identified them!

Now nearly two years into treatment, sessions admitted a two-way, to-and-fro dynamics, though she took care to keep up in front. On entering the office, she showed me two "princess" dolls – she is much interested in this theme – saying: "*iá pinzezas, as pinzezas*" ("look at the princesses, the princesses"); finding the small table a bit out of place, she rearranged it and jumped up on her chair before I sat on mine, exclaiming "*te gané*" ("I won"). Opening the four puzzles' case, she took the Memo pieces and enthusiastically put them together precisely; she applauded when she finished and took out another puzzle, the dolphins, chanting "the dolphins jump, the foam, the mother dolphin, the baby dolphin". After completing it, she passed to the other two puzzles, the sharks and the sea horses. She lacked the piece of a shark's tail, searched for it, found it in the case and laughingly said "Here it is".

After finishing the puzzles (which are a main sequence currently), she took out Barbie and Ken (which are at a time mom/princess and dad/prince), two girls and a baby. She conveyed, partly by pointing, partly in her baby talk, that mom had pink earrings, Lila had no earrings, the girl had no earrings: she looked directly at me, and her comments were addressed at me, whereas months before they seemed not to be. Suddenly she took a small pot, put it over her ear, ran to the couch at the other end of the office and said: "*hola aity hola*" ["Hello Maity hello"]; as I did not respond immediately, she came, grabbed another pot and gave it to me, saying "This phone" and ran back to the couch. Again she says "*hola aity*", and I responded: "Hello, Lila, how are you?" and she said: "*bem, etó acá*" ("Well, I am here"); I asked her where she was and she said "*acá, illón*" ("Here on the sofa"). She took a small jar and two little cups, saying "*tomá eche*" ("Drink milk"), and she served both cups and gave me one; she 'drank' and so did I, thanking her; I commented it was tasty and wanted more, and she served me again.

She played for some minutes with the princesses and the girls and then asked for the "*momomono*" [hippopotamus], found it, asked for the baby hippopotamus while I commented she wanted the mother and the baby hippopotamus to be together. She searched, was unable to find it, and when I saw it I gave it to her as I have usually done, but she seemed mildly annoyed and then mixed it in the pile of animals saying: "No, Lila searches". She took it out once again saying, radiantly "*acá tá, acá tá, Lila encontó*" ["Here it is, here it is, Lila found it"]. Minutes later she asked to play ball, which she did with precision; as she stood up with the ball in her hand beside the lamp, she said "the light". Betting on her expanded tolerance for more complex narratives, I said "This light is very important, sometime ago you realised how to turn it on and off and you liked that very much"; she seemed to be attentive and responded "Yes, Lila lights on, off, on, off, now let's play ball". As the session ended, I told Lila "I'm going to call Mom", and she said "No". The mother took her up in arms against some resistance; however, as they entered the lift, Lila said "Bye-bye *aity*" and saluted me by shaking the hand that held the "princesses".

Quite contrarily to what happened initially, Lila's sessions had become lively, and she showed a sense of humor and irony. She used the pronoun "I" as well as her name, "Lila". Affect flowed freely: returning to the office after a two-week break due to a trip by the analyst, she came in radiantly shouting my name and jumped upon me, putting both arms tenderly around my neck in a long hug; from then on, she hugged me when she entered.

Presently, the mother commented on how well she sees Lila doing. At a kindergarten celebration, Lila took part in a dance with ribbons and did it all very well. I commented that she has made much progress, and that I had just been rereading some initial notes, in order to refresh my thinking on how she then was. Recalling her own panic at that time, the mother interrupted, her face in horror: "I will never forget that time!". Both parents commented on new things she named, and the father said:

> She is quite cunning. I ask Lila "who is she?" [referring to the mother] and she responds "the Princess", then I ask "and Bob?" [the brother], she says "the Prince", and then "who am I?": sometimes she responds "the Beast" and escapes running, laughing; at other times she says "the King" and embraces me lovingly.

A playful scene indeed, which evidences Lila's pilgrimage from the wastelands of autistic encapsulation to the emotional greenlands of childhood Oedipal games.

Comments on technique and the 'quality of attention'

It is indeed difficult to describe the unfolding of the process in the treatment of autistic children, especially non-verbal ones. But, having traversed the emotional wastelands of the extended clinical narrative, the reader has contacted the difficulties in attending work with encapsulated mute children, the barrenness of which hits directly on the analyst's identity. Inasmuch as these children reject the analyst's humanness, treating her as inanimate, it is only through an awareness of – and an unflinching effort on the analyst's part to bear – being treated as non-existent, that one can keep the mind attentive to what goes on. That few occurrences come up as comment along the course of the clinical narrative is the effect of a sustained void of ideas, brought about by the bane on the analyst's capacity to think and phantasise while being dealt with as inanimate. A late Meltzer statement in his Barcelona seminars endorses that work with these children "has a clouding effect, one of flattening out one's thoughts, of not leaving any material for thought. Your mind doesn't work, as there is very little material to observe" (Meltzer 1995, pp. 48–49). Winnicott put it poignantly: "Therapeutic work with autistic children is maximally exacting, and constantly makes the worker feel: is this worthwhile?" (1967b, p. 221).

A question now: should the felt demolition of her humanness and of her capacity to think on the side of the analyst count as countertransference? This issue can likely be answered in both ways. It might be theoretically not amiss to hold that the analyst is projectively identified with an inanimate, shut-out mother: in a context of outright reliance on the concepts of projective (or adhesive) identification, it might be a given that the analyst's mental state be called countertransference, as is done by Meltzer et al. (1975) as well as by Alvarez (2010), who gives much emphasis to putting to action countertransference urgency. However, inasmuch as encapsulated autistic states, being asymbolic, display no workable transference, it might be better not to speak of countertransference. This is the stance we opt for on the eminently practical grounds that a workable countertransference is expected to eventually lead to useful interpretations: this is not the case for the 'void countertransference' long signing the 'shut-out' state of the analyst's mind, which must be endured rather than interpreted to the child. Only as the treatment inches along, moving away from the encapsulated state proper (of which a fleeting instance was presented at the fourth month), the analyst comes to be felt by the child as a human being, workable projective identification starts to operate, a transference comes to be established and interpretation is able to take more usual routes.

Much in Kanner's (1943) wake, to Tustin encapsulated autistic children do not relate to people, and at the start of therapy they lack empathy, are bereft of imagination and fantasy, do not relate to the therapist and do not play, all of which are essential for psychoanalytic treatment as usually practiced (1988a, p. 39, 48). As was explained, despite not having a sense of self, their greatest threat is losing their sense of existence, which leads them to construct a protective covering of "me" sensations in order to keep the dreaded "not-me" at bay: as a result, they feel continuous with the unacknowledged outside world in a primitive "identicality". She steadily holds, and we concur, that intrusion by premature interpretation of the transference forestalls progress.

To Tustin (1988a, p. 36), the analyst's 'quality of attention' is at the core of therapeutic success in the treatment of autistic states, stating that whereas she was unable to help recover encapsulated patients she saw at the Clinic, she became able to do so when she started seeing them in her private office, where she felt more at home. As she explains in a final paper, autistic insulation is not absolute:

> Autistic children have a peculiar fringe of awareness of what is going on around them, and at times seem to have a sixth sense about the state of mind of people who are close to them. This is the "chink in their armour" which enables us, by degrees, as they begin to trust us, to show that we understand and can help them with their suffering and with their feelings of helplessness. This will help to break the vicious circle of "repetition compulsion" that has held them in thrall.
> (1994a, p. 124)

Behind their autistic shell, these children are highly vulnerable and hypersensitive: whereupon one should, she avowed, be much firmer with them because they are very frightened and have held themselves together with autistic manoeuvers, which they will not renounce if the therapeutic situation does not hold them firmly; our language, she holds, must be commonsensical, simple and direct (1988a, p. 37). The firmness requested by Tustin stands in contrast with the overriding permissiveness as regards physical contact with the therapist in touching, looking, smelling and tasting that Meltzer et al. (1975, p. 15) advocated, and his co-author Isca Wittenberg (1975, pp. 71–72) gallantly put into action on the assumption that the role assigned to her was that of a mother who was impermeable to the baby's projections – a permissiveness she came to decry.

In line with Tustin's advice that in addressing the autistic child our language must be commonsensical, simple and direct, Anne Alvarez set apart in addressing these children a descriptive level (the 'whatness' of experience), a more complex explanatory level (the 'whyness' of experience) and a more intensified, vitalizing level ('reclamation') that insists on meaning, involving not a 'why', nor even a 'what', but a kind of 'hey' (Alvarez 2012, p. 2).[1] Aiming to further detail Tustin's emphasis on the 'quality of attention' autistic children require, Alvarez's notion of *reclamation* stands, she holds, in contrast to "a more neutral or containing psychoanalytic stance" (2012, p. 1). Reclamation, a notion she came to while treating her hugely passive, ameboid autistic patient Robbie, relies on the idea that mothers must function as alerters, arousers and enliveners of their babies (Alvarez 1992, p. 60). This type of 'cheering up' needs to be distinguished from the kind of manic reassurance or denial of depression, which could encourage the development of a false self. To her – and this fits snugly into what Winnicott deems the area of play – the mother should be able to muster sufficient *aliveness to attract her infant to the real enjoyment of her face and voice* (1992, p. 65, italics original). To Alvarez a core aspect of the analyst's task is to actively anchor the patient's attention to her, to the point of coaxing or begging in order to obtain it, though she admits that "It is not easy to strike a balance between being too intense and therefore intrusive, and being too remote or too weak" (2012, p. 5). Anyhow, an ameboid autistic child, as was Robbie with his sluggishness and passive hooking to his objects, is in many ways at the opposite end from shell-type, encapsulated children such as Lila.

On our side *recognizance* is the main initial aim of technique, because as the autistic child comes to find himself recognised by the analyst, the primal dialogue with its mutual emotional mirroring is reinstated. This raises the need to clarify the distinction between reclamation and recognizance. While reclamation involves an insistence on meaning on the side of the therapist, an intensified level of intervention responding to a countertransference sense of desperate urgency (Alvarez 2010, p. 863), putting the accent on the analyst's active, at times forceful search for contact, recognizance as we understand it highlights *meeting the child half-way on her own track*, which gradually ushers in receptive mirroring as the way to emotional contact. We do not think in terms of enacting a state of mind of desperate urgency: these children's uncanny sensitivity to the analyst's state of mind, on which authors coincide, requires as much of a receptive, tranquil even-minded attention on the analyst's side as is feasible under the circumstances. While as quoted, Alvarez contrasts reclamation to a more neutral or containing psychoanalytic stance, to us the analyst's psychic stance approaches as best as possible the time-tested, benevolently neutral state of mind evincing no anxiety or anger advised by Strachey in his classic paper "The nature of the therapeutic action of psychoanalysis" (1934).

An effective, quite initial instance of recognizance came in the second session with 19-month-old Lila as she was sitting on the analyst's rotating chair, which allowed the analyst to fleetingly catch the girl's attention for the first time: this differed from reclamation in that no pressure was put on Lila to respond. Recognition involved in this instance the analyst's moulding herself to the child's action, and in such sense is at odds with Tustin's emphasis on firmness on the analyst's side. We in no way endorse outright permissiveness, but in fact undue bodily intrusion upon the analyst was not a feature in Lila's treatment, nor with our other children in the autistic spectrum. We found no need to be firmer with these patients: for example, should the moment come in which they ask to take a toy home between sessions, this is usually allowed, just as we do with other children. An even-minded, receptive firmness lodging in the analyst's state of mind has been both requisite and sufficient to sustain proper limits.

Now, a question: can the work of recognizance be considered interpretive? In the widest sense, yes. In the sense in which the "primal dialogue" between baby and mother is mutually interpretative, at the level in which ethologists refer to "mind-reading" (Griffin 1992) as a basic ability of higher mammals: the level at which, as has been amply studied, the vital, primarily non-linguistic baby–mother "primal dialogue" goes on between chimpanzee babies and their mothers, as it does between human babies and their mothers. It is of course far removed from the verbalised intellectual complexities involved in psychoanalytic interpretation in the usual sense, as put by a founding father of Latin American psychoanalysis, Enrique Pichon Rivière: "here, now, toward me as it was elsewhere, in the past, with others" (Ahumada 1997a, p. 145).

In what follows we shall do our best to amplify on the analyst's 'quality of attention' as it unfolded in Lila's treatment, taking support in René Spitz's concept of the 'primal dialogue' (1964), which is missing in autism and needs to be reowned, as well as in Winnicott's notion of maternal "mirroring" (1967a). Additionally, this clinical material illustrates what Justin Call (1980) highlighted about the baby-mother interaction in the early stages: that the infant is the initiator and the primary architect of reciprocity, while the mother (and the analyst) is the follower. Meeting the child's spontaneities halfway gives due place to Winnicott's (1963, p. 181) notion that the object must be felt to be created by the infant in order to be discovered.

The early stages – which lasted, in slowly diminishing fashion, for most of the treatment – were heavy going. I ended up exhausted on being unable to elicit a minimum of interaction, which risked leading me to isolate myself from Lila as she did from me: again and again I had to force myself to keep attentive and try new ways to get in contact. Absence of feedback led me to fly forward into my own thoughts, which was grist for the mill of Lila's non-contact. My attempts at gesturally and verbally 'mirroring' her were akin to trying to walk a narrow path, with Lila constantly escaping to one side or another: in the initial stages she did not look at me, only *through* me, with no lalling, just her "*e,e,e,e,e*" which, though at times expressing feeling states, was mostly a vocalised "autistic shape" (Tustin 1984) rather than an attempt at communicating.

The first sign that Lila's encapsulation was not impenetrable came soon, in the second session: her anguish upon her mother's prompt leaving. My going on my knees moulding to her, picking up the falling car, was the first occasion where she fleetingly detected me and smiled at me. Her "discovery" of the light by accidentally stepping on its interrupter was a turning point, leading to an incipient "moment of contact" with her analyst. Thereafter, for many sessions she established a sequence, when coming into the room, of putting the light on and off: here my "mirroring" comments were "heard" by her and established a connection that had been lacking up to then, evidenced in our laughing and applauding together. These enacted "moments of contact" set the scene for her first vocalised term ever, "*uz*" [light]. As time went on, the initiatives she brought in, which I accompanied, settled into sequences such as going to my empty chair and making it turn, or opening the furniture's doors. A relevant sequence came into play later on, bathing the doll in the lavatory, leading to our first look at each other in the mirror with quite some intensity, as well as to our laughing together whenever the doll would happen to fall head first into the water! Some time later the emotional experience allowed by such fleeting "moments of contact" on my following and accompanying her initiatives, expanded into "moments of sharing", which acknowledged the analyst's responses and participation, such "moments of contact" and "moments of sharing" being steps in the buildup of what Tustin calls a "context of togetherness" (1986, p. 303). Thus Lila accessed an expanding emotional acceptance of her analyst, rescued from the theretofore wholly rejected "not-me"; in other words, she, little by little, entered a "primal dialogue", at first unilaterally directed from her to an analyst who was ready to grasp, hold, and comment upon her flickers of spontaneous initiative: only much later it made place for a two-way dynamics with increased acceptance and receptivity on her side for the analyst's I-ness and initiatives, that is, for the analyst's identity and spontaneity as a separate person. In such a fashion, we surmise, she reworked and made up in the analytic link for the emotional experiences she did not undergo as a baby.

"Moments of contact" and, thereafter, evolving gradually as the process went on, "moments of sharing" allowed the up to then 'not-me' analyst to be *felt* as emotionally receptive and therefore as human, enabling the child to use a mirroring object whereby her own self comes to be acknowledged. The unfolding of this process by which the autistic child's I-ness comes to experience herself in the mirror of the analyst is, as clinically illustrated, labourious indeed. But, when treatment is undertaken early enough by an attentive analyst willing to bear the wear-and-tear, it can, as shown, lead to quite gratifying results in a reasonably short time.

As concerns the capacity for symbolisation, as cited Tustin stresses that shell-type autistic children are initially asymbolic. Lila's capacity for using symbols evolved in a maddeningly slow way, following step by step upon an evolving tolerance for affective contact. As illustrated, a year into treatment she only attended to, grasped and responded to the analyst's pointing and naming the objects Lila encountered in the course of her action sequences. She ignored more complex narratives that meant nothing to her, which shows that she was still far from having a psychic place for grasping elaborate interpretations. As her tolerance of contact increased further, she started naming people, first those closest to her (Dad, Mom, her brother Bob), which the analyst would draw for her; only some time later she came to include other human beings such as "girl" and "baby". Up to then she had never responded to her name, never voiced "I" or her name Lila. It was only after the second summer vacation that she responded to my question "Where is Lila?", putting both palms to her chest while saying "here Lila, here". From then on, having found herself, games and naming evolved at a rather swift pace.

Our technical distances with Meltzer and Alvarez focus on how meaning evolves out of the barrenness and the lack of symbolisation signing the clinical process. Says Meltzer in his Barcelona seminars: "In this kind of work you have to make sure to leave the therapist's imagination free and talk as much as you can" (1995, p. 56); and he adds, upon the conviction that in the face of the emptiness of his fantasy the analyst is to perform the alpha-function for the child:

> This kind of work consists of filling with meaning something that is void of meaning. With children who have not developed and with autistic children you have to do this constantly. While giving them meaning, you are also giving them symbols, until they're capable of forming their own symbols. One supposes that this is what the mother's alpha-function does.
> (p. 58)

Now, this is a far cry from Bion's (1962) notion of alpha-function, as well as from Justin Call's (1980) idea that the baby is the initiator and the prime architect of the primal dialogue. To us, meaning must be sought for and gained from the interaction rather than purveyed: attempts to fill the void of meaning by unending verbalisation backfire, as these are highly intrusive to the child. As regards Alvarez's stance on reclamation, to us a sense of anxious urgency on the side of the analyst is also bound to be felt by the child as intrusive: Lila's avoidance of her distraught anxious mother's approaches during the initial evaluation and sessions serves as an example. We attentively wait and help meaning accrue by 'holding' and amplifying upon the spontaneities the child comes to provide: only quite occasionally, following upon such spontaneities, can a bit of urging fit, as happened after Lila accidentally stepped on the light interrupter.

Our child patients Axel (Chapter 2), who began treatment at age 2 years 9 months, a few months after autistic retraction started, and Lila, starting at

19 months of age, both out-and-out encapsulated children, have been our most surprising patients in that autistic retraction lifted in a short time span, less than one year in the case of Axel and two years in that of Lila. Mainly, they have been quite surprising in that once autistic retraction lifted, a lively child emerged unscathed from beneath. Our other children, starting treatment at a somewhat later age – children who Tustin would deem confusionally entangled rather than encapsulated – were involved in their diverse restitutional pathologies, which took longer treatment spans in order to be resolved. This is a strong motive for the therapeutic "window of opportunity" to be used as early as is feasible.

On saying that in both cases of out-and-out shell-type autistic dynamics a lively child emerged unscathed, we do not purport to make a definitive assessment, just to state what we can observe at this point. Nine months after termination, Axel insisted to his parents that he wanted to see the analyst again, and he came in gleefully. We worked for a number of sessions on some "bad dreams" that were troubling him, and he departed calm and contented. Lila still continues her analysis, but she is thought by everyone (including the analyst and the other children) to be presently a child like any other. We are aware though that a definitive evaluation of the results obtained must wait until they traverse the turmoil of adolescence and arrive at the tasks of young adulthood.

A brief comment on parent work, that analysts such as Mahler and recently Angela Joyce deem "a *sine qua non* with the individual treatment of a young child" (2010, p. 176). This is not so for us, and was not so for Tustin; we see the parents during the initial evaluation and thereafter occasionally: once or twice yearly, and whenever difficulties arise or in case they ask for an interview, and for final interviews when the end of treatment is outlined. This is how we usually work with children; no changes were incorporated for treating autistic ones. Work with the autistic child is maximally demanding; attending to both child and parents is to be at the crossfire of two conflicted scenes, which would go against the privacy of the 'quality of attention' on which, we agree with Tustin, the evolution of the analytic process depends. This caveat does not apply to parent work done by another therapist, but a need for this did not arise in our cases. So in our set-up, work with the parents has not been part of the treatment proper, which relies on bearing the brunt of the refusals, the anxieties and the intimacies of the psychoanalytic interaction. In our experience, reawakening of the primal dialogue in session translates seamlessly to the family ambience; we can surmise the parents have been relieved that the analyst spared them the wear and tear, and they have certainly been grateful for being returned a child they can love and live with.

Emphasis on the central role played by the reawakening of the primal dialogue, that at some point had been interrupted and is in need of being reinstated, does not mean that we put blame on the parents. In the wake of Bettelheim's "refrigerator mothers", psychoanalysts are often accused of putting the blame on parents: in our cases, parents have certainly been "good enough" parents, able and eager to accompany, receive and enjoy their children's progress as it came about. None of our mothers can be described as cold; also, no child showed an initially observable non-response, which might be tagged as innate. Why, then, the upsurge of autistic spectrum disturbances? As shall be taken up in Chapter 8, Spitz had warned in 1964 about alarming changes in child rearing. In media culture, the privacy of the baby–mother link is, as happens with privacy generally, under multifarious impingement; currently many, if not most, mothers interrupt nursing their babies in order to return to work. That little span is allowed to "primary maternal preoccupation" does not help babies!

Note

1 Precedence of the 'whats' over the 'whys' harks back to Aristotle's five questions guiding enquiry: 'what', 'how', 'where', 'when', and 'why'. While the first four questions indicate successive descriptive frames, 'why' attempts a conjectural causal level. Precedence of the 'whats' over the 'whys' regularly occurs when children learn to speak, and in chimpanzee babies learning from their mothers the ASD gesture language used by deaf-mute children (Fouts 1997; see Ahumada 2006). Some measure of descriptive grasp, verbalised or not, is requisite in order to attain the level of causal conjecture.

Chapter 3

Treating encapsulated autism soon after trauma: Axel

Axel came to consultation aged 2 years 9 months. He was born of dedicated young parents working abroad, up in a mountain European village; they described his first year as "normal", responding well to stimuli. A sister was born, and the mother did not note anything unbecoming, but the next winter, at which time she felt "lonely in that frozen world", she noticed that Axel retracted, did not respond and avoided her gaze; she acknowledged having felt badly depressed when Axel's sister M. was born. After inconclusive consultations, they returned home, where both parents have extended families – a process that took months. The mother said Axel "has strange behaviours, different from his cousins; he is nearly mute, is always on the move, coming and going, his sister is already more mature than he is"; he was still in diapers.

The mother stayed at the diagnostic interviews. Axel came in running, did not look at me (LBA) or respond to my greeting. He stepped with no seeming register on toys lying on the floor, circled around the consulting room and hit the bathroom door delving to open it; he smiled with a void smile. The mother tried to interest him in some toys, to no avail. He pointed at the games up on the table, and I gave him a Memotest having chips with drawings on them. He mentioned some: "girl", "car", "cat", and the mother insisted in correcting how he pronounced. Finding two alike chips, he hit them one against the other, and I think he recognised them as equal because he briefly seemed to seek akin ones. Then he resumed running, smiling as usual, and at times he ran on tiptoe; he stepped on the Memotest cage, so the mother reprimanded him for this. The next diagnostic interviews went much the same; the mother intervened, trying to lead him to perform better. As summer vacations were upon us, we arranged to start treatment thereafter.

The initial sessions in his twice-weekly schedule were mostly business as usual; on entering, he glanced at me and I seemed to intuit that he recognised me. In the second session he pointed at the Memotest. I gave it to him, and he seemed glad to see the chips, mentioning some; he pronounced better and had a few new words, and at times he sought the two equal chips. My interventions were limited to mentioning what he did. After a month and a half, he brought a quite simple, sizable red rocket, keeping it under his armpit for the whole hour. In the meantime he started kindergarten, being assigned a special teacher; he likes to be with the kids but – according to his mother – bothers them because he copies them or walks behind them quite close, nearly touching. As time went by, I noted that he ran less and spent a bit more time with each thing, especially the Memotest. He had never sought his playbox, so I displayed its contents, giving their names; sometimes he took up one, repeated its name and then left it. In the fourth month of treatment, he noticed a big red marker that was upon the table from the start, took it and showed it to me enthusiastically, saying something I didn't grasp. I told him he liked the red marker, he gave it to me, I took it, got its cap off and drew some lines on a white office wall that serves as a drawing board. Axel took the marker and drew more lines, repeating what he had said before; then he ran, marker in hand, for the rest of the session. In the next session, he fetched the red marker; I uncapped it while telling him what he did, he drew some lines and then resumed his usual activities, marker in hand. This continued for some three or four sessions, and then I recalled – upon the similarity in colour – the rocket brought a couple of months before. When he again took the marker, I told him that it seemed to me he much liked the red marker because it resembles his red rocket; this led nowhere, but in the next session I repeated this while drawing a very simple rocket drawing with another red marker. Axel gladly pointed to it, repeating the syllables uttered in relation to the red lines, which now I grasped as "rocket". Soon after, in an interview with the parents, I asked about the "rocket". They responded it is Axel's favourite toy, but it then came out that he does not play with it, he just carries it around (which makes me recall his carrying about the red marker in the session); he uses it on going to sleep – "hard and big as it is" says the mother – and also when he is scolded. He had it from age one year and a half on, but his "using" it came about later, before returning to Buenos Aires.

From the time "rocket" came about, ushered in by the marker's colour, the vertigo of the sessions lessened; there is no play, but his movements are slower and at times he stops for a few moments in whatever he does: moving cars, kicking the ball, looking for Memotest pairs. Sometimes he gets behind the curtain: once I told him "Alex is behind the curtain, coo-coo Alex", and now he repeats it, getting behind, coming out a bit, till I tell him "coo-coo", then he hides laughing. This came to me spontaneously such as happens with a baby, and perhaps his response points to past experiences with his mother in their good, initial bond.

In the next month he grabs the red marker each time he comes into session, and sometimes instead of drawing lines he traces circles; at times he gives me the marker and I draw a quite simple "rocket". When the marker gets spent, he hits the wall with its point, insists, shakes it, insists again with a serious face, then throws it away. I told him he got angry because the marker does not work and we cannot have "rocket" with us. There is intense muscle discharge, up and down the couch. In the following session he tries to draw lines, but only a pale pink line results: he throws the marker away and throws himself on the floor on his belly, his face down and his hands beside his eyes. I tell him that "rocket" is very important and now that he cannot draw it, he is sad and angry. He seems to be listening, at least he keeps there quietly. I tell him "rocket accompanied you while Mom took care of M. and you were feeling alone, just as you feel now"; it seemed relevant to mention sadness, which he had felt as collapse. I do have an extra marker, and I doubted whether to give it to him or not; despite my feelings, I decided to wait an extra session. I repeated what I had said using different turns of phrase, and after some time he sits, in a sad mood; I don't want to overcome him, but he seems more receptive.

On entering the next session, he seeks the spent marker, attempts to draw with no success, hits the wall with its point harder and harder, quite angry, saying "I want rocket". He throws the marker and throws himself on the floor. I tell him "Axel got angry but I think you are also sad, you love rocket, and as I think it is very important I brought you a new marker". He raises his head, sees the marker I offer him, his face lights up, and he takes it and draws big red circles. Then he gives it to me, asking "draw Lulu" (the feminine person in "rocket"). I draw a figure inside the circle and Axel starts jumping, saying "Lulu there, Lulu there"; he grabs the red marker and runs around, going up and down the couch. Minutes later he calmed; after I mentioned what it meant for him having "rocket" again, be it as a drawing, so that he can do those other things the real "rocket" accompanied him to when mother was busy doing other things, he seeks the Memotest figures, looks for couples, nominates them, and others he has them walk, as do the cat and the dog. Then he plays with the cars, keeping the marker in one hand. The mother comes to seek him, and he goes to the lift grabbing the marker; the mother tells him to leave the marker at the office, and Axel looks at her, surprised at his having the marker; he doubts but upon mother's insistence he gives it to me. I tell him I'll take good care of it till he comes back.

After the three-week winter vacation, on coming in he looks at me, smiling. He goes straight for the marker, and the session follows akin lines. In the next session he for the first time draws lines not only on the wall but also on a paper; he gives me the marker, and I draw on the paper just as I had drawn on the wall. I tell him that now that we have "rocket" on paper we can keep it, we don't need to erase it; when he goes out I offer him a folder to keep it in. (I used to erase the drawings on the wall, only then I realised what happened to Axel as concerns his rocket's disappearance and his dire *need* to re-draw it in each session.) Presently he consistently looks and smiles at me on entering, and he sketches a hand salute on leaving.

By that time, at age 3 years and 6 months, a school report announced advances in all areas, which led his enchanted parents to vouch for less frequent sessions! However, I pointed out that (a) he lacked an ability for reflection, especially as concerns emotions; (b) there was no proper play, just motricity: moving, pushing or pulling his toys; (c) his "best friend" at kindergarten, who wanted to monopolise him, was a problem child (he was later diagnosed with Asperger's).

He brings in two puppets from the rocket's crew, asks me to draw, besides Lulu, one having glasses; he draws circles on the wall, mentions "propellers" and something else which I understand as meaning a sort of turbine having "rocket" on top. He is always asking me to put in personages. I'd take the occasions to ask on the emotional, human aspects of these personages, whether I should draw their face as happy, sad or angry: he would always respond "happy". If I asked though "how does Axel feel?" he did not answer, and in case I mentioned several possibilities he repeated the last mentioned; importantly, he seems unable to identify his moods, while personages must always be "happy". Little by little, affective shadings enter his games: a car is sad because it lost a race, a lion is angry and must be covered with cloth so that he does not bite. For the first time, he mentions his sister.

Initially, all was a haphazard mess, aimlessly running, jumping, moving, picking up objects or verbalizing; as the year goes by, his drawings of "rocket" get better defined, and the same with what concerns himself. "Rocket" was our initial point of contact as well as his first intentionally defined object, sustained along the process. Now at times a game goes on with the ball, there is his hiding game behind the curtain, and his taking up a toy based on a decision rather than on being in the way. Whenever able, I strived to bring in the diverse emotions and the ability to be sad. He started saying "Axel is glad" with a somewhat forced smile, and we assisted to a growing complexity of Playmobil games with animals and puppets. In some sessions "rocket" did not come up. He puts two cups upon the table for us to take tea, then seeks cups for two puppets, a prince and princess who are invited; in another session we must feed the animals. Cars must load up fuel, and we assist to an upsurge of family relationships among animals and puppets. His vocabulary has expanded mightily in the last months while impulsivity has lessened. Sometime later, he drew up a rocket "having many wheels".

We arrive to the year's end, and he has a good report from kindergarten, so the parents are satisfied and eager to end treatment. Anyhow, I ask to meet Axel after the summer. He comes twice then, and he's happy to come; he asks me to play with him with the animals, and he builds up families with them, requesting me "to handle the moms" walking with the children; there is also a father around. Then we play with the cars, and I must handle the gas station where the cars come for fuel. He draws up "rocket", asks me for help in cutting it out, and then keeps it in his folder. At the parents' request we finish treatment: to my eyes such ending was premature, but the fact remains that at that time Axel was no longer autistic. This is shown at the end of the year when, at his prompting, the parents brought him to see me: he is a lively boy who plays enthusiastically in his interview. As mentioned in Chapter 1, he came in gleefully, we worked for a number of sessions on some "bad dreams" and he took off calm and contented. To his teacher "there was a breach with the other children: now he is a child like any other".

Let's stop at this point. This clinical case is at the opposite pole from Bettelheim's severest, long-drawn cases requiring full-time institutional treatment for many years. Axel's is a fresh case starting treatment at a quite early age, only a few months after the clinical picture began: twice-weekly sessions sufficed to solve the autistic disconnection within a year of treatment. Here psychoanalytic treatment of autism potentiates its "window of opportunity". Meltzer and Tustin assert that treatment should start before age 7; this case, as well as others, evince that the earlier, so much the better.

How to enquire a bit further into the dynamics of the cure? As mentioned, Tustin gives central place to "the quality of attention" in repairing the disconnection of affective contact: in Axel's treatment we find that it was the analyst's intuiting, recalling and mentioning "rocket" – based on the held marker's redness – that allowed Alex to traverse his autistic disconnection, opening the way to her being felt by Alex as "human". In such manner the "primal dialogue" (Spitz 1964, p. 773) – that is, the mutually-mirroring, affect-driven action-dialogue between baby and mother, starting at birth if not before, and long antedating verbal dialogue proper – was reinstated. Despite its being hard and big, as his mother had noted, his "rocket" fulfilled for Axel the function and value of a transitional object, as is shown by the fact that it often accompanied him, consoled him when he was scolded and accompanied him on going to sleep. It can be surmised that on the analyst's intuiting his link to "rocket" by way of the red marker he held in hand, Alex felt affectively recognised by the analyst, which in turn made him able to acknowledge the analyst as animate, thereby re-starting in session the affectively meaningful "primal dialogue" he had become disconnected from.

Chapter 4

From mimesis to agency
Clinical steps in Sophia's work of psychic two-ness

Psychoanalysis was built on findings from the study of adult patients: reconstruction of the early stages grounded the model of neuroses. Child analysis came later, prompted by Ferenczi urging Melanie Klein to enquire directly into the infant mind. Its findings modified the insights gained from the neuroses: mainly, an in-depth understanding of the pre-Oedipal stages, symbol-formation and psychic evolution.

The neuroses were, then, our privileged field; psychoses were collateral while autism came later. In the line of thought emerging from "Introjection and transference" (Ferenczi 1909), the primal object-baby unity suffers a trauma of rupture conceptualised in terms of a bipersonal psychology. A year later, in the "Leonardo" (1910) paper, Freud introduced narcissistic identification on a bipersonal model, where the rupture of what he calls the "highest erotic bliss", the traumatic loss in weaning of the fusional oral link with the mother, leads to an alteration of the early ego (Ahumada 1990); here, he is close to the Budapest metapsychology, which concerns an initial fusion of baby and mother and the ego rupture on weaning. Thus, nearly a century ago, there emerged a nodal point in shaping the reality principle, which, under different names, presided over later conceptual developments: primary identification (Freud), symbiosis (M. Mahler), dual unity (I. Hermann, M. Little) and archaic reality-less egotistic love (Alice Balint), while the rupture phenomena were conceptualised as weaning (Freud, Abraham, Melanie Klein), autotomy (Ferenczi) and psychological birth of the human infant (Mahler). Based on Imre Hermann, Frances Tustin (1981) again took that Ferenczian line, holding that, to the baby, *his body flows into the mother*: awareness of bodily separateness institutes a psychic catastrophe, a crisis of two-ness anteceding psychic birth and the Oedipus complex. The everyday form of the crisis of two-ness is that sempiternal hideout of the Furies, the explosive eruption of the tantrum or the caprice, leading to rage – narcissistic rage, in Kohut's (1971) terms – or trauma. Discussing his 18-month-old grandson's game of the bobbin in 1920, Freud provided a long-standing model on how the baby works through in play his early separation anxieties in the road to symbol-formation. But for Balint (1968), Freud's line of "primary love" coexists with two other stances on psychic origins, namely, primary autoeroticism and primary narcissism, which dominate his theoretical writings.

Psychic evolution involves, in the Budapest metapsychology, a process of differentiation starting from an initial symbiotic unity; Ferenczi (1932) also thought out the basic dynamics of autism, *autotomy*. Leaning on Mahler, Searles (1965) developed his ideas on the processes of symbiotisation and individuation in the psychotherapy of schizophrenia, while Bleger (1967) and Sydney Klein (1980) reworked, in terms of autism and symbiosis, their clinical findings in neurotic patients.

The case we present expands on the working-through of primary loss and emotional (and intellectual) differentiation evolving conceptually in Tustin's work; mainly her understanding of the attainment of psychic two-ness as essential for psychic growth. We shall also take recourse to Eugenio Gaddini's ideas on the 'precursor object', the object of primary identification sustaining the baby's imageless illusion that the baby is the mother and the mother is the baby, at a stage with no differentiation of outside and inside (R. Gaddini 1995, p. 219). Imitation belongs at that level: here, failure involves the agonies of loss of the self. But, instead of limiting the precursor object to the thumb or the pacifier in an initial stage where the union of mouth and nipple abolishes separateness, we centre it on the maternal object as psychic breast at the level of the gaze. Such dynamic operates as precursor object beyond the early stages; our clinical material illustrates the intense corporeity of psychic symbiotisation and differentiation.

We will clinically approach the dynamics of autism in a girl age 3 years 10 months who is regarded by her family, quite acceptingly, as being genetically dumb. The initial contact was done by the grandmother because, while the girl's mother had in her youth tested at an IQ of 70, which supposedly backed a genetic condition, something might perhaps be done psychically. As her problems impinged on knowledge acquisition, we shall call her Sophia.

The initial interviews

The mother took care of the house and children, and the father was an employed professional. Sophia's feeding, motor development, sphincter control, and sleep patterns seemed adequate, while her language was limited (she missed 'lalling' and 'babbling'). She did not recognise colours, was unable to count, had no initiatives and was incapable of choosing between proposals: she responded "I don't know" as a cliché. The parents pointed out that "she's very close to her elder brother Paul [aged 7]; they adore each other and they never fight". My hunch (LBA) was that the elder brother was her translator and interpreter of the world. To give an example, when there was a choice of dishes, Sophia did not voice what she wanted; at some point the elder brother conveyed "her" wishes, she lighted up and repeated what he announced! She also got on well with her 18-month-old brother. She had had no problems adapting in a preschool for 3-year-olds: to the teacher, Sophia "is lovely, she is never a bother", and she follows another girl in all activities; however, a written report remarked that she did not act on her own or attain basic goals. Her parents then attempted to teach her using didactic toys and games, but in vain: she could not resolve games meant for 18-month-olds. To the parents, Sophia is a "dummy".

The mother added that she has overprotected her: she spoon-fed her so that she would not get dirty, and now she must continue to do so or Sophia will not eat. The poignant issue of maternal mind-blindness comes up in her spontaneous remark that she did not talk (or sing) to Sophia when she was a baby "because, anyhow, they do not understand".

I decided to evaluate Sophia, a smallish, likable girl who had no trouble staying with me – as often happens with autistic patients. She was kind of absent, and did not seem to register her environment very much. However, and importantly, at times her face would brighten and her gaze sought mine expecting me to take initiatives; when I did not, her gaze veiled and she took on a devitalised look.

Her vocabulary was limited: I counted some 20 to 25 words, all badly pronounced except mum, dad, water and a few others. She did not invent words; I realised that she just said the last one or two syllables of any given word, so that it was not difficult to grasp what she said. However, when I did not understand, she repeated only once; had I not grasped then what she had said, I had to wait until I caught it in another context: Sophia reacted to insistence with mutism and retraction but no open anger.

Play was poor and stereotyped: she did not attribute names or roles; there was no agenda and no process. For example, she would put some dolls or animals arbitrarily beside each other; feed them "*opa*" (*sopa*, [soup]) one after the other and then serially clean their mouths from first to last with a napkin, which she carefully folded and put away, and would thereafter put them all in the toybox. She did not ask me to participate. At other times she undressed them all and had them pee; her difficulties flared up when trying to dress them again, despite an apt ability of movement: she could not put on a dress right side up; she tried to pull the pants up over the arms, or she put the legs in the pants wrongly. Spatial organisation was a big theme.

In the diagnostic interviews she attempted to cut paper: she held the scissors with both hands leaving none to hold the paper with, whereby it ran off and she could not cut it. She then requested, by gestures and some words, that I cut it for her, which I did silently with no comments or indications: she stared, intensely attentive to how I held the scissors, and then asked me for them. Though she is left-handed while I am right-handed, she took correctly both scissors and paper, cutting it now with no trouble. Despite her ceaseless cliché, "I don't know", this incident led me to trust that Sophia would eventually be able to know.

After the diagnostic study, I suggested that, as we might be dealing with a psychogenic entity, it was best to start treatment because in such a case each month lost was an opportunity missed. Treatment would show whether what went on was indeed psychogenic and in principle modifiable, or an organic malady. On this understanding, twice-weekly treatment was started. After the first summer holidays, based on her progress, the parents agreed to a third weekly session.

Some points on her evolution in the first 18 months of treatment

Often in the initial sessions Sophia did not utter a word: she took some element from her toybox, then another, often waiting for me to take initiative; at other times she was distracted with no objectives of her own. To questions she responded immediately "I don't know", giving herself no chance to listen and grasp what was being said. On taking up some puppet, she would angrily make it shout "hello" and, if I responded or asked a question, an "I don't know" followed on the spot. Then she would leave the puppet, developing neither sequences nor organised play.

Shortly thereafter, she came to a session accompanied by her older brother. Sophia insisted that "*Alito*" (Paul) come into session, although she had never requested that her mother do so. I decided to accept. Paul sat at the table and started drawing. Sophia sat beside him, adoringly. What followed was a totally synchronised scene: while Paul talked, Sophia would repeat, as if an echo, the last syllables. She did not seem to get the meaning; she was only intent on repeating. And, when Sophia said something, Paul engaged in simultaneous translation. When Paul silently drew, Sophia followed suit, repeating each line, but her drawing was totally incoherent.

With few variants, repetitive games and drawings went on and on in the first months: she would repeat a drawing of a child while saying "*aeza, ojo, oca, a ena, ota ena*" (head, eye, mouth, a leg, another leg). The result at times approached a human figure, while at other times the elements were scattered throughout the sheet. The impression was not of a genuine attempt to draw on her own, but to repeat mechanically something "learned": the confirmation, I think, of such drawing being a sort of perseveration came about when she said that she was going to draw a house, and then did exactly the same drawing that she had done when drawing a child: eyes, mouth and nose included.

After the first three months, the weight of the handling of the gaze became evident: Sophia constantly looked at my eyes for approval, and her vitality, or conversely her crumbling down, were the responses to the visual interchanges. She expressed this through her puppets in a session at the time when she was already playing with them to some extent; she took out the tiger, who saluted me in a friendly way – as happened from now on – and then put him to rest because "*a aza ele, a omi*" [*la panza duele, a dormir*; belly hurts, go to sleep]. She repeated the sequence exactly with a lady puppet and a fairy. Then she took one who might be an old man or a witch and, holding it in front of her face, she said, "*no me mía, miáme, miáme*" [It does not look at me, look at me, look at me]. Then in her first fit of rage in a session, she threw the puppet forcefully to the floor and went angrily to a corner, crossing her arms. She came back and, picking it up, again put it in front of herself, shouting that it should look at her, then again threw it to the floor with all her might and went for a long while to the corner. Thereafter, she took the tiger, the lady and the fairy, saying that they were her friends, they all look at her. In the meantime, she kicked the old man/witch puppet saying, "He's bad, he does not want to look at me, does not look at me, bad bad". Thus, she displayed toward her puppet a fit of fury that rescued her from crumbling down (later on, after she left, I noticed that the old man/witch's eyes were, in fact, almost closed).

Sometime later, she stopped drawing repetitive "copy" figures and started making colour stains and outlining her own hands; after that she came back to drawing human figures, now, I surmise, more on a personal initiative as she incorporated apt elements distributed more logically. On referring to numbers, she would always raise three fingers (from the time she was aged three), naming indistinctly "*osho, uno, tes*" [eight, one, three] or whatever. During these first months, it showed that her mispronunciation had nothing to do with phonetic problems, that she aptly pronounced many words she learned at the consulting office. That this happened also when these were more difficult to pronounce comes out better in the original Spanish:

P: "*A aca, ota aca*" [*una vaca, otra vaca*: a cow, another cow].
A: "Yes, this is a cow, but this is the son of the cow, the calf [ternero]."
P: "*A aca, un ternero*" [a cow, a calf].

A month later she brought further clues of an incipient distinction of levels and hints of fantasy. On coming into session she noticed that her toybox was slightly open. For the first time she commented on this and then closed it down. I told her that she always kept the dolls closed down and I wondered why that was. She tried to open the toybox, then said that she could not. I did not offer help, and she opened it herself. She took out all the dolls (Ken, Barbie and the two babies), undressed them and set them belly down on my thighs. She shouted at them that they must sleep; she hit them and she got angry: "*A omí, a omí*" [*a dormir, a dormir*; go to sleep, go to sleep]. She hit them with a tray, saying that they must sleep, that they misbehave by not sleeping: I told her that she seemed to want to be alone with me, with no mom, no dad, no daughter, no other daughter (that's how she refers to them). She agreed. She put the tray on top of the dolls and hit on it, shouting "*A omí, a omí*", and got angrier and angrier; she threw them into the toybox, wanting to close the lock, which got stuck, and raged against it. She managed to close it, then got the toybox to the farthest corner and shouted to it to stay there. She came back relaxed. I told her that, now that all those people are not here, now that she is alone with me, all is well. She nodded her agreement and then fetched her markers. She "wrote" *dad*. Inadvertently she painted her own finger, and she fearfully said she had got it dirty. I calmly replied "yes . . . a painted finger". After looking at it with some surprise, she painted her fingers and palms, and asked me to paint Paul on one palm and Santiago on the other. Then she went to wash them. Thereafter, she looked for more markers and found a pack of cards. She volunteered that we were to play and distributed some six or seven cards to each of us. With the airs of a seasoned player, she told me to start. I placed an uncovered card on the table and she placed another; I placed another one and she did the same. This went on until the cards ran out. I asked who had won and she said "I won". I asked her why. With a mischievous grin, she responded "I don't know, I don't know how the game is", and on this she laughed.

What first appeared as a mirror imitation of a game of cards with no attempt to invent a game or inquire on it gave way to some acknowledgment of the existence of rules external to her. A distinction of levels is here adumbrated. Such initial glimmers of a game or a fantasy came to nothing unless I took up the game or made up some proposal, in which case she accepted it with no conditions.

A session at five months of treatment further illustrates the dynamics of the gaze, the importance of which had been hinted at on the occasion of the puppets looking and not looking at her, and now came roundly to the fore in analytic work. She came to the session in a happy mood. I greeted her and asked her how she was. For the first time, she responded "*Bem*" [Well]. We were both sitting on our identical small chairs, with the table between us as usual. She looked at me expectantly with bright eyes. I realised that she took my exact posture, just as in a mirror image: I had my right elbow on the table, with my forearm upright and my chin on my hand; I noted how she was copying my posture when she slightly corrected how she supported her chin on her hand. I was waiting and so was she. After some moments, I changed my posture slightly. Sophia seemed to lose her support, her gaze became veiled, and without changing posture she started collapsing. She looked at the floor and then slowly started looking at me again, this time with dull eyes. My vivid countertransference image at this point was that Sophia was my marionette held by strings to my eyes, utterly dependent for her existence on being held alive by my gaze. I felt the need to modulate this tension, asking "But what are we doing?". Her eyes brightened a bit, and she seemed to wait for some proposal on my side. As I did not forward it, her gaze started again roaming across the floor. I waited, as this seemed to be the only way to make space for her to have initiatives on her own. We both seemed to feel the tension in the air. After three or four minutes she looked at me, and I smiled but did not speak. Her gaze went slowly over my face and then over my hands. I told her that it seemed to me that Sophia cannot think of what to do because she gets afraid to do so, and thus has to wait for me to tell her. Her face glowed; she stood up and approached her case, saying "*vo a sacá íere*" [I am going to take the puppet out]. She took the fairy out and she approached with a smile, saying "hello". I responded to her by addressing the puppet: "Hello. What are you doing?". She answered "I don't know". I asked her for her name and she said "Lola". For the first time she was giving a name: Lola, that of the preschool friend she followed everywhere. I asked her what she was going to do, and she said, "*vo a bujá*" [I am going to draw)]; she was still talking as if she were the puppet.

Sophia then sat the puppet on the table, took a sheet and a blue pencil, and drew a human figure while enumerating what she did, apparently speaking for herself rather than on behalf of the puppet: "*Vo a bujá a Lola, a abeza, a mano, a pé, a naí*" [drawing Lola, the head, the hand, the foot, the nose]. I told her that it seemed that Lola had decided to draw and now Sophia is drawing also. She looked at me in the eyes, her hand holding the pencil in suspense; she seemed to be reflecting on what I'd said. She drew some hair around the head, said "It's Mum", looked at it silently for some moments, then said, "It's Iago" (Santiago, the younger brother). She drew his hair more and more forcibly. She made scratches and then scratched his face, grabbed the pencil with her whole hand and stuck it in the paper, breaking the pencil's point. I told her that she had drawn Mum, then Santiago, and then she had grown angry with Santiago, maybe because she wanted to be Mum's little baby. She nodded in agreement and ripped the sheet to pieces, drawing in each little piece a small Santiago, which she then cut to bits. I told her that she may be afraid that mom might have more babies. She put the paper bits together, got out of her chair and threw them into the wastepaper basket, picked up each little piece from the floor until they were all in there, and then looked at me with a triumphant air.

I told her – putting the accent in the term "drawn" – that she feels she can throw those little *drawn* Santiagos into the bin. She then got up from the chair, chose two big markers of different colours, saying she was going to use those – one was orange; she said she didn't know what colour it was but it was the same as the scissors – and she asked me, "*É oló é?*" (What colour is it?). I told her "orange". She said, "*Y ete é azul*" [and this is blue], which was right. She drew a sun, then another, which she kept in her folder. On another sheet she drew Santiago again, then asked me to draw her mother, which I did. She again drew a Santiago, a very small one. She got a small piece of Scotch tape and asked me, "How does it go?", referring to which side the glue was on. I told her that I did not know, as I was not touching it. She looked at me fixedly, bewildered at my lack of response. I told her, "You seem to be afraid at finding out for yourself how it goes". She kept on looking fixedly at my eyes seeking support, and at the same time she touched the tape with her fingers, without looking at it. There was strong tension. Finally, she looked at the piece of tape stuck on her fingers. She unstuck it, turned it around and stuck it over the small drawing of Santiago, saying softly, "*Así va*" [thus it goes]. She cut another little piece, touched it on both sides, looked at me, all of this done in a slow and deliberate pace, and said finally, "*Así va*"; the sequence was repeated several times at an increasingly faster pace, and she laughed. I told her she was glad at having been able to realise by herself how it goes. She did not tear to pieces this drawing of her brother "immobilised" by the Scotch tape; rather, she kept it in her folder.

After seven months in treatment, devitalisation and crumbling had lessened and, importantly, it was possible to engage in dialogue with Sophia; she still pronounced badly, but her vocabulary had expanded hugely. Furthermore, after the summer holidays her parents were worried because she had started to fight with her elder brother; in what seemed to have been her first personal stands, she was against him all the time; in fact, she often took misguided stances in the urge to cross him.

A communal scene after the holidays

Sophia now attended the preschool for 4-year-olds, and she was to be evaluated later to discern whether she was ready for the kindergarten course. On coming in she seemed glad. She took some pillows, and leaned them against the desk legs, thus constructing a house. She got inside the house she had built, said that we must sleep, and asked me to lie down, out in front of the "house's door" with my belly drawn against it, so I did. Sophia had done this once before, and I had said then that in this way she felt safe like a baby in the mother's belly, and we rested in silence for some time. Seen retrospectively, we would gather that this scene, where the house she rests in is a direct continuation of my belly, seems to be a re-enactment experience in the line of what Tustin (1986, p. 210) called a womb-like communal situation. Then she got out, saying she was going to draw.

She took a sheet and said she was going to draw me: "*Eta o vos*" [this is you]. She wrote my "name" up in the sheet and hers on a side. She said she was drawing my *belly*, hands and hair. She took another sheet and drew Santiago; of what looked like a big open mouth she said, "*Una ota naí*" [another nose]. She turned the sheet over and copied the outline of her hand, and she asked me to put my hand down as well and copied its outline, repeating these actions many times. She then took the green marker, made a line and said, it's "*Iago*" and started sticking her marker in it: "*Andate, andate, no queo a Iago*" [Go off, go off, I don't want Iago] – then angrily threw the sheet to the floor. She brought in the tempera paints and diligently painted her own finger. She said it was all green now, then she painted a nail black and asked me which colour it was. I said, "Perhaps you know what colour it is, but knowing is something you leave to others". She looked at me mischievously and said "Yes". Now she painted all her fingers until she got out of paint and stuck them on the sheet. Only when the paint became dry and cracked did she go to the lavatory for washing.

When she came back, she sat on the couch and told me to sit beside her. As she had been unwell and had not gone to the preschool for the last few days, it occurred to me to ask her whether she had gone today. Automatically, as she used to, she responded "I don't know" and started doing stunts on the couch, with her head resting on it and her legs up on the wall.

A: It's easy for you to answer 'I do not know', but if you try to think perhaps you may know and be able to reply.
P: (after continuing with her stunts) But I don't want to think. [After a silence she came to sit beside me] *No é, ecí vo, é e no ero pensá* [I don't know, you say it, I don't want to think].

She then suggested that we play a game where I was the mother and she was my 2-year-old daughter.

A: If I am your mother, I must think for you.
P: (laughing) *Ale, uamos* [Come on, let's play].

She got down to the floor to make herself small, pretended that she was weeping and touched my knee, asking,

P: *Eche, eche* [Milk, milk].
A: You want me to be your mother who knows where the milk is and how to give it to you, while you are a 2-year-old baby that does not want to think.

She went on crying and asking for milk. I got her a cup from her toybox. She "drank" all the milk, got up and got me by the hand.

P: *Aoa amo a paseá* [Now we go for a walk].
A: Now this baby is bigger and knows how to ask to go for a walk.

In the following session, she inverted the roles: she played the mum who taught me how to put together a puzzle.

A session at 14 months of treatment

She came in happy, as was usual by this time, asking what I wanted to do. I told her to say it herself, and she responded "the doctor", which was now her cliché game. She was the doctor who had a daughter named Caroline. My own daughter had hurt her hand with the chair. I was to get her to be cured, to have a bandage put on. It was unclear how, but she ended up not being the doctor anymore but Caroline's mother. She served us coffee and the game seemed to be ending. Then she saw the blackboard. She lit up and took the "best" chalk, saying that she was going to write "Caroline" (up to now, on announcing that she would write, she just made some scrawl; she had learned the letters of her name at home or preschool, which she at times wrote in session in haphazard fashion). She asked me to tell her how it was written. I showed her the letters and she copied them laboriously, then asked me whether it did say "Caroline". I told her yes, and she seemed happy and asked me to write something. I wrote Sophia. She looked at it and said "I do not know how to read". Suddenly, she lighted up and said in a surprised tone "Sophia!". I told her yes, and then she wrote "So-phi-a". She was quite happy. She showed me the numbers in a chart and recognised them quite correctly from 0 to 9.

When she finished doing this, something both intense and startling happened. She was happy and loose until she realised all that she had done by herself. Then she became anguished; her gaze turned opaque and she came into a full-blown crisis of two-ness in the form of a temper tantrum. She had a muscular discharge, turning around violently whatever was in the toybox, got on all fours and went around the office barking. I told her "What happened? Did it happen that you know how to do things, and then when you realise that you did them you get afraid?". She sat on the floor, looked at me very seriously and maybe sadly, and with a small voice she said, "Can we play that I am a small baby and you are my mum?". I told her that it seemed she got scared of being independent and so had to come back, if only playing, to be a baby having a mother who cares for her and who takes charge of everything. She listened, looked around and insisted, "Come, play". We heard the voice of her small brother in the waiting room, who had come with her mother to fetch her. Sophia said, "Mum has come" and took off. On my arrival there, she was sitting in her small brother's pram and looked at me triumphantly – perhaps mockingly also – as if to say, "Look where I am".

As things stand, Sophia has acquired a delightful spontaneity. A few days ago, when I was returning a call from her mother for a change of schedule, she took the call and we had a nice talk in which she enthusiastically told me she was then eating salad with fish. And indeed the family commented on how lively she had become.

Conceptual comments

We will strive to keep our comments as near as possible to the observational findings. Freud demanded of psychoanalytic enquiry that it remain "close to the facts in its field of study" (1923a, p. 253).

Is Sophia a bona fide case of psychogenic autism? We believe so, based on both the initial diagnostic impression and her analytic course. Though not at the sickest side of psychogenic autism, nonetheless her inhibition in learning, and more generally her pathology, condemned her, however benevolently, to the unbecoming status of a "dummy". And, though in all likelihood it was good for her to have available an elder brother providing a fraternal symbiosis she could make use of, which enabled her to set up mimetic links (with her friend Lola at the preschool and with the analyst as well), such satellised submissiveness opened no viable path to emotional growth and psychic maturity.

To us, Sophia's is an everyday case of autism; that she was born into such a doting family does not make things any better. No early traumas are discernible: she was hospitalised at 1 year old for pneumonitis, but this had no detectable impact. It is relevant that her history shows no trace of a transitional object. There is, however, an early trauma in her mother's life – the sudden death of her own father in her early infancy – but how this trauma has contributed to the mother's mind-blindness (we mentioned that she does not sing or talk to babies "because anyhow they do not understand") can only be conjectured. However, it can be assumed based on the available clinical evidences that, despite abundant goodwill, maternal mind-blindness seemingly shaped, for Sophia, a cumulative trauma conducting to mimesis and pathological symbiosis. We here use the term "symbiosis" in the sense in which it was employed in Budapest at the time of Ferenczi's death and came into the wide psychoanalytic literature in Margaret Mahler's landmark paper "Autism and symbiosis: two extreme disturbances of identity" (1958), rather than in the sense introduced by Bion in 1962 on distinguishing the commensal, the symbiotic and the parasitic links. As used by Mahler, the term *symbiosis* involves what in Bion's terms would be both parasitic and symbiotic emotional links.

A pathological symbiosis was perhaps enacted first with the mother and, subsequently, with her brother Paul as her overall world interpreter; later on with her friend Lola, her leader and interpreter at the preschool, and finally with her analyst as part of the transference. In fact, it was mind-blindness as a parasitic component of the pathological symbiosis that, after an initial period of rather absent-minded rambling and perseverations, had come first to the forefront in her enacting on her dolls as the mind-blind, mechanical mother. As we see it, the mimetic/symbiotic component is the healthier part of her psyche opening the way to analytic progress.

After a first stage of psychic absence and perseverations, she centrally enacted in session the psychic blindness as the parasitic component of the pathological symbiosis, acting on the puppets in the role of the mechanical mother. Thereafter, two main dimensions were clinically discernible, whereby through a number of "moments of contact", it happened that the "primal dialogue" was reestablished and a "context of togetherness" (Tustin 1986, p. 303) came to evolve.

1 A mimetic relational frame is then established in session, mainly in eye-to-eye and more generally through visual contact with the analyst, whereby Sophia would seem to recover her place, as Tustin masterly puts it, in the "womb of the mother's mind" (1981, p. 79). At this level, mimetic mirroring re-establishes primary identification with the analyst-as-mother.
2 Within that mimetic relational frame of contact with the analyst, Sophia, in the role of the mind-blind mother, continues to handle the dolls and the animals serially, with no individual distinctions.

This conveys, in Ferenczi's (1932) terms, the zone of trauma in an "identification with the stronger victorious opponent". As lack of empathy rather than overt aggression on the side of the maternal object is here involved in the main, in discussing autistic processes these terms seem preferable to the more widely used ones Anna Freud introduced in identification with the aggressor. Such enactments might correspond, in terms of the scheme Bion forwarded in "Transformations" (1965), to the realm of transformations in hallucinosis, where learning from experience is not bearable nor attainable. These ongoing enactments, which in our terms (Ahumada 1980) shape up a transposition of self and object, are a bulwark of *un*knowing erected against contact with the tearing apart signing the crisis of two-ness; however, in case they happen to be contained and eventually resolved in the analytic link, they can be part of the royal road to attainment of psychic two-ness.

In Tustin's diagnostic terms, Sophia is not a shell-type encapsulated autist nor an entangled, schizophrenic-like one: in her family's words, she is a convivial, attractive, submissive "dummy". The initial diagnostic appraisal meant distinguishing "stupidity" from "pseudo-stupidity", which had daunting consequences: in the first case, she would be only trainable, whereas in the second case a wide perspective opened up by way of analytic treatment. In fact, ability to use the analytic situation clinched the issue to prognostic hopefulness.

However, given that she does not fit in as a shell-type encapsulated autist or as an entangled schizophrenic-like one, where does she fit? Mahler's advice that symbiotic psychoses may go into a secondary autism (Mahler et al. 1975) does not fit either, because she has not been and is not psychotic: here we find, as Tustin avows happens in autism, "very little mind", a void of fantasies, and an "obstructed" transference (1988b, pp. 103–104). The symbiotic component is clinically secondary: it is the healthier part of her psyche opening the way to analytic progress.

Is at issue a deficit pathology or a conflictive one? Being a "dummy" daughter to an unempathic though loving mother evokes the idea of deficit pathology. However, distinction between deficit and conflict pathology should not be pushed. Here deficit and conflict are to our mind entwined and, importantly, in access to conflict within an emotionally holding link – through "moments of contact" evolving to a "context of togetherness" – progress is made. Much, if not most, of such holding initially happens in a mimetic transference mirroring with the maternal object, so that Sophia's case may be described as a 'mimetic autism'. Autistic phenomena and mimesis correspond to two polar moments of the structure.

Let us go back to Eugenio and Renata Gaddini's concept of the precursor object, namely the object of primary identification (we prefer to speak of primary identity) sustaining the baby's imageless illusion that she/he is the mother and the mother is baby, at a stage with no differentiation of inner and outer (R. Gaddini 1995, p. 219). At this stage, failure precipitates the agonies of self-loss. However, rather than limiting it to the pacifier or the thumb, and considering it solely or mainly as pertaining to a primitive stage, we see fitting to extend the concept to the psychic breast/mother evident rather centrally in the mirroring gaze, which continues to function at a deep unconscious level far beyond the earliest stages.

Such extension seems warranted by Freud's concept of primal identification and by his final and wider concept of an unrepressed unconscious, as well as by Matte-Blanco's (1975, 1988) ideas on the operation of the unconscious in terms of propositional functions rather than in terms of individuals. In the Mattian frame, it is no surprise that the analyst's receptiveness – or the elder brother's – incarnates from core emotional-relational viewpoints more of Sophia's "mothering object" than her willing but emotionally stunted, empathy-deprived real-life mother manages to do. In the session, this comes up in the vicissitudes of imitation and mirroring, where Sophia poignantly depends for her integration and her feeling psychically alive on being recognised by the analyst's gaze as overall frame, oscillating from a rather mimetic liveliness to dejection.

From what can be clinically discerned, a significant step occurred at about three months of therapy, signaling the establishment in session of the precursor object in our extended sense. By then, as said, Sophia constantly searched the analyst's gaze for her approval and depended on her recognition for liveliness or dejection; besides, she started greeting the analyst in a friendly way by way of the tiger puppet. In that overall frame, she went on, enacting on the tiger puppet, and then on the lady and the fairy puppets, her traumatic identification with the mind-blind mother as "stronger victorious opponent": she serially "interpreted" them in bodily terms with no cognisance of individual differences, and then sent them all to sleep. Coincidentally with this transference, establishment of the precursor object (which to us includes the functions of the "base" described in 1968 by Money-Kyrle; see Ahumada 1984) emerges a split of two psychic universes, those of friendly good objects and persecutory bad ones – the old man/witch that withholds recognition by not looking at her. As part and parcel to the emergence of persecutory objects comes Sophia's first raging outburst in session, addressed to the persecutory old man/witch. What divides the friendly good objects and the persecutory bad ones is their granting or withholding recognition and, noticeably, her rageful fit provides an alternative to her usual dejected crumbling down.

A second step, again involving mimesis enacted at the level of the dynamics of the gaze, marking the approach to the crisis of two-ness, comes up in the scene at five months of treatment. In what is likely an ongoing development of the precursor object in the transference, the bond to the analyst is now more resilient as to the analyst's absence between sessions, and Sophia responds "well" to her greeting. The effort at visual fusion mirroring herself on the analyst's posture is too obvious for comment, as are her taking her analyst as the source of all initiatives and the agonising tension when guidance is not provided as to action. Mention of her fears of her own thinking and her dependency on the analyst's initiatives helped Sophia take the initiative on her own, which includes giving, for the first time, her puppet a name, "Lola", the name of her mimetic partner at the preschool, which she impersonates.

We want to highlight her drawing the mother and immediately her younger brother whom she attacks: first with the pencil, then by tearing the sheets to pieces and carefully throwing them into the wastepaper basket. (As we can see in several scenes, side-by-side with differentiation from the analyst/mother, her baby brother Santiago comes up as a main persecutory object she attacks.) A new drawing of the mother and a very small Santiago follow, and this in turn is continued by the far-reaching scene with the bit of Scotch tape, with the – to Sophia – stunning finding that the analyst cannot know which side of the tape the glue is on given that she does not touch it. Sophia then starts to differentiate her own actions from the analyst's initiatives, and presumably her own body from the analyst/mother's, in a definite eureka process of discovery, which she studiously repeats several times.

Further steps in discerning herself from the primary identification enacted with the analyst, marking the step-by-step, resistance-plagued and laborious passage from use of the analyst as precursor object to her being used transitionally on the way to separateness, would seem to come just after the summer holidays, at six months of treatment. There she ascribes the analyst a name which, surely enough, she "writes" in her copy-cat manner. We would consider painting her own fingers and hands as a way of differentiating herself, both concerning her own actions and her own body, from the mother's unspontaneity as another relevant, perhaps less apparent, eureka process of self-discovery. The discovery of both spontaneity and bodily separateness leads to a tirade of stunts while brandishing her cliché slogan "I don't know". However, her voicing "I don't know, you say it, I don't want to think" shows that she now can think further about her cliché. Thereafter, she transparently dramatises the motive for her anti-thought stance, asking that the analyst be the mother and she her 2-year-old daughter, and openly asking for milk.

For reasons of space, we shall now leap forward to the session in the 16th month of therapy, retracing at a higher level of self-discrimination and symbol-formation the processes and the huge resistances observed in the session at the fifth month of treatment. In the "doctor" game, as mother of her daughter Caroline, Sophia suddenly spotted the blackboard, lit up, asked the analyst how the name Caroline was written and carefully copied its letters. In this emotional context, when the analyst then wrote "Sophia", she came for the first time to really read her name and then to write it. Emotional turmoil and enacted regression followed once again on the eureka discovery, including massive muscular discharge, her going on all fours and her acting as the barking dog. She was soon, though, able to regain containment at a level of play, asking the analyst to "come, play".

The shift toward transitionality of phenomena in the analytic space and expansion in Sophia's personal space coincided with a lessening of persecutory anxieties. As Christmas neared, the once intensely persecutory witch/old man, which she had thrown to the floor in a fit of fury because he didn't look at her, came to be included in the play/celebration, metamorphosed into a Santa Claus.

This clinical presentation has kept its bearings on the transference installation of the analyst as precursor object and the evolution of the analytic link toward the predominance of mimetic and then transitional phenomena on the road to two-ness and, in Alvarez's terms, to agency over one's mind (1995, p. 242) – on what merits being called the "work of two-ness". Discovery of separateness and spontaneity, the accomplishment of symbol-formation, and the access to agency over one's mind brings emotional turbulence because progress in the work of two-ness involves renouncement of unity at the level of the mimetic link.

May we mention in passing that Sophia's unhooking from her symbiotic link with the elder brother did not go unheeded. Whenever he comes with the mother to fetch Sophia, his resentment toward the analyst is quite noticeable.

Let us end with a hopeful note: three years after finishing her analysis, Sophia is well advanced in elementary school, academically holding her place solidly in the middle of her class. Socially she is well regarded and has plenty of friends, which, if we recall that at age 3 years 10 months she could not solve programs designed for 18-month-old babies, should tell something about the potency of the psychoanalytic approach to the autistic spectrum, when treatment starts early enough.

Chapter 5

Autistic mimesis in the Age of Media

Juan, a screen-bred animal-child

In what from McLuhan on is known as the Age of Media, we inhabit a global sociocultural milieu where, holds his heir Neil Postman (1985), media impact sets the model for the life-world. However, despite some consensus on the changes in psychopathology in the last decades, there is a dearth of clinical psychoanalytic papers detailing the psychic impact of media upbringing. To Christakis et al. (2004), attention-deficit/hyperactivity disorder (ADHD) affects between 4% and 12% of US children and is the most common disorder of childhood; in their prospective study of more than 1,000 children, they find that early television exposure at ages 1 and 3 strongly associates with attentional problems at age 7. Similarly, Landhuis et al. (2007) in New Zealand found that children's television-viewing time at 5, 7, 9 and 11 years old stably correlated with later attention disorders in adolescence. This being so, we find pertinent to share our experience with Juan, a boy coming to consultation at age 3 years 10 months fulfilling the DSM-IV criteria for "autistic disorder", sent by a phonoaudiologist who thought his troubles were emotional rather than linguistic.

The initial interviews

In the initial interview, the analyst (LBA) found the parents agreeable, willing to help and intellectually awake; emotional grasp was poor, insisting – unaware of his games' stereotypical quality – that Juan played a lot. So it is not easy to know what they meant by his infancy being "normal" except for some prematurity resulting in spending a day in the nursery. The mother was home till his sixth month, taking then a 12-hour-a-day job, leaving him in the care of an employee; the father, coming home briefly during the day, would find Juan sitting, looking at the TV, while the employee did her chores, but as Juan was quiet that did not worry him. On evaluation for preschool shortly after Juan's second birthday, the mother was told he was unlike other children and could not be accepted: the mother then left her job in order to take care of him. Thus, Juan was mostly television-bred from six months on to his second birthday. After his third birthday, on entering preschool he adapted difficultly, mother accompanying him for quite some time. Bizarrely, while others exchanged places and roamed around, he stayed at the corner where he had sat the first day, refusing to move and getting furious when insisted on. He participated only when themes involved animals. Also, while the other kids were toilet trained and freely used the bathroom, he refused to forego his napkins (diapers) and use the bathroom, though he would come home with dry napkins.

In the first diagnostic interview, I met a sad-looking boy, with veiled eyes and a restriction of spontaneous movement in a context of emotional flatness. He was not curious about me or the toys offered; only when the mother gave him some animals would he put them in a row, making them walk or run on the desktop. Concerning speech, he uttered just a few intelligible words: "Daddy", "Mom", "water", and some syllables with no identifiable referent; mother attributed sense to them, but likely these were guesses since none was repeated in the sense assigned. It dawned on me that the mother went beyond Juan, putting him in the role of the leader; thus, upon his interest in animals, the parents bought him all kinds of animal toys. The parents bent to make Juan lead, and his coming home with a dry napkin brought me, before treatment started, to advise them to take the initiative in taking out the napkins, which to their surprise led him to pee in the water-closet (bathroom) at short notice. As to defecation, he went napkin-less to the kindergarten and, once home, asked for the napkins and defecated standing in a corner.

The sessions

It is not easy to describe his hugely repetitive sessions. From the beginning he took cars, trucks and animals – mostly animals – from the box, put them up in rows and moved them on from first to last. No distinction was made between the animals, aligning them as he had grabbed them; once or twice in the hour he had them run on the desktop, making noise with their hooves, which brought him ecstasy, head to a side and eyes turned, not responding to my interventions: to a lesser point, this happens today when he is anxious. On observing this, a scene from the movie *Lion King* came to my mind where all animals run in stampede; later I learnt from the parents that, jointly with shows on the TV channel Animal Planet, *Lion King* was his usual TV fare.

After a month, his vocabulary began to increase; when I didn't get a word and asked him to repeat it, he mostly retracted. He vocalised awkwardly, his vocabulary and intonation mimicking so-called neutral Spanish on TV; while children use it on playing roles from TV or films, this was his only language.

He had *no term to refer to himself*; after three months he started referring to himself as "to me"; with a single exception soon after, over a year passed before he started referring to himself as "I".

The parents said Juan did not stand celebrations or songs, at home or at the preschool, where he would put his hands to his ears. When after two months, on his fourth birthday, I tried singing "Happy Birthday", he on the spot shouted "no, no, no, it is dangerous".

Peculiarly, from the start on he took home some animal or other, bringing it back the next session, and then got another home; I told him he seemed thus to keep me thinking about him and he thinking about me. During a third-month session, he grabbed the black tempera paint and made a jotting saying "two monsters", took some animals seemingly at random, had them walk and dabbed paint on their backs and the underside of their hooves, and then on his own soles. Upon the desktop they left their steppings, the same as his steps on the floor. Thinking that he thus equated himself with the animals, I tell him this, and he nodded and responded "we leave the marks".

He missed the following session, and on the next session the father commented that for the first time Juan did not want to come. He entered willingly, grumbling because he cannot open his jacket (he never asks for help), but now he accepted my help. He took out the animals, showing me the black spots. I told him "yes, they have spots: who painted them?" and for the first time he says "to me". He sought the animals having black spots (two elephants, a female kangaroo, a cow, a giraffe, a hippopotamus and a goat), adding a sheep having no spots with a cart tied by a string; to my question he replied "it has a white spot". A horse got tangled by the leg to the string, and he strived unsuccessfully to untangle it; he did not ask for help, using the sheep and cart as if the horse were not there. He cleared chairs out of the way, whereas up to now he had circumvented obstacles. Also, for the first time an episode came into the animals' run: he let the female kangaroo fall to the floor, and the sheep with the cart brought her back (relevantly the kangaroo had a baby in her pouch, and a few days before I learnt that Juan's mother was pregnant). I heard him mumble about "help", he raised the animals to the table, the kangaroo sustained herself with her forelegs at the table's edge and with effort the sheep and her cart raised her to the table; she carried the kangaroo on the cart and then on her back. I told him the sheep helps the kangaroo just as I help him; they walk on the table and then the kangaroo jumped to a chair where Juan left his bag. He said it has hurt her leg, then it slipped under a bag's band and he said it's trapped; again the sheep goes to help her. I told him that he also is somehow trapped, there being things he cannot do, such as playing with other children, and I'm trying to help him as the sheep does, so that the kangaroo can join the other animals and he can share and play with the children at the preschool (this being the first time I mention preschool without his shouting: "no, no").

The above session adumbrates some openness to protagonism and containment, while the following material, at the end of the third month of treatment, evinces the anxieties attending protagonism, as new situations emerged amid the stereotypy and emotional flatness. His mother had mentioned that he couldn't use scissors; he tried them in session but was unable to cut paper. Now he took them with both hands and stuck them with some effort into the sheet of paper, then gave me scissors and paper for me to cut it, which I did; again he took the scissors, this time correctly, managed to cut the paper and then cut around the borders of the sheet. At that time the mother came in, saw him cutting and exclaimed: "He is doing that! What son of a bitch! He doesn't do that for me". In the next session he painted a "monster" and then a "circle", saying that it had eaten the monster. He took the scissors and seemingly at random cut a tip of the paper; he was surprised when it fell down and then, very seriously, he cut another tip; quite moved, he looked at both tips, let the scissors fall down, and for the first time threw himself, belly down, upon the couch. I told him he became afraid on cutting the tips; he looked at me, listened and sank his face in the couch. I repeated what I said, and he stayed silent for some time, then he got up and lie down on the floor, his head under the desk; he asked me to lie similarly on the other side. We stayed face-to-face under the desk; casually or not, the cut tips rested between us, and he took them up and put them in my hand. I told him that he needed our staying together to assuage his fear of what he had cut. He nodded, so we stayed together silently for some minutes. Then he got up and started playing with the black-spotted animals (the elephant, the giraffe, the tiger, the sheep with the cart), the animals fell down, the cart rescued them and brought them to the table, which he repeated many times. He had the animals run upon the couch, which didn't suit him because they made no noise.

Two weeks later, close to summer vacations, it turned out about his thought disturbance that while he recognised numbers and letters, he could not put letters together forming words. Also, although he was unable to build a tower using coloured cylinders as smaller children easily do, he discerned – which other children don't – the figure of a lightly sketched animal at the bottom of each cylinder, immediately remembering which belonged to each of the 16 cylinders. Then he "discovered" in his playbox the Power Rangers, which were there from the start. He asked me to help him place them upright on the desk: he had them walk and was ecstatic about the noise. Suddenly, he pointed at me, making the noises of a firearm shooting (he is marvelous about making noises); unwillingly I make a gesture of fear, raising a hand to my face: he looked surprised, and then pointed at me again with even louder noises,

I repeated my gesture of fear and he started laughing loudly, as never before. He re-enacted this game with the other Power Rangers, again I showed myself afraid, and again he laughed enthusiastically. After some eight or ten repetitions, I no longer showed myself fearful, and he insisted "be afraid". We do it again, he laughs, and the next time his expression changes and impulsively he embraces me strongly as if he were a little monkey, saying "are you afraid? I am not afraid". *This single use of the term "I"* does not come up again for 14 months. I told him I thought he was very much afraid; he embraced to me for some moments, listened to a plane and told me "we listen?". I asked him what was it, and he said it's a plane. Then mother came, he refused to go, and he fetched a marker to take home, which he had not done for some time. I told him that he gets something from here in order to come back, because he was angry at leaving. We came to the end of his first year of therapy lasting five months, August to December. By that time progress at the preschool allowed him to be promoted to the four-year-olds class.

The summer interruption (January–February) brought in havoc: his sister was born, and the parents said Juan showed no impact. However, this second year of treatment was highly stereotypical for months on end, continuing his "run" of animals with no winners while graphics were restricted to colour blots: he kept up, though, and indeed increased his achievements at the preschool. When I mentioned his sister, he was blunt: "don't have any sister". Amid the reiteration and poverty of the material, the hooves' noise in the unending animal "runs" made him ecstatic; now sometimes he asked me for help in making them run: I passed him the animals, and he ran them and then piled them up. Were I to suggest, for example, that the lion might eat the sheep, he angrily shouted "no, they just run". He's mostly sad, and leaves the session saying that he goes to mom's room to look at Cartoon Network.

After one year in treatment, he speaks fluently, has sphincter control, and interacts some with other kids at the preschool, is more plastic in games and shared in the "family day" celebration. He brought a ball, saying we were going to play baseball; he smiled and sometimes laughed when able to catch the ball, and also when I failed to catch it, saying "you failed"; proposals to play ball had to come from him, otherwise he rejected them. As the year went on, he mostly took the role of various animals and ended up on the floor feeling stuck, saying "listen, Maity (my nickname), you must help me"; I gave him a hand and, relieved, he said "that's it". I told him once and again that he did not know what to do being Juan, so he passed on to being an animal that walks and makes noises. After several such sessions, he sat over the glass desktop and for the first time drew his family upon it. To my mind this marked his birth as Juan; some yellow details in the drawing are shared just by Juan and his father.

At the start of the third year, at 5 1/2 years old, Juan brought a pack of Pokémon cards; each of us turned a card, I read the name, and he mentioned it by heart; sometimes I won, sometimes he won, for no reason at all. He then fetched the Power Rangers, made a stereotypical war, and told me "let's make the Pokémon screen". I asked "what was that?", and he gestured with both hands a square in the air. To my question "like that on TV?" he replied "of course". We were going to play with the animals of the playbox but deformed, just like the Pokémon: the elephant and the dinosaur fought, one won and the other lost, and so on.

Some weeks later, he asked for a computer; on my telling him I didn't have one, he said "we have a problem, we have no screen; then we build one" drawing in the air a square. He asked me to choose a monster, but I told him I didn't see any. He replied angrily "I know! . . . take this one, it's an xxx" (he gave me a bear, which he named after some Pokémon), took an elephant, chanted music and noises seemingly from the TV show Pokémon, turned the elephant against my bear and said "I won" (by this time he started to regularly use the pronoun "I"). The game went on and on, leaving me out, and I found myself more and more uncomfortable, wondering whether this came from the lack of even a minimal story coming from somewhere and leading somewhere. One won and the other lost, there was no history, future nor objective, even destruction or death were just fleeting, everything came back. I told him that he found himself quite comfortable in the screen, where the others seemed to be and where events happened (my idea being, though I do not voice it, that he has lived mostly in the screen rather than in a human context). He answered "of course" (which might be a stock answer rather than an acknowledgment, since he used it on being countered); he said "please please let's play together", which may also have been a stock answer, to which mimicking him I replied "please please please let's play together". Surprised he looked at me, impacted. He said "aren't we playing together?" I replied "I think you are playing by yourself in your imaginary screen". With a "monster" in each hand, he turned thoughtful, looked at me, and something seemed to go on in his head. Two sessions later, amid the stereotypical play, a crocodile fell from his hand and he asked me to pick it up; as it was at his feet, I asked him why he didn't pick it up by himself, and he answered "don't you see I cannot get off the screen?"

While the second year of treatment, after the trauma of his sister's birth, was signed by daunting stereotypies, this third year evinced bursts of emotional vitality. Toward the end of the second month of this third year, he came in angry and did not salute me; sitting on the couch, he embraced himself strongly, looking sad and angry. To my mention that he came quite angry, he responded "yes I want to go home and look at TV". I said that he felt so lonely that he embraced himself, and he responded "yes, I want to be with the TV who is my mom, Carmen (his mother) is Lisa's mom". I told him that feeling angry and sad he wanted to stay with the TV, and he just nodded. We keep silent for a long time, some 20 minutes; then he asked "where's the fish?", and I answered it must be in his box. He fetched it and said: "he wants to swim", then went to the bathroom, filled up the lavabo (sink) and had it swim there. When the lavabo filled, he drank water from the edge; I told him he had turned small and drank water like a baby. The fish swam ever more lively, and I commented that though he had not looked at the TV that put him well, having the fish swim made him think the fish is well; Juan got animated, and the fish jumped "as dolphins do". He got more and more lively, sucked and splattered water and said the fish was happy. I told him "and so you are" and the session ended.

What follows, months into the third year, shows heightened tolerance of anxieties, allowing me to better confront him. After some repetitive games, he proposed to play checkers. Even in simple games he tended to forego rules, using them his way. Putting up the checkerboard he took the red chips, and I took the black ones. He said "I choose three elephants", softly knocking the chips on three black squares counting "one, two, three", and asked me to choose four lions; I did as he had done, and he says okay and chose four zebras; I said "five dogs" and he countered anguished: "no, no, you must choose a wild animal". So I said "five tigers", asking "how's this game? who wins?" and again he got anxious: "stop, stop, it is thus, it is thus". I told him that my speaking about rules or about winning and losing gave him ill feelings. He nodded, saying "they must just walk" (he reiterated the noises, not with the hooves but with the chips, which must correspond to wild animals). He said "let's leave apart the box and paint", and then he fetched some paints, brushes and water. I asked him about the paper and he replied: "no, no, let's paint the wall" (paper seemingly reminded him of demands in the preschool and at home, which made him cross).

He then told me "close your eyes, I paint an animal and you tell which one it is"; he drew a face with members sticking out of it as jots, and as I opened my eyes he recited "a head, an eye, another eye, a tail, some legs" and "some horns", and then "your turn". I drew an elephant, and he applauded saying "an elephant" and then "my turn". He made exactly the same drawing, and when I opened my eyes said "a fish"; I asked him "with legs?" Putting his hand in front of my face in a gesture of rejection, he said "stop, stop, yes, yes". I drew a cat, and his anxiety went up and up, saying "no, not a cat, a wild animal, it must be a wild animal", and some tears rolled down his face. I decided to wait, feeling that for a long time I had let him evade his anxieties and should let him contact them, and I said "wild animals such as in *Lion King*". His face lights up, whether by my comment or by his occurrence: "a wildcat, now my turn". He made an identical drawing, saying it is a lion: to my mind the drawing was not his production but something learnt; then I drew a tree, and he got anguished, perhaps on noting the difference. Soon after he drew an adequate tree, painted a rainbow, a fish with "spots" and "lines", and then said "it's all inside a great circle". I thought this was the second time – the first one was his drawing the family – where his drawings showed intentionality; he was happy, looked at it from afar and says "it's a great painting", which might refer to its size but also to it as achievement. He went back to his reiterations: "now the bears, the tigers and the monkeys will run". In the next session he proposed to put up the initial letter for an animal and that I drew it; he drew a P and I drew a penguin; an I, and I drew an iguana; an E and I drew an elephant, then a B and I drew a bear, and then he asked me to write the word bear.

Four weeks later, aged 5 years and 10 months, a tolerance of an ability for linking and relating, as well as for rules, continued to adumbrate. Coming into session he looked at the pile of table games, saying "you have 10 games, can you fetch me that one?", pointing to the Guess Who. I gave it to him, and he was enthusiastic on noting the figures on the boards (some 40 in each, with a human figure and the name below it), gave me a board and kept the other. He put the cards right side up (instead of down), saying "I choose this one", and started looking until he found it, and then said it's my turn (starting to use local speech instead of TV one). I told a characteristic, black hair and glasses, and he found it and was happy about it, then chose himself a characteristic, adding the first letter of the name and asked me for the name (as said, he long recognised letters but could not link them even in his name). When a figure was named Pedro like his father, he was enthused.

Office space provides just two places to hide; we had sometimes played hide-and-seek, so Juan knew them. Let me add that *he still thought that when he does not see, the other does not see him*. Some weeks after, he asked that we hide alternatively under a blanket, he or I standing, with the blanket on. When he was counting, at which time I should put the blanket upon me, it occurred to me to leave the blanket upon the seat where he had left it and hide behind the desk. Opening his eyes after counting and noting I was not under the blanket, he called me anxiously twice, staying at his place; he got paralyzed and did not manage to look for me. After a few seconds he again called, quite anguished; I came into view and told him that he got so scared because on not seeing me he had thought I was not there, just like when he was small and did not see his mother because she was not there. Next session he asked me again to play hide-and-seek with the blanket, asking "but if I don't see you, will you still be there?" I assured him I will and rather anxiously he managed to enjoy the game.

From these sessions on, changes were noticeable, opposite to the months after vacations when no improvement occurred. His drawings conveyed more meaning and greater variety: trees and water turned up, while animals started to get bodies from which tails and legs sorted out. While he kept rejecting drawing on paper, he painted on the wall using markers and tempera. His sixth birthday came, he accepted our singing "happy birthday" and soon after accepted for the first time to put on a disguise for celebration at the kindergarten. On the evaluation to enter first grade, he was approved on social behaviour but not on academics: he did not do well on the Bender test, did not write his name and his drawings did not reach a proper level, but based on his progress, a final decision was postponed.

The fourth year of treatment showed advances in symbol-formation with a foregoing of seriality. He saw a Playmobil pirate handling a map, which he described in detail: "there is an island, there are trees, at the 'X' the treasure is buried, and there is a giant guarding it"; "let's play pirates". I was left in the role of spectator, but he addressed his comments to me; the dinosaurs were to be the pirates. He "hid" the coffer under a couch pillow and Sully (from the movie *Monsters, Inc.*) was the giant guarding it. About what he was going to draw on the desk, he said "we must do a pirate ship in my favourite colour, purple; a half-moon, a mast and a triangle for the sail". He tried to draw a half-moon but did not manage to, and said "listen, Maity, can you help me?" I drew the hull, and he added the mast and thrice attempted to draw the sail, which wouldn't come out; he said "a triangle, this way" and drew it correctly up in the air but on the desk it was too long and narrow. He took up a monkey, which got command of the marker, and a good enough triangle resulted. He then, imaginatively and coherently, built a story of "pirate dinosaurs" who go seek a treasure, defeat "the giant that guards it" and come back home with a treasure, which they deposit on the desk saying "it's for us". I told him he was happy with the story he built and that he wanted us to share what he did.

Switching games, he started organizing a repetitive "run of animals", but finding a smaller animal from another set said: "listen, this is a baby, I have an idea!; a baby's race". He joined all the smaller animals – the babies – with some big ones, allocating for the first time family roles and relationships: "a mother giraffe, this elephant is the grandfather"; heretofore they were just "animals". The babies will race, and the mothers and grandfathers are spectators. Once the babies were in the starting line, he said "but there is a serious problem; how will they cross from the table to the bed?" He sought a pelouche (plush) female rabbit with big sneakers on its hind legs found in a desk locker, to which he had paid no attention: "the rabbit is going to help them". Asked whether mothers and fathers were going to help, he responded "no, they don't know; the rabbit knows". I wondered whether I might be that rabbit, someone outside the family helping him jump to go out.

That a caring mother is now part of the emotional context came through some weeks later when he said "let's play at the wild animals and Bu that walks through the jungle, and the mother guards her and saves her" (in the *Monsters, Inc.* film, monsters terrorise children making 'Bu': the protagonist is a girl aged 6, who is not scared of the monsters' noises and finally becomes their friend). He put the elephant behind a tree, making noises, and asked me that Bu walk approaching the tree; she was afraid of the roars and I, the mother, was to hold her in arms and calm her, which I do. This he repeated with several wild animals, and then he took a polar bear but then said "listen, this is not a jungle wild animal, it is a polar bear and lives in the Pole" (the jungle seemingly derives from *Lion King*). He had the animals walk, run and roar as in the film, and I told him that this is as when he was looking at *Lion King* and mom was not there (this I had told him before, but as said now a caring mom is part of the context).

Once and again come Bu and the animals scaring her while I was to protect and calm her; she never entered the game when he played with the real monsters. Bu needing to be protected and held seems to stand for his own scared infantile self, and use of the animals rather than the monsters likely recalls the efforts to master his early anxieties attending to *Lion King* while mother was absent. For the first time he drew the analyst: face with eyes, nose, mouth and the four limbs, but not a body; in a corner of the same sheet of paper he wrote, also for the first time, his name, Juan.

Soon after the baby-race reruns: the mothers were busy, so the female rabbit with big sneakers helped them "triumph over obstacles"; once back he sought food – sausages, hamburgers, pizza, which theretofore he paid no attention to – feeding the babies one by one, and he ate too. The next week aggression surged more realistically: for the first time he opened the box with soldiers, which confront with cannon and tanks, shooting till the point came that he decides one side won; now he firmly stated that when hit "they die, they cannot fight any longer".

The next week he brought the Pokémon cards, and he took them and mentioned their names, which he mostly knew by heart; he asked me to read those he does not know. I read some and then tell him that as he knows the initial letters, he could read them himself. Turning angry and tearful, he said "I know, I know" in order to stop me, adding "I don't know how to read, I don't know how to read". I told him that he knows the letters, but what is difficult is to put them together; he got angrier and said "if you don't shut up I'll draw my face", then grabbed a marker and made lines on his face. He stopped suddenly, seemingly surprised, and went to the bathroom to look at himself. I followed him, as he was drawing some more lines on the mirror upon the reflection of his face. He looked at his reflection in the mirror, and his anger seemed to have passed. He asked "do I have more lines on my face?". I told him it seemed to me that they are upon the mirror; he looked again, at the lines on the mirror and those on his face superimposed, and he said "look, don't you see that they are here upon my face?". I replied that they were upon his face in the mirror; while he kept drawing upon the mirror, he replied "Here! Here! Upon my face!; now all my face is painted". I told him "I think that you mix up your face and that on the mirror"; he looked at me, then looked at himself in the mirror: having moved somewhat, the lines on the mirror no longer coincided with those on his face. He touched his face, saw his hand in the mirror, he touched it with his other hand, touched the mirror and then again his face; he erased some lines with his finger and said "they are no longer on my face" to which I replied "on your face in the mirror". He again looked at me, he looked at himself and said "come here", pointing to his side, which I did, and in so doing my face appeared upon the mirror. He touched the mirror and then my face, involving some work of recognition; after some minutes and without further comment, he went back to the office and sought the game of serpents and stairs, which he had always handled in his own way, hitting the board with the chips: again he did this and then said "I'm bored". I tell him that he gets bored because he plays just as a baby would. He was somewhat angry but then asked "how is it played?". I explained the two basic rules, he accepted them, we played and he got enthusiastic when his turn came to go up a stair: for the first time we played a game according to the rules.

On the next session he asked to play baseball; having no bat, I made up one with rolled cardboard; he hit the ball quite correctly, and I asked whom he learnt it from. He replied "from my friends". To my question, "which friends, those at the kindergarten?" he countered "I have no friends at the kindergarten; my friends are at TV, they teach me baseball, tennis, every sport. They are my friends and I talk with them". I again asked "and those at the kindergarten?" and he emphatically replied "I have no friends there, these are my companions, I told you my friends are at TV". A couple of sessions later, he found a new set of crayons upon the desk, he got enthusiastic and said he was going to draw. He asked me to draw a giraffe, which I did, and he added some spots and hooves. He drew a bear and then asked me to write their names; he said "giraffe with a j", but when I wrote it as "jiraffe" he said "no, it goes with a g"; I wrote "giraffe" and then he wrote the o for *oso* (bear) and asked me to complete it. Expecting a rebuttal I told him he can do it, and he accepted and wrote it – his first written word.

The next week he drew an accomplished hen on the glass desktop, saying "the crest, the beak (drawing another one upon it), the feathers, the legs; it's the farm's hen". He sought a cock, a horse, a hog, a rabbit, and a bull saying it's a cow. While his left hand "walked" fingers down along the "farm", his right hand moved the bull-cow; his left hand "asked" "we need milk". I asked him what did his hand stand for, and he replied "my hand; don't you see? It's my hand" and he went on "the cow has no milk". I said the cow had no milk because it was a bull, and he exploded angrily, hit the bull-cow and shouted "it's a cow! it's a cow!". I did not insist, so he calmed down and repeated "the cow has no milk. Goes to the supermarket to bring us milk". A week later he proposed we play hide-and-seek, but he just covered his face with a small pillow. I told him "There is Juan who hides his face with a pillow"; angrily he insisted he was hidden and I can't see him. I told him his face is hidden but not his body, so he put his hands on his face, angry and tearful: "I don't want you to see me. You cannot see me". I volunteered that the fact that his hideaway behind the pillow being not what he wanted it to be made him very angry.

Bringing a pack of Yu-Gi-Oh! cards, similar to Pokémon, he asked me to read their names; at some prompting he attempted to put letters together, which he managed for some simple syllables: he was surprised, laughed happily and started concentrating to read other syllables. Suddenly he recognised as part of a card name his name, Juan, and jumped astounded: "look, it says Juan, look, look!". I told him that knowing what the letters said made him happy. When we finished the game, he said "the winner is Juan", pointing to himself.

After summer vacations, 3 1/2 years into treatment, he came smiling, hands at his back. After mother left he said, his face full of expectation bent to surprise me: "look what I brought", showing a Ken-style figure dressed with T-shirt and shorts. I told him "you brought a man", but he replied "no, it's a man-animal". I asked what is that, and extending the arms he made it fly saying "you see, it's a bird"; then, putting its arms along the body, he made it swim saying "thus it's a fish, look at how it swims" and furthermore, he put its arms to the front and left it upon the desk saying "now it's a lion, though it lacks a tail". He again put the arms to the side and made it lie face up on the desk: "now it's a man, but he's dead". I asked whether when he is a man he is dead, and he responded: "yes, now we are going to do a jumping race". And he dutifully got into a series of races where everybody wins.

As shown earlier, Juan offered brief transformational sequences, which he decisively interrupted, taking refuge in stereotypies, repetitive games such as the Power Rangers confrontations or races where everybody wins. After a comeback to the unending fights, in the third session after vacation he sat on the desktop, saying "come, I have something very important"; as I got closer, he embraced me strongly and for a long time amid a climate of silence, which I chose to respect. Soon thereafter, he suggested playing *Lion King* and quite elaborately built up and enacted the scene in which the Wise Monkey presented the Baby Lion to the ensemble of wild animals; in the midst of the representation, on making the animals walk toward the Baby Lion, he started falling into a trancelike state. I commented at this point that this makes me remember something, and he then asked "when I had the animals run?". I asked in turn "what do you think?". He reflected for a moment and said "this might be so", and he got out of the trance and resumed his role as play manager where he directed the scene rather than being a wild animal himself; contrasting with the previous emotional flatness, events became intensely dramatic.

Coming to session after summer vacations, at 4 1/2 years of treatment, he was furious and threw himself upon the couch: "I didn't want to come because I cannot look at the Power Rangers program". He was also angry with his father who brought him in. I told him that during vacations the Power Rangers were there on schedule, while I wasn't there for the whole time. He got up and went under the table, sighing deeply; he fetched the Power Rangers and put up their act during the whole session. In the next session he again was angry and did not speak for a long time; then he said "I do not want to ever come again, nor to go anywhere, nor go to school, I'm going to tell my mom", some tears running down his cheeks. I told him that he had missed the program once again, and he nods and lies upon the couch hiding his face. I told him "yes, it is a problem, that you only want to look at the program and do no other thing such as going to school or seeing friends". He interrupted me saying "I do see my friends; they are the Power Rangers". I asked "and those at school?" and he responded "they are not my friends, they are my companions"; he again put his face against the pillows. He said "it is a secret, a great secret, and a great problem"; I asked whether he can tell me what the problem is, but he responded "no, because it's a secret and I cannot tell secrets". I waited, and after some time he said "there are two secret problems". After a long silence he added "I want to have a TV in my room, close the door, put up a poster saying 'I'm the king of the universe' and never go out"; that was said softly, his mouth against the pillow. We stayed in silence for some 10 minutes, and then he said "I'm going to tell you the problems"; there is another silence, I waited and then he volunteered "one problem is that I cannot enter the screen"; there was another silence and then he went on "the other one is that they cannot get out of the screen". I told him that he wanted to be the king of the universe to get together with them and never go out.

His being unable to enter the screen did not come up again for several months, but he enacted the screen-games in session, totally absorbed in his fights with the Power Rangers. That he did not bear losing led him to avoid playing with friends: at school he refused to participate at sports. Sometimes he proposed "normal" games such as playing ball or hide-and-seek, but there must be no winner. Some six months after, at a time in which sadness came to the fore, he entered session and threw himself upon the couch, got up after a few minutes and in a serious tone said he did not want to go camping. I asked him what he meant, and he responded that "yesterday we did a pre-camping all day long, it's boring" and then, furiously, "I don't want to go!". I asked him why it was boring (by boring he often means angry), and he replied "there were games and more games and my team lost four times"; I said it must have been ugly for him to lose four times. He went on "every time, every time my team lost, and camping will last two days"; he got under the table, embraced his knees and added "at the campings children eat marshmallows after they put up the tents, and they never play football, I want to go to those campings". Asked "are these campings those of your TV friends?" he agreed and said "but do you remember that I told you I cannot enter the screen? now I can never enter the screen". I told him "yes, you once said that was a great problem" and he added "and now they don't see me", to which I replied that this makes him sad. He sighed and stayed under the table for a long time, then he got out, saying we are to play hide-and-seek. He fetched three animals and told me to close my eyes; he hid them and I had to seek them: I found them in different places. Then I asked whether the tiger, which I found last, was the winner; he replied that they all won because I found them all. I asked whether to be found is what is important rather than to win, and he agrees. I add that this might have something to do with that presently he cannot find ways of meeting his screen friends.

After finishing second grade, the school reports that he does well socially as well as academically, mixing with other children. In session, though, he keeps to his distinction between his TV "friends" and his school "companions". In a recent scene, bored, he started one of his unending fights involving now two firemen and a diver: he acted out blows, jumps and flying kicks amid varied noises. Feeling thoroughly left out, as so often happens, I told him it seemed to me that he makes me feel left out grasping nothing of what goes on, such as he feels when children at school play and he feels left out. Interrupting his game, he looked at me thoughtfully; then he resumed his game but with a variant: amid the diverse blows and noises he says "he hit him on his prick, again he hit him on his prick"; also, instead of going on and on as usual, the game soon stopped. Then he fetched a bag of food he had not used for a long time and put up food arranged by colours rather than kinds: he fetched animals coming to buy food, but they come back and return it.

Some sessions after the last vacation he showed me his new sport shoes, saying that they are for the sports at school, which he doesn't like; they play football there, but he is not good at it, nor at running: he is only good at quadripedia. Asked what is that, he responded that it is running on all fours, and he is fast at that. I commented "running as animals do?" and he responded "yes, don't you remember when I was an animal?" I asked "were you an animal?"

and he told me "yes; no; that is what I thought, I don't know. But that was before, now I am Juan (he straightened up) and I am a boy".

Commentary: on the humanisation of a media-bred animal-child

Frances Tustin (1986) noted that to autistic children their body flows into the mother's: they feel continuous with their environment in a state of imitative 'identity', connected not with others as such but with self-generated auto-sensuous sensations felt as part of themselves; on approaching contact with the terrifying "not-me", they retract or arrive at the unmitigated furies of the crisis of two-ness. Tustin stresses that while in the schizophrenic child, projective identification is quite active and there is some acknowledgment of an inside and an outside, that is, of objects different from himself, the autistic child connects with sensations rather than with objects as such. A primary sense of "me-ness" needs being well established in order that a stable consciousness of a "not-me" be tolerable. What we describe as "mimetic autism" is outside the realm of psychoses and entails other beings in an imitative 'identity'. In Sophia's case (Ch. 4), such 'imitative identicality' entailed an older brother and a girl at the preschool; in Juan's case identity mainly took place with screen-mediated wild jungle TV animals. Thus, while we put together Sophia and Juan under the label of mimetic autism, there are relevant differences in how the transference was enacted: Sophia showed a full-blown mimetic transference while Juan's transference autism allowed for just brief moments of contact.

Tustin sustained that a primary sense of "me-ness" needs being achieved in order that a stable awareness of the "not-me" be bearable. However, autistic isolation is not an all-or-nothing affair. Issues of contact and of personification (the emergence of a sense of self) interweave, step by step, throughout our clinical narrative, as shown by Juan's from the start taking home some animal to keep contact with the analyst and the sessions. What singles out Juan's case is that he allots his core self-identity to an animal identity built upon a screen-mediated mimetic identity rather than to a human one; so we deal with counterpoised subjectivities and life-worlds, in the screens and in everyday life. We shall strive to trace in this complex material how psychic development and the processes of subjectification in Juan's dual life-worlds proceeded under the thrust provided by the analytic space.

An enacted first step in the development of his sense of "me-ness" is discernible in the third month of treatment when, after dabbing paint on the underside of the animals' hooves and of his own soles, leaving their respective steppings upon desktop and floor: to the analyst's suggestion that he thus equates himself with the animals, he nods and responds "we leave the marks". Beyond his equation with animals, "leaving the marks" appears as a neat, spontaneous first feat of personification, of a sense of "me-ness"; likely not by chance after a session missed, he accepted help from the analyst; responding to the question of who painted the marks, he for the first time referred verbally to himself as "to me". Now he cleared obstacles out of his way, and for the first time introduced a libretto into the animals' run, evincing in displaced ways his need for help, the white sheep helping the kangaroo with the baby in her pouch; damage and pain come into the picture when the kangaroo hurts her leg and must be untrapped.

Soon after, the risks entailed by a more protagonist attitude come to the fore when he learns to use scissors and cuts the two tips of paper that fell to the ground, which after a silence led to his lying on the floor under the desk, asking the analyst to do likewise; there we stayed face to face in what Tustin calls a scene of intrauterine communion; he put the cut paper tips in my hand, and nodded when told he needs our staying together in order to assuage his fear. Clearly, here his own protagonism and its upshoot – the cut paper tips – bring him into fright; clearly also, this brings him to seek containment. Kanner (1951) noted that for autistic children wholes must be preserved in their entirety, as they are greatly disturbed at the sight of anything broken or incomplete: here, importantly, the paper tips get broken on his own protagonism. However, he did not fall into unmitigated terror: he sought and received psychic holding in a momentary passage from autistic dynamics into a communicational use of projective identification allowing psychic containment.

These protagonism/containment issues dramatically shine through some three weeks after, close to the end of this short, five-month-long, first year of treatment, when he suddenly pointed at the analyst making firearm noises, and the surprised analyst made a gesture of *genuine* fear, which he then asked her to repeat several times, bringing him to an enthusiastic laugh. When she stopped responding, he insisted, and after the next time they did it, he embraced the analyst while saying "are you afraid? I'm not afraid" this being his first use of the term "I", which did not reappear for 14 months. Successful communicational/gestural use of projective identification of his fearful aspects into the analyst as container led – amid his embracing the analyst – to verbal distinction between a "you" and an "I". In the frame of moments of psychic intimacy (at-oneness), he discerns between his own self and the object, allowing for veritable symbol-formation: this required a *genuine* emotional container, a fearful analyst that quickly mitigated and fitted her genuine fear into a playful game.

What precedes illustrates a double dimension, and therefore a double function, in psychoanalytic work: on the one hand, a dimension of *contact/holding/*

reverie, coming out in moments of emotional contact with the analyst, where the analysand foregoes autistic dynamics and bears mind-to-mind awareness (after Bion, Antonino Ferro (2007) speaks of being *at-one*). On the other hand, we meet a dimension of *discernment and self-discernment*, which in the case of Sophia's mimetic transference (Ch. 4) took place as crises of twoness in the relation with the analyst; Juan alternates periods of transference autism with brief moments of *at-one* contact. In both cases *it is in the frame of moments of psychic at-oneness that the hardships of self-discernment and objectal discernment are tolerated*, ushering in genuine symbol-formation.

That the unfolding taking place in the initial five months of treatment collapsed in the first summer vacation upon the birth of his sister Elsa evinces that Juan's steadfast avoidance of the not-me did not immunise him from massive trauma, which signed his devastatingly monotonous second year of treatment. The third year of treatment showed a renewal of process, or more precisely, an inmixing of moments of process into the prevailing non-process. In this third year he came to use the term "I" instead of "to me" on a stable basis, though speaking from animal personifications. When such personifications were confronted, he drew his (human) family upon the glass desktop. By non-process we mean that he was mostly immersed in a media-like fleetingness of mimetic identity playing by himself in his imaginary screen, where everything can be and not-be at the same time. It was up on *mirroring confrontation* by the analyst: "please, please, please let's play together" that inroads open between his screen-world and his real-life world, leading him to respond "don't you see I cannot get out of the screen"; that when angry enough he volunteered that he wanted to go back "with the TV who is my mom, Carmen is Lisa's mom" and then to an unusual 20-minute silence evinces that the atemporal screen-world was parasitically adjoined to the role of a substitute mother. Heightened tolerance of symbol-formation appears in his proposal to write a letter and that the analyst using it as the initial letter drew an animal. Then confrontation by the analyst hiding behind the desk instead of under the blanket ushered in terror, which he reincorporated, quite anxiously though, into the game. His drawings got richer, and he pleasurably built a narrative on the pirates and a treasure; importantly, the animal babies came into the picture, the female rabbit with the sneakers helped them while mothers and fathers, not knowing how to help, stood as spectators.

Advancement in the process of humanisation is evinced by the coming into the scene of the first human actor, the girl Bu, needing to be protected and calmed by the analyst-as-mother. It is a fair measure of Juan's terrors that she was exposed to frightening jungle animals but not to the real monsters, likely reenacting his own efforts to hold his anxieties by watching *Lion King* in mother's absence. In such context he drew the (body-less) analyst and wrote for the first time his name, Juan; also for the first time he fed the baby animals, and ate too. And for the first time soldiers fought realistically; foregoing fleetingness and reversibility, he admitted that when they die they can no longer fight.

We have more questions than answers concerning the scene where, angry at being unable to read, he made marks on his face and then, surprised, went to look at himself in the mirror, drawing further lines on his reflection. The ensuing mixup between the reflection of his face on the mirror-screen and his own face required, in order to be sorted out, more than the analyst's verbal confrontations: it needed his looking and touching the analyst's face and his own face;[1] our impression is that the analyst's presence was effective mainly at the level of holding/containment, furthering his enacted piece of ostensive discernment involving both sight and touch, his own confrontation by touch likely playing the essential role. That something crucial did effectively happen came up in his asking about rules and for the first time accepting and enjoying a game played according to rules, in that soon after he wrote his first word, *oso* (bear), and in that a bit later he recognised as part of a card name his own name, Juan, leading him to a jubilant cry, "the wiiiiinner is Juan".

Again, what to say of the "surprise" right after the next summer vacations at 3 1/2 years of treatment, his bringing in, likely evincing a transformation in his sense of "me-ness", the Ken-style manly figure? He on the spot, though, denied Ken is a man, turning him into a bird, into a fish, into a lion, fleetingly voicing why: when he is a man he is dead. Why soon after, after a flight into his stereotypies, did he bring in as something "very important" a long, silent embrace with his analyst? Despite defining himself as an "animal-child", meaning an animal not yet grown, he can now act as drama director of *Lion King* instead of being an enthralled wild animal, so we can feel confident about his progress. By this time he had entered first grade, held his place academically and interacted more with his companions; the second-grade boys, though, call him "Martian" because of his weird intonation. In session he was often in a working mood and his productions got more and more varied. After the next summer vacations, at 4 1/2 years of treatment, we assisted to what may be seen, on the one hand, as the furies of a protracted "crisis of two-ness", and on the other hand, amid a veritable weaning from his screen life-world and his screen self-identity, as the pangs adumbrating what in Kleinian terms is the "depressive position". He did not want to come to sessions because this precluded him from looking at the Power Rangers and he forcefully avowed, tears running down his cheeks, that he did not want ever to come again, nor go anywhere nor go to school. That he verbally expressed that "I want to have a TV in my room, close the door, put up a poster saying 'I am the King of the Universe' and never go out" at the time illustrated the omnipotent control put to play in his inhabiting his screen-world, and the felt threatened loss of such world; shortly thereafter he acknowledged two newfangled problems: that he now cannot enter the screen and that his friends cannot get out of the screen. In the next months he enacted on and on in session his screen games, absorbed in his fights with the Power Rangers; on his not bearing to lose, he avoided playing with his companions or participating in school sports. Then, six months into the analytic year, at which time he was notoriously sad, came out the scene where he was furious at the pre-camping in school, his team having lost four times in a row: going under the table and embracing his knees, he longed after the campings of his TV friends, but he verbally acknowledged that he now cannot enter the screens and his screen-friends no longer saw him, to which the analyst responded, noting that this makes him sad.

Let us now get, if only tentatively and controversially, into another track of the complex experience of Juan's treatment, relevant for this case but also as concerns the ample topic of the all-pervasive impact of visual media culture. As far as we are aware, there are few descriptions of phallic dynamics in the literature on childhood autism, this being no doubt true of Tustin's work, but it is the case that overt phallic rivalry played a conspicuous and often dominant role in the dynamics of Juan's screen-world, and that phallic anxieties played a relevant role in his emerging real-life world.

As mentioned, Juan's screen-world first came into session as an ecstatic sensuous state, the noise of the hooves in the wild animals' run: this seemed to set the stage for his first personal protagonism, dabbing paint on their hooves and his own soles and saying "we leave the marks" and, when asked, his voicing for the first time a self-reference: "to me". The wild animals' run recurred once and again and eventually incorporated in a libretto personal elements in displaced forms, evincing his need for help in rescue games (the white sheep with the cart, the female rabbit with sneakers). A daunting fear of (phallic) aggression came up in the real-life context when, learning to use scissors, he cut two tips of paper, dropped the scissors and then dropped himself first on the couch and then on the floor under the table; he asked the analyst to lie on the other side, they stayed together face to face, and then he put in her hand the two paper pieces: after some minutes, once his fear was assuaged, he resumed his rescue games. Again two weeks later, phallic aggression at the analyst after discovering the Power Rangers bluntly came up in his pointing at her in mock firearm shooting. The trauma of his sister's birth during vacations put an end to such displays.

The contrast between his screen-world and his life-world came to the fore in the third year of treatment when he fetched the Power Rangers, put to act a stereotypical war and said "let's make the Pokémon screen". His screen-world was the privileged place for endless games of phallic rivalry, coming from nowhere and leading nowhere: an animal, a Pokémon, or a Power Ranger wins, the other loses, with no plot; destruction or death are just fleeting, as everything comes back. He played by himself, leaving the analyst out, only on being countered by the analyst he put to words his inhabiting a screen-world in session: "don't you see I cannot get off the screen?". Soon thereafter, lonely and angrily embracing himself, he avowed: "I want to be with the TV who is my mom, Carmen (his mother) is Lisa's mom". Nearly two years later, at which time distinction between his screen-world and his life-world had progressed to the point that he felt that he no longer could enter the screen nor can his friends get out of it, he further made clear that "I want to have a TV in my room, close the door, put up a poster saying 'I'm the king of the universe' and never go out".

So what is to be surmised about Juan's link to his screen-world, to – in his words – his link to his substitute "Mom"? Such link is a defense against trauma as well as a result of trauma of mother's absence from ages 6 months to 2 years; it entails a parasitic link in Bion's sense, given that this Never-Never-Land where mind operates as mind-as-muscle (Bion 1962) sustained unlimited omnipotence ('I'm the king of the universe'): it worked in the main on a phallic level, and it effectively obstructed the emotional developments linked to mourning and the depressive position.

This huge link to the screen-world-context-as-"Mom" resulted from trauma occurring long after Juan's bodily weaning from the breast, so let me add at this point what Justin Call (1980) brings in on the dynamics of infant–mother dependence: in the early stages the infant is the initiator and primary architect of reciprocity in the visual and sound games constituting what Spitz (1964) called the "primal dialogue", while the mother is the follower; visual reciprocity is an organizing feature of the mother–infant dyad. In the "visual violation" experiment described by Tronick et al. (1978), the mother looks above the infant's head instead of into his eyes; after attempts to recapture the mother's gaze visually, the infant becomes distressed, reaching out for contact using his arms, legs and body, and finally he gives up and lapses for a few seconds into a collapsed postural attitude of withdrawal; after renewed attempts to contact the non-reciprocating, blank-faced, distant mother, the infant again collapses. Similarly in "oral violation", which Call (1964) described, the mother removes the breast or bottle from the hungry infant one or two minutes after initiating feeding, and there results an intensification of approach, attachment and sucking behaviour, which are the infant's contribution to mutuality and reciprocity with the mother. Call (1968) had remarked that the infant's play "responds only to an object which will reduce his discomfort", that "the capacity for social play in infancy is developed only in the presence of a reciprocating party" (p. 375) and that "the element of mutually enjoyable, playful interaction is missing in the relation of autistic children to their parents" (p. 376). This quite obviously took place in Juan's infancy, leading to cumulative trauma and the defences against it.

What can be surmised about Juan's relatedness to his substitute "Mom", the TV set, it being the case that the "dumb box" as an alternative set-up is quite unable to afford emotional reciprocity? We can only conjecture about what went on at home in mother's absence from age 6 months to age 2 years: our evidence comes from what happened in session. The initial finding on his substitute Mom, the screen-world, which persisted though mostly in the background, was in the nature of an ecstatic sensuousness, built upon the noises and movement of the run of the wild animals: such ecstatic, atemporal "mimetic sensuousness" already transpired his core identification as an "animal-child" on the model of the wild animals in *Lion King*. It is from this mimetic animal impersonation that he evinced his first verbal expressions of the emergence of a sense of self: "we leave the marks" and "to me". It is unclear that the two instances of personification that follow next correspond to such "animal-child" core identity: first his cutting the paper with a scissors leading to fright and his seeking a face-to-face "intrauterine communion" with the analyst, and second, his frightening the analyst with firearm noises right after "discovering" in his playbox those humanoid figures, the Power Rangers; that while embracing the analyst saying "are you afraid? I'm not afraid" he referred to himself as "I" might likely be a step, fleeting as it was, toward accepting a human personal identity.

After unrecognised trauma struck in the first summer vacation, when his sister Lisa was born, we assisted, as stated, to the protracted emotional flatness of his second year in treatment. In the third year, his screen-world landed neatly in session with the "Pokémon screen", and so did the unending, atemporal stereotypical phallic games with animals, Pokémons or the Power Rangers – games where no one lost and everything was reversible – whereby he brought into and inhabited in session the realm of the screen-mother leaving the analyst out.

So allow us to enter into an excursus on the double dimension of phallic dynamics, which corresponded to the commencement of the Oedipus complex in the classic psychoanalytic literature: we might recall that Juan started treatment at age 3 years 10 months, well into the chronology of the phallic phase. We shall start at distinct but related statements of Freud. First, his avowal in *Leonardo* (1910) on that suckling at the mother's breast is "the highest erotic bliss, which is never again attained" (p. 129); that such blisses are not untinged comes up, though, in his ascribing to the *Mona Lisa*'s smile in Leonardo's painting "the promise of unbounded tenderness and at the same time sinister menace" (p. 115). Second, in *Inhibitions, Symptoms and Anxiety*,

Freud attributes castration anxieties in the phallic phase to the fears emerging from earlier situations of danger, adding that

> The high degree of narcissistic value which the penis possesses can appeal to the fact that that organ is a guarantee to its owner that he can be once more united to his mother – i.e. to a substitute for her – in the act of copulation. Being deprived of it amounts to a renewed separation from her, and this in its turn means being helplessly exposed to an unpleasurable tension due to instinctual need, as was the case at birth.
> (1926, p. 139)

This is the original object-related dimension of phallic dynamics, which according to Freud exposes every one of us to the persistence, even in adult life, of the anxieties attending the link to the mother in the *ab initio* oral dynamics.

The other dimension of the phallic dynamics comes about, also according to Freud (1926, p. 138), precisely upon "the loss of object as a determinant of anxiety"; i.e., upon the traumatic effect of the anxieties involved in the trauma of separateness resulting, in the case of Leonardo da Vinci, in a *splitting of the ego*, compromising his sexual identity (Ahumada 1990). In the case of Juan, the trauma of separation brought a splitting between his screen-world and the human life-world. But quite apart from trauma, it can also be said that every toddler oscillates between moments of tender closeness to mother and excited ruptural impulses, which are observable, for example, when the infant is in the process of learning to walk: after joyfully rejoining mother, he quite soon departs from her in an exalted run (Ahumada 2006). The state of exaltation associated to the rupture is at the basis of the phallic attitude, as masterly described by Wilhelm Reich in *Character Analysis* (1933). In the phallic attitude, psychic hardenings are at the core, at the service of keeping at bay the tender feelings that are part and parcel of acknowledged contacts with emotional dependence.

Juan's stereotypical phallic games may be deemed to be enacted, mitigated equivalents of what Tustin described at a sensation-bound level as "hard" autistic objects; dealing with them in session requires direct confrontation, such as "you are playing by yourself in your imaginary screen". His turning to the analyst for shared playing happened stringently in the frame set by his screen-games, with no one winning or losing, no rules and no process. Thus, sessions involved a years-long pull between the robotic-like phallic attitude ruling his screen-world and an emerging, life-world human relationship with the analyst. When phallic castration anxieties took place in what was felt as the real-world scene, it was quite another matter, from the forceful emotional impact of his cutting with the scissors two small pieces of paper during the initial months of treatment. Such anxieties might well have grounded his daunting fear of celebrations, which were there before treatment started; also, that the first definitely human personification in his games was a girl, Bu, rather than a boy, might well have had to do with a need for distancing from massive castration anxieties.

The inner impact of his relinquishing his screen-world in favour of a human one in the last phases of the clinical material transcribed followed closely the line of Melanie Klein's (1935) initial description of the depressive position as a melancholia *in statu nascendi*; this can presumably be grasped as the interweaving of an objectal loss (the loss of the 'TV-Mom') and a self-loss (the loss of omnipotent thinking and omnipotent control). Though fusional anxieties and the emergence of self are not part of the Kleinian conceptual apparatus, the beautiful quote that Ron Britton (1999, p. 37) and Hanna Segal (1952) take from Rilke "Beauty is nothing but the beginning of terror, which we are still just able to bear" (Britton 1999, p. 37) fits here, as does Tustin's emphasis on the unbearable quality of ecstatic states (1986, p. 147). Tender emotional contacts with the analyst, from his impulsively embracing the analyst in the first year of treatment, were once and again fleeting: after those moments of intimacy, Juan soon took a flight into stereotypical games, which discloses an intolerance to felt contacts with the object's goodness (Ahumada 2004, 2006); it seems to be the case that fusional anxieties, kept at bay by the phallic antics, come to the fore as soon as emotive human contact is achieved, which can lead to claustrophobic anxieties. In a Janus-faced dynamics, effective containment opens the ground for moments of *at-one*ness; such moments bring forward threatening fusional anxieties, which in turn lead to a reinstating of primitive defences – the stereotyped unending games – effectively forestalling relationship.

This analytic process illustrates how clinical emergence of a sense of "me-ness" occurs in moments of genuine *at-one*ness within the analytic link, and that the evolving sense of "me-ness" in the contexts of *at-one*ness builds a place for moments of confrontation/discernment furthering symbol-formation and the distinction of self and object. As stressed by one of us (Ahumada 2005), psychoanalysis involves a double work on the evidences – on the side of both patient and analyst. We hope this chapter sheds some light on the primordial emotional and protagonistic stages of such a process.

Note

[1] It is interesting to compare this mirror scene with Sophia's at five months in treatment, when the analyst realised that as they were seated in their identical small chairs, the girl exactly mimicked her posture waiting for directives. In both instances, Juan's and Sophia's, we assist with the hardships of differentiation as part and parcel of the emerging of a sense of self.

Chapter 6

Clinical notes on a case of transvestism in an autistic child: Jaime

This chapter illustrates the reversibility of disturbances in sexual identity through the treatment of a patient brought in for consultation when he was nearly 6 years old. I will present clinical material, including drawings. The goals of the presentation are to describe in detail the process's evolution through its five years and to illustrate that psychoanalysis leading to structural psychological change is still possible despite the likely limitations of a restricted framework.

Betty Joseph (1971) noted the scarcity of detailed clinical material on cases of perversion, and the same appears to be true when the patient is a child. Given that the classical theory of perversions, including transvestism, is fundamentally derived from the analysis of adults, the lessons of this child analysis are well worth considering. Folch Mateu (2001) recently emphasised the need for broad clinical observation of incipient object relations in severe pathologies. As to theory, the basic conceptual dilemma would be whether to keep to the classical psychopathology of the Oedipus complex or centre the case on oral trauma and the dynamics of autism.

In the framework of classical psychopathology, the principal source is "The psychology of transvestism" (Fenichel 1930). As the author summarised in *The psychoanalytic theory of neuroses* (1946), the basic feature of transvestism coincides with that of homosexuality and fetishism: it is the refutation of the danger of castration. While the male homosexual replaces his love for his mother with identification, the fetishist will not accept that the female has no penis. There, the Freudian notion of phallic monism provides a broad conceptual framework, where the phallic mother has fundamental importance as reassurance for castration anxiety.

In the case I present, the traumatic situation occurred right in the oral phase during the first year of life. The symptom of transvestism was precocious, occurring towards the end of the second year, just at the beginning of the classical chronological order for the phallic phase and the unfolding of the Oedipus complex; this reflects Klein's (1952) notion that the beginning of the Oedipus complex must be traced back to the middle of the first year, coexisting with the oral phase, and that the early Oedipus complex sets the stage for subsequent Oedipal experience. I intend also to rely on Jones (1933), for whom the child's projection of his/her oral anxiety triggers an increase of castration anxiety. Birksted-Breen (1996) made a precise distinction between the phallus and the penis-as-link; Ferraro (2001) found that 'phallic logic' was characterised by intolerance at the limits and by suppression of the experience of need, and thus of contact with the infantile self.

From another conceptual viewpoint, Greenson (1966) underlined the role of 'as if' magical fantasies, where to imitate the mother is tantamount to becoming her; he considered dressing like the mother as a transitional activity (Winnicott 1953) stemming from a failure in individuation and operating as a defense against separation anxiety. The clothes are like the skin of the mother and play the same role as the kangaroo's pouch plays for her young. As we will see, this encompasses certain aspects of the case, though it evades the central importance of both unconscious delusion and role reversion.

Clinical material

Jaime's pediatrician referred him because his parents were afraid that he would evolve into homosexuality. A year previously, they had taken him to a hospital for consultation, but he was considered too ill to be treated there. He was spending an extra year in nursery school, having been rejected for primary school because of immaturity – he did not play with other children or respond to directions; instead, he would roll himself up into a ball on the floor in a corner and suck his thumb. At the club on weekends, he remained close to his mother; he would swim in the pool, but alone. Despite his father's efforts, he would not play football with him or with other children.

Jaime is the fourth of several siblings. He used a comforter until the age of 2 when he was toilet trained; he had no identifiable transitional object. His great pleasure was to be included by his sisters as one more girl, and he liked dolls quite a lot, especially Barbies. The mother gave the girls her cast-off clothes to play with and, as far as she can remember, Jaime loved to dress up in them for hours on end: garments, rings, necklaces and women's shoes all played a part in his feminine personifications. An older brother called him '*puto*' (male whore), until their parents forbade it. He enjoyed the long hair of his mother and sisters and took any opportunity to stroke it pleasurably, which led his mother to cut all their hair quite short.

His favourite feminine turn involved tying a long-sleeved T-shirt around his brow with the shirt tail and sleeves trailing down behind like long hair. He would then ecstatically shake his 'shirt-hair' in front of his sisters or alone. These games took place at home and not at public places like the nursery school, but there he would run into trouble with girls when he stroked their hair, for it wearied and annoyed them.

At the initial interview, the father admitted that Jaime's feminine behaviour exasperated him and that he was angered by Jaime's refusing to play with balls or cars or any other male game. He could only experience closeness to Jaime in card games. The mother was not greatly disturbed by the feminine behaviour. What disturbed her was the boy's violence when meeting with any opposition, and also a rhythmic head movement when going to sleep or in situations of anxiety.

After beginning therapy, I discovered that a few months after Jaime was born, the mother had become pregnant again and had wanted to have an abortion. Her religious convictions made that impossible, and she felt that God had betrayed her. After a spontaneous abortion, she became severely depressed and left to stay with relatives in the US. Jaime, who was about 12 months old, received no explanation. At the airport, on her return, the child became agitated. Suddenly the thought came to her that, during that interval, he had possibly believed that she had died.

Because of financial and scheduling constraints, we began with a restricted setting of two sessions per week: in fact, one of this presentation's goals is to show how the process managed to unfold even in such conditions.

At the first session, I had Jaime come in with the mother. To the question of whether he knew what he had come for, he offered no answer. Leaning against his mother, he sucked his fingers. Addressing Jaime and me, the mother said that he is coming because of his tantrums, and that in the preceding week, angry because there were noodles for lunch, he had given the matrimonial bed a heave and had made it come apart. Jaime laughed but stuck close to her. He did not approach the toybox in this or the following sessions. He did accept a pack of cards I gave him because it was the way he related to the father. Lying face down on the couch, he played cards with an invisible friend – he cheated and always won. Afterward, he did come in by himself but continued playing with his imaginary friend. Days later, saying that the invisible friend had gone to France, he began to play with me: when I pointed out his cheating, he accepted it but carried on. After a month, he approached the toybox, picked up the ball, proposed that we should play and passed it to me (a hand throw). His first drawing was of a house and two toboggans, one blue and one pink, noting that blue is a boy's colour and pink is for girls.

The stage of the "cacas"

After about two months, he began to play with plasticine (modeling clay). He made 'little sausages', stood them upright and measured them. He said they were families and that the biggest ones were the papas. He also said they were 'cacas' (faeces). He sometimes bathed them, and at the end of the session they died, and he threw them into the wastepaper basket; at other times they became food. At the following session he would make new ones. In general, when he began something, it would go on for some time, in what he would later call 'stages'. This, then, was the 'stage of the cacas'. Feminine voices and attitudes appeared only in the second year of analysis.

After about two months, as if just noticing it, he picked up the Barbie, saying, "This one, I don't use it because it's for girls". He continued playing with plasticine and drawing. He took to kicking the ball, trying to make a goal – but quite awkwardly. He never used animals, cars, blocks or other things from the box. He drew tall houses full of children in a chaotic environment. 'It is a mess', he would say, 'everything is missing there, from food to window panes', then, 'The sun is cold'. My feeling was that in referring to this congealed chaos he had a sort of a perception of evoking something internal, something there was no way of ordering. He made dinners, teas and breakfasts. Play dramatisations of the primal scene appeared, with Barbie and Ken under the couch or in the bathroom, narrated in an undertone. I heard some words like 'kisses' or 'walks'. Ken was very muscular and taller than Barbie. Jaime played with Barbie's hair: little by little he cut it, until one day, saying that she was dirty and a fool and that he did not like short hair, he tore off her head and arms, shredded her clothes with scissors and – calling her 'Irma' – said, 'She died and those who die go to heaven and never come back' in what seemed an impulsive attempt to eject his feminine identity. He threw her into the rubbish, from where I later rescued her. Days later, he asked, 'I threw that Irma away. Did you keep her?'. For the first time he felt anxiety, asking 'When will my mother come?'. I said that he became concerned about his mother, seeing how he had left Irma broken and quartered – dead. After the interpretation he calmed down. I added that once, when he was little, his mother had gone on a journey. He answered, 'When my mother went to the United States I didn't think *that*, that she had died'. A little later he asked for another Barbie. He named her Florencia. He continued playing his games but did not cut her hair.

Trying to clear up his sexual confusion, he threw away the pink felt-tipped pen, saying 'I don't want it because it's for girls', adding, 'I don't want to become a woman: they're all witches' and 'You, you're going to be a man'.

The stage of the "little tablecloths"

About eight months into the treatment, he entered the 'stage of the little tablecloths'. He folded a sheet of paper several times and cut the edges into a sort of fretwork, laughing as he showed me the little rhomboid holes. Aiming at his castration anxiety, I suggested that when he cut the points off the paper, little holes were left. On one side of these 'little tablecloths' he painted pink girl cars and, on the other, black boy trucks (Figure 6.1 shows two sides of a single sheet; at this 'stage' he used both sides of the paper only when defining gender). One day I told him that he made a black truck of a boy like himself and a pink girl's one like a girl he sometimes wants to be; that he confuses himself because he has a willy like Dad but sometimes he wants to be a girl. He answered, 'When I dress up like a girl, I believe I am a real little woman'. He crumpled the tablecloth/drawing into a ball and threw it on the floor, saying 'Better let's go and draw grass. How high it is'. As he drew, he named things: 'A sun and clouds, a flower'. He crumpled this up too and threw it away, saying 'I'll give it to you. The sky came out too high', then 'I'm going to make another. The house is pink like my willy'. He wrote his name, making a mistake with one letter and laughing as he looked at what he had written. I asked him what he had wanted to write. He answered 'Lulú'.

At the following session, he tried three times to write his name and made mistakes each time. I said that he was getting into a problem because of his boy's name, maybe because he wanted to have a girl's name. He answered, 'D'you know what the girls in my class are called?' and recited several names. He wiped his nose with the paper and gave it to me, creased and folded. I mentioned that he must not like his name very much for he had used it to wipe his nose. He then wrote the letter 'J' (his initial) and, after asking if I was a J, said it was a 'wicked' J: 'Can't you see that it's the upside-down world?' I answered that the upside-down world is the problem he has because of being a male and, perhaps, wanting to be a female. At this point he managed to write his name correctly, then pasted on the strips of fretwork and painted them girl and boy colours and neutral green.

Days later he drew a blue truck – a boy's one – and then crossed it out and threw it away, saying it had come out badly. I told him that boys' things came out badly for him and that was why he wanted to throw them away. He answered that he was going to write a story: he drew a flower/house and, in a climate of growing incoherence and agitation, read 'Once there was a birdie who fell from the tree and was crying. . . . No, that wasn't the story. It was about a lady with hair curlers, and another called Chucha. And there was a girl playing with a doll [he started to get more agitated], and they fight. And Mrs.

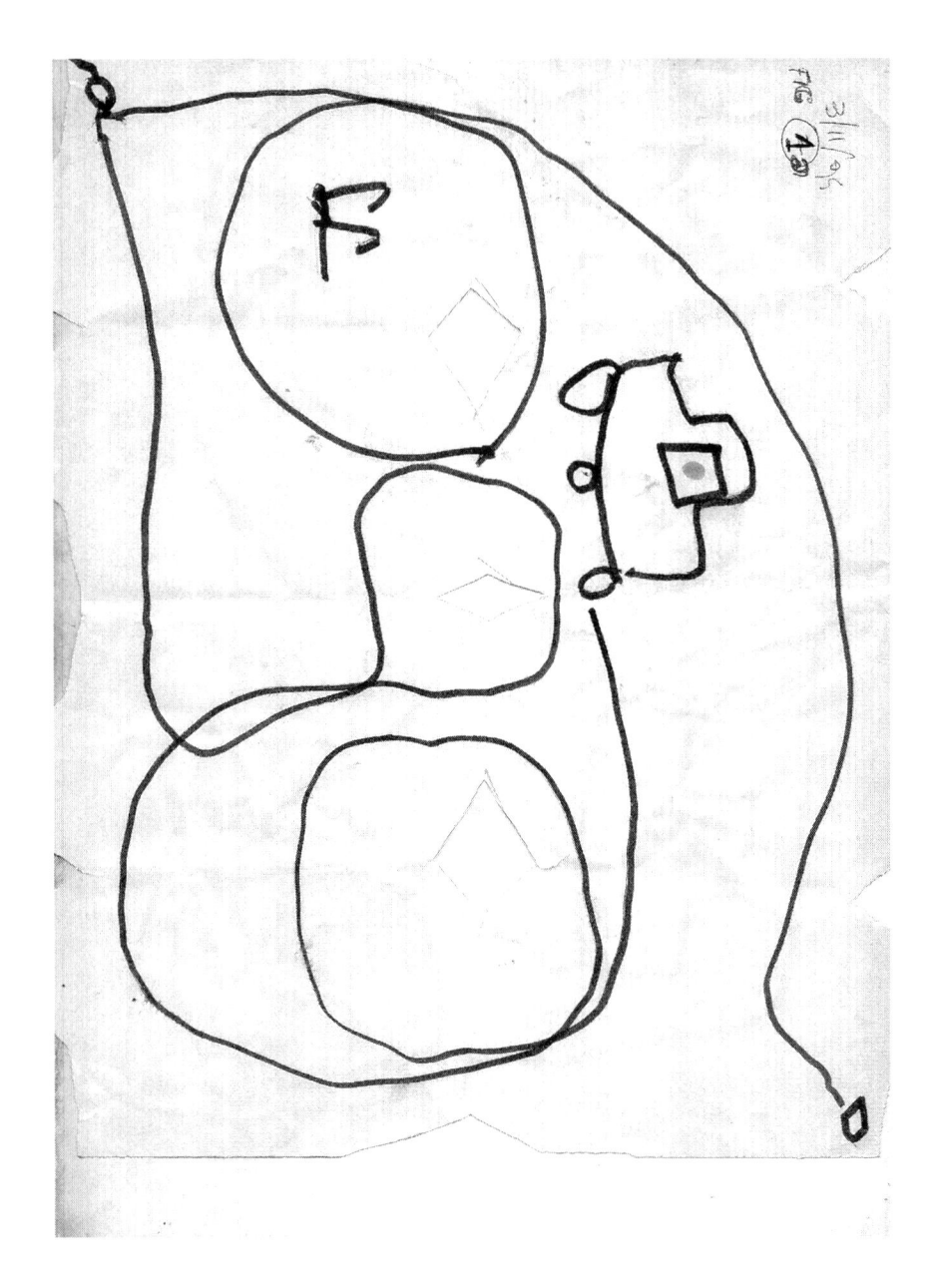

Figure 6.1A The little tablecloths

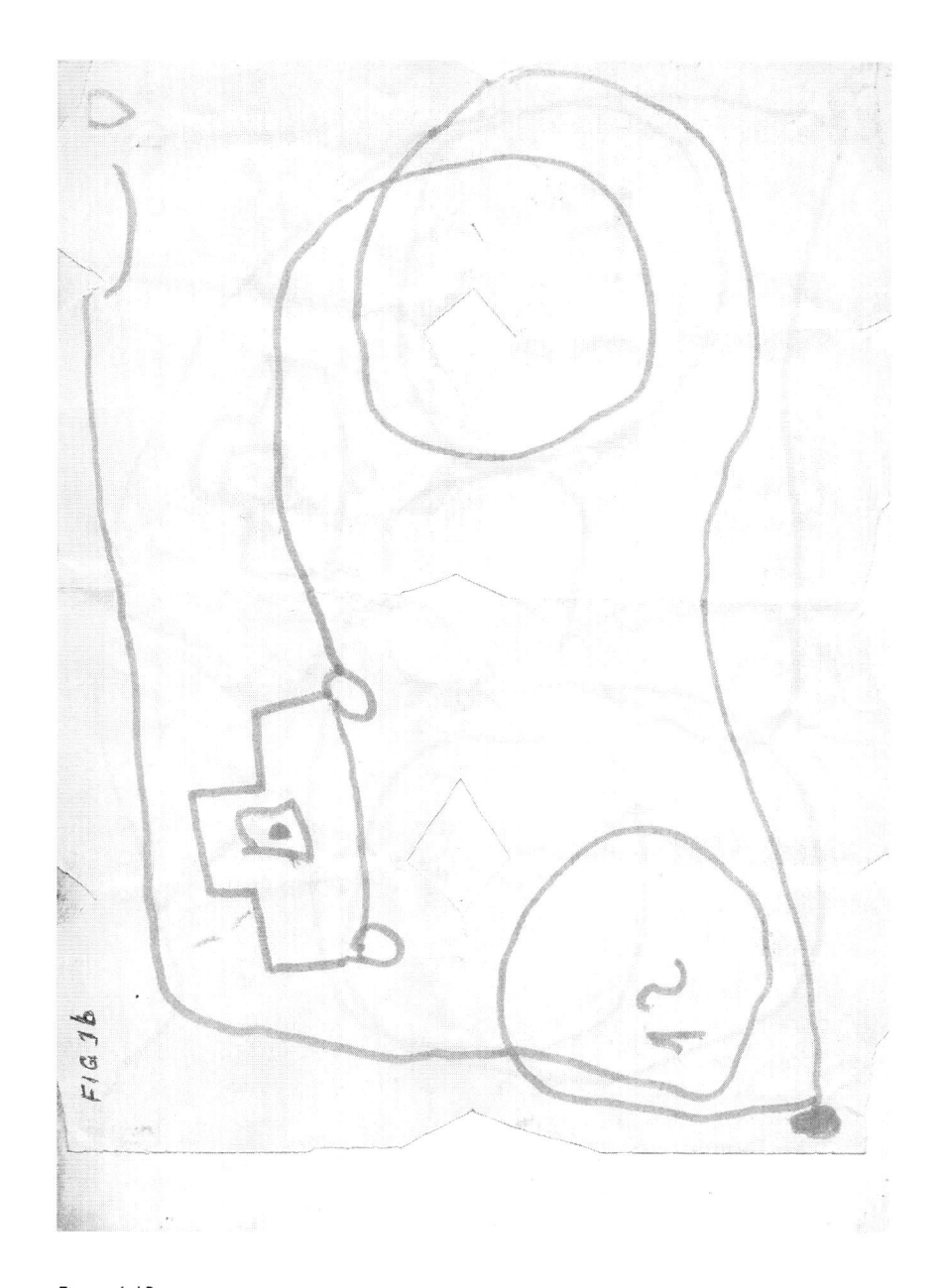

Figure 6.1B

Chucha said to her, "Shut up". And the lady with curlers said "We are going to sing a song: How lovely it would be to fart and not say who did it, and go to the toilet and not find paper and wipe myself on the wall"'. Then he segued into, 'My lovely little globe, painted blue . . . [a song from the nursery]'. Finally, he said, 'I want to pee' and when he returned, calmer and more coherent, possibly through the bodily evacuation of his aggression, he said 'I'm going to play with Barbie. I haven't taken her out for so long. I've missed her so much'. Jaime stroked her hair and then, with a sad air, gave her back, saying 'Here, give her to your sister or your daughter, I don't want her in my box anymore'. This was the first time that he acknowledged that I have children. Later, he wrote out in fancy and confused ways his initials, his name, letters and numbers, asking in turn, 'What's this? . . . What's this?'. I answered that he was asking me and asking himself who he is and what he is like.

As Christmas and the school holidays approached, he contentedly made gifts for me and my husband and children. However, in the last session, as he quietly drew a Christmas scene with snow falling, he became frightened because the snow was increasing until it froze the entire universe. (My feeling was that after having installed himself with great intensity in the treatment, the holidays implied a return to the cold universe, and that this was beginning to register.) After a moment of terror, two suns appeared and began to thaw out the world, implying, I believe, a measure of hope. He remained quite drained of vitality and lay on the couch gazing at the ceiling. After a while, he fixed his attention on an orifice at the centre of the ceiling fan in the consulting room. He perked up a bit and said that he wanted to put a felt-tip pen into that hole. When I said that he wanted to insert there his felt-tip pen – his willy – he felt very relieved and when he left he seemed more integrated.

During that first year, there were changes in his behaviour at school. He stopped withdrawing into corners, mixed with other children and stopped stroking the girls' hair. He was able to pass into the first form, work at his desk and learn to read and write. Even so, he did experience moments of withdrawal.

His games in sessions at the beginning of the second year of treatment featured the black (or brown) boy's car and the pink girl's car (always drawn on opposite sides of the same sheet of paper), which had to go through the small holes of the little tablecloths to reach the wheels or balls on the opposite side. One day, he took out the Barbie, greeted her, caressed her and put her away again. He referred to himself as Lulú frequently, but also said that when he was big he was going to be able to put his felt-tip pen into the hole in my ventilator. Around the middle of the year, he invented more structured games, though he cheated and twisted the rules. Behind my back (so that I would not laugh, he said), he played with Barbie and Ken.

The stage of the "Señorita"

One day towards the end of the second year, when he was already able to read and write, Jaime came into the session, sat in my chair and said in a theatrical voice that he was Señorita (Miss) Norma Beatriz, the teacher, and I was the pupil, and that we were in class. He spoke about himself in the feminine gender (more obvious in Spanish than English): Norma Beatriz was not a game, not make-believe, but a certainty. He scolded me a lot for being a bad student and said that I would not be promoted if I did not do things properly. He taught me some letters from a non-existent alphabet he had invented, changing what he had learned at school – and not through uncertainty or ignorance but as part of a process of changing things round. Thus, he drew a building and said 'This is a house', and then he drew a house and said 'This is a building'. Every so often he would say 'Now it is time for the break' and, after becoming Jaime again, would play 'secretly' with Barbie and Ken.

One day, when I mentioned something about 'your mother' he retorted indignantly, 'Don't say "your mother". I *am* a mother; I have children'. Before the holidays, he came in with a bad stomach, vomiting. He was apathetic and did not play, and asked 'When is my mother coming?'.

After the holidays, he picked up the Barbie and cut her hair a little, saying that it would grow back. In later sessions, he was sad to see that her hair did not grow back, and he tried to paste on the hair he had cut off. Then he again became Norma Beatriz, with exaggeratedly feminine gestures and speech that sounded like self-parody.

Sessions then alternated: some were more depressive and others more manic. Thus, he drew a boy he called Lucas and then Lacas, with breasts and a penis. He invented a confused song, with stories of loss, theft and recovery: 'There was once a woman with big tits [he laughs] and then a girl touched her tit. Oh, how horrible! And a man came and touched her willy (Laralá-la, hahahá-ha), and then Lacas came and touched her cap (heeheehee). A thief came and stole her tit and the willy, and then the girl began to cry and she had no tits, and when she had a baby it couldn't drink milk because she had no tits, and then she recovered her willy and tits and Lacas came and they kissed on the mouth'. I did not interpret, because when he was agitated he would evacuate contents. Like a beta screen (Bion 1962), he did not listen then and any attempt of mine to get him to do so would exacerbate the agitation. During the following session, I asked him, 'Do you remember that Lacas had a willy and tits?' I told him that he wanted to have a willy and tits; be Jaime and Norma Beatriz or Lulú. He answered, 'better I'll call myself Maria, which is a girl's and a boy's name [in Spanish]. I really want to be a boy with long hair'.

In the months that followed, he enacted in sessions the delusional identification with the role of Norma Beatriz, showing me the invented letters of the language of a country we would go to: "Poquea". He made a drawing of this country, where trees have curls for leaves and houses were the shape of fancy bows, complete with other feminine embellishments that he described in a laboured, effeminate way. He said, 'It's a very special country, but imaginary'. He drew its map, saying it had the shape of a penis. Finally, he decided on a journey to "Poquea", with me sitting on the table and him standing on it, directing the voyage. He resolved to change the destination and travel to China, then fell into an agitated anxiety, saying that his head was getting confused and was mixing everything up.

At that point he made a drawing of his brain to better explain this (Figure 6.2). In the inner circle he wrote YO (myself) in capital letters. When I said, 'There, you have put yourself', he wrote VOS (you), thus including me in the situation. At the front of a second circle he placed the BARBIES and MUÑECOS (male dolls); on one side of the head he placed FUTBOL (football), BIDEOS (videos) and PLATA (money) and, on the other, MI CAMA (my bed), CHI (children) and LUISA (myself). Behind came COLEGIO (school) and even further back, out on a third area, NORMA BEATRIZ. Then he crossed her out, saying 'She went to China and is inside another man'. I said, 'And you wanted to go to China and that was when this whole mess happened? It's not easy for Norma Beatriz to go . . .'. He interrupted, 'But I don't want her to come back! She's no longer in the back of my head', adding, in a reflective tone, 'Yesterday I played with the Barbies, alone, but I was myself; I wasn't Norma Beatriz. Afterwards everything got mixed up for me, and then I began to think about football – at school – because the winter holidays ended, and I didn't play anymore'. This last sentence was said in a depressed tone. I felt that with a measure of sadness he was gradually accepting his condition of being male and abandoning bisexuality and the gambit of femininity as ways of arming himself against chaos.

Towards the end of the third year, Norma Beatriz no longer appeared. After considerable time he took Barbie out and, seeing that her hair was still short, said that now he realised that her hair was not going to grow. Then, two weeks before the holidays, in a more depressed period, he showed me some accounts with the felt-tip pens, adding and subtracting by 'ones' to provide a firmer support for his thinking. He remarked that he was big and understood that dolls' hair did not grow back, adding that we could throw Barbie away because he was not going to use her anymore. Later, and after looking at her with affection, he put her away in his drawer.

The day before the holidays, in a more reflexive moment as he played with the felt-tip pens, he again saw the hole in the middle of the ceiling fan. He

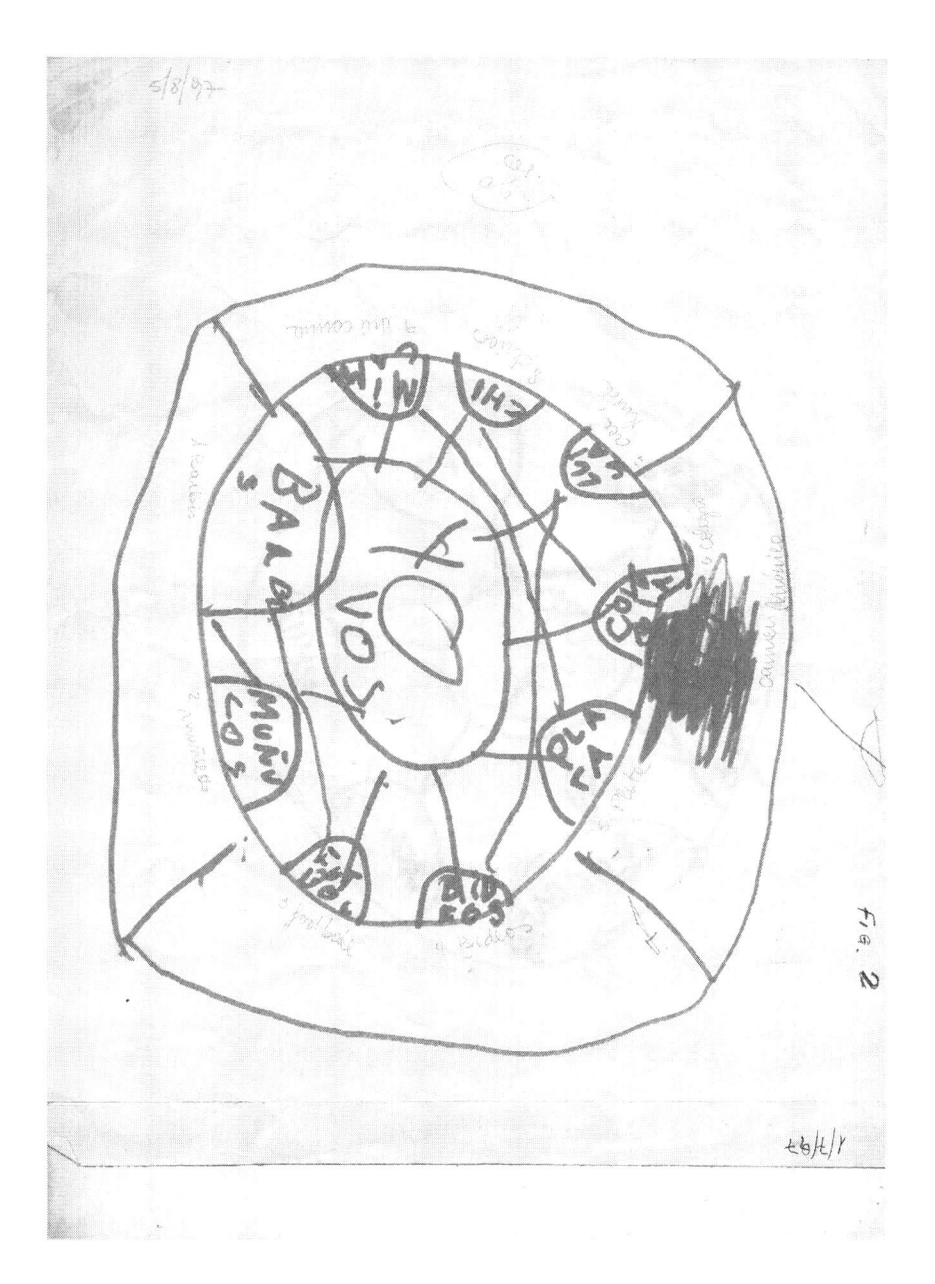

Figure 6.2 My mixed-up brain

taped several pens together in an effort to reach it but did not manage and said that he still had to grow more, that maybe after the holidays he would reach it.

The stage of the "Titanic"

When analysis resumed, he connected right away, playing hide-and-seek despite the consulting room limitations. He gave himself male names but added female endings, with Ezequiel becoming 'Ezequiela', for example. I told him that this was a bit like Jaime/Norma Beatriz, who is a boy and adds something of a girl. He then proposed to change the game, saying that we would go in little boats to Uruguay. We made two paper boats. He called one Luisa (it was for me) and his was Jaime. He told me to follow him because he knew the way down from the table to the floor: 'Watch out for the ocean . . . go along the river . . . in the ocean there are sharks that can eat you'. The boats collided – first his and then mine – and their points broke off (he cut them off with scissors). 'But we can sail on'. I mentioned his fear of sharks that can eat your willy, because the boats lost their points, possibly their willies, in the crash. The game continued. 'Now it is night-time', he said, turning off the consulting room light. 'How scary. We have to bring the boats together'. Then he began to call one of them *Titanic*, and so inaugurated a central stage: that of the *Titanic*. He taped the boats together. 'It's going to sink, it's crashing against a mountain of ice!'. Then he asked, 'You, what do you prefer, to die in freezing water or be eaten by sharks? Well, they could be dolphins or whales, there are killer whales too'. He made the *Titanic* crash against the mountain of ice. It broke up and he threw it away. 'Did you see the picture *Titanic*? I didn't, but I saw when it crashed, thousands of people died, but some are saved'. While the fear of annihilation continued to be present, a chance of being saved was beginning to surface.

In the next session he drew a 'more better' *Titanic*, with windows, very tall. He asked me to draw the windows, 'Mine are not good'. He called it 'Tita-nic', 'because that's the way it is' (Tita is a woman's nickname in Spanish). He pasted another paper onto it, saying with strong gestures and a strong voice that the glue is like the cement of the boat and that he wants the boat to be 'really hard and really big'. He turned off the light 'because it is nighttime'; I was to pilot the boat while he guided me. We came down from the table through cataracts to the river and the ocean, and then he took the boat and crashed it against a table leg. The boat broke up. 'The whole ocean is full of blood that is blue because it's frozen'. He tore the endpoints off the boat and threw them on the table, while two other pieces sank into the ocean (he placed them under the rug). Then he said, 'We're going to make another *Titanic*, not as big but much stronger, to go and get the one that broke'. He drew it, asked me to cut it out, then pasted it up. He picked up the point of the previous *Titanic*, said it looked like a willy and placed it over his genital area, then said, 'No, it doesn't look like it', and threw it away. Now time was up. He was sorry not to finish the game: 'Well, we'll continue next time'.

He continued making bigger, stronger versions of the *Titanic*, with added features, and, since we always collided with the iceberg, the *Titanic* would lose something with the shape of a penis: I noted how dangerous the crashes were, because the boat lost its willy or the sharks ate it. He set off the shark alarm, saying 'It looks like a willy'. Then we crashed against an island: 'It's very, very hot, bodies are melting and becoming just juice'. I said that Papa and Mamma crash; they are together when they make babies. He answered, 'Yes, you know how they must sweat when they are so together'. I said that perhaps he felt that as being dangerous, and he answered, 'Houses have something like air-conditioning; cold comes out from the walls. If they are in there they are saved'.

In another session, he made an even bigger boat with four sheets of paper, paste and tape, three storeys up and one down, and told me, 'With this one, we are going to be able to travel much more; look how hard it is'. He asked me to cut it out, saying, 'While you cut it out, I have a free period'. He got up on the couch and sang and danced very well, quite in the style of a girl. I told him that during the break he allowed his girl part to appear. He answered, 'Like before, when we sang songs, D'you remember? And remember when I've made *cacas* with the plasticine in the water and that was in the first form, no, in nursery school, and then it was the Barbie and then Norma Beatriz?'. He said that he had invented the song himself (he sang something about the soft wind of the Caribbean and returning or not returning, with dancing and gestures).

After cutting out the *Titanic*, he made me touch it to see how hard it was: 'This one is really hard and strong; this one is not going to break'. I said that I believed that the stronger, harder and bigger, the less danger he felt – more secure. But I knew that I was missing the point: the danger was there and the solution was to be feminine, and this was what happened during the 'free periods'. I did say that possibly it reassured him to do girl things in his free period. He finished the boat, we travelled to the United States and crashed against its coast, but with this *Titanic* being so strong, nothing happened – the point got squashed, but he said that was nothing.

Following this phallic-genital crescendo over two months, a more regressive stage recapitulated the treatment's early period. He declared that he had had enough of the *Titanic* and of school (because they made him study) but that he did like the breaks. Once again, he gave me cookery lessons, often in the laboured style of a TV-lesson, making little faecal sausages in the guise of cannelloni, which he called *riculines*. 'Actually', he added, 'they are *culines*' (unavoidably an allusion to *culo*, Spanish for arsehole), but so good that they are *riculines.* (A meaning for *rico* in Spanish is 'good to eat'). He sang and danced, pretending to be in a ballet and acting partly male and partly female – something that I mentioned. He remembered the episodes with the fan, asking 'D'you remember when I wanted to reach that hole and couldn't, and taped all the felt-tip pens together and couldn't reach, and stood on the cushions and couldn't either? Let's see if I can reach now'. He got up on the table with the *riculín* 'sausage', but it sagged and he laughed. I noted that it seemed that the *pitulín-riculín* (note the mixup of zones: phallic, oral and anal; *pito* is 'willy') still couldn't reach the hole, and that he wants to get there like Papa, with his willy, gets to Mamma's little hole. He got down from the table, remarking, 'Well, okay, now we have to cut the *riculines'*. He took the scissors and began cutting. 'Come on, cut, you too. No, wait until I finish. I'll give you the scissors'. I said that it looks like the long *pitulín-riculín* was no good; that it had to be cut and that, perhaps, that was what he was afraid would happen with his. He said, 'Go on, we have to eat them'. He speared them with a pencil and pretended to eat, saying 'They all have to have a hole, else they are not right'. He said he was going to bless them, placed them in water, declared that they were blessed, pulled them out in twos and made them sing, chanting 'Lará, lará, lará, the *concha* (both cunt and shell, here standing for 'vagina') of your mother'. Then, in twos, he threw them into the wastepaper basket and told me I had to sing. I asked him what the *concha* of his mother was. He didn't answer and asked for more plasticine for the next time.

The stage of the "interplanetary journeys"

Coinciding with the football World Cup in France (he was always thinking about countries and trips), he declared that the stage of the *Titanic* had ended and that he was going to build a rocket to travel to France; then it became an interplanetary voyage. He drew the rocket, painted it blue and red, and put his name and mine on it, saying that it was very hot because it was very close to the sun. He drew the solar system with considerable precision and added other galaxies. He said that we were traveling into space to conquer other worlds and explained to me the solar system in relation to other galaxies: 'One called *Cola* (a vaginal-anal conflation) is close to a black hole that sucks everything up and makes it disappear' (Figure 6.3). I ventured, 'Looks like the black holes are very dangerous', to which he replied, 'Yes, yes, if our rocket goes out of the solar system and passes close to the black holes. Yes, the black hole then sucks it, swallows it, dies and makes it disappear. But if from *Cola* and another galaxy next to it (he explained with drawings) they fill and fill the

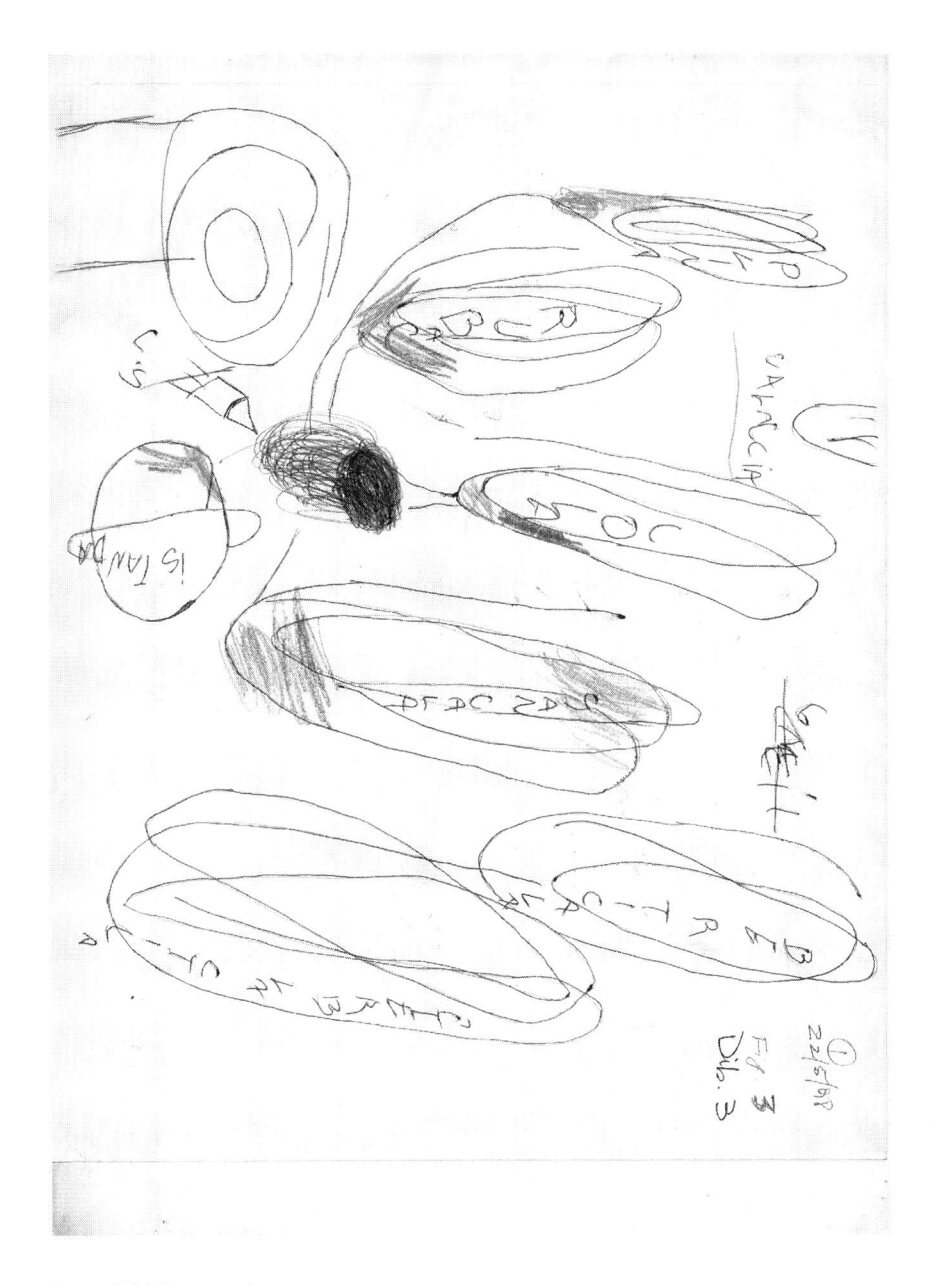

Figure 6.3 The interplanetary journey

black hole, then afterwards they are not so dangerous and we can pass. That's why I'm testing you: you've got to know the way so the black hole won't swallow up your rocket'.

One day, he said that a knot in the wood of my table was the black hole. He used a felt-tip pen as a rocket to fly low over it. He said the hole was swallowing up the rocket, and he made the pen/rocket disappear by throwing it back behind him. He explained what black holes 'with teeth' are like (by placing his fingers in front of his mouth like enormous teeth). I said, 'The rocket is like your willy and the black hole is the hole in girls, which is very dangerous: it bites and swallows up willies'. Then he went back to drawing and said, 'There's also a blue hole: these are not as dangerous; they don't have teeth, they have little mountains and you can go in and come out. They've become brothers for life, the black hole and the blue hole' (Figure 6.4).

We traveled through space, skirting around black holes that swallow and kill. I pointed out to him that, because of the intense way he was experiencing this, it was a real situation for him, not a game.

Days later, after going to an amusement park, he came in and was quite agitated, with effeminate attitudes and remarks. I told him that it looked like Norma Beatriz had returned. He answered that she was in China, and then, 'Yes, yes, she came back for a little bit, but she only comes here; she never comes to school, or home either' – this all in his boy's voice. Then, with exaggerated feminine tones and gestures, he said that he was going to dictate to me the games at the amusement park. Laughing, mocking and effeminate, he corrected me and made fun of me because of things I didn't know; at such manic moments I would feel the brunt of his devaluing me. Then he threw himself on the couch, saying 'While you write, I'll tell you about Norma Beatriz: she went to China but she comes back for a bit and then she goes further, to Japan, and then she will go through space in a rocket to the black holes. But the rocket is not going to be sucked in; it'll turn around and come back to Japan'. Again, I took up his fear that the willy/rocket would be destroyed by the black hole of girls – the holes of women – and so he prefers to be a woman – Norma Beatriz to whom nothing happens with black holes – and that he feels more secure that way. He answered, 'I'm going to do some exercises', then jumped from the chest of drawers to the couch and turned somersaults. He wanted to turn on the fan, saying that it was very hot, and then said, 'I'm going to see if now I can get to the hole in the fan'. He piled the three large cushions on the table, asked me to help him keep his balance, and nearly reached the hole with the felt-tip pen. Very excited, he threw himself back onto the couch.

At the following session, he said he wasn't going to draw the attractions at the amusement park and drew a pirate ship in the form of a canoe (he liked

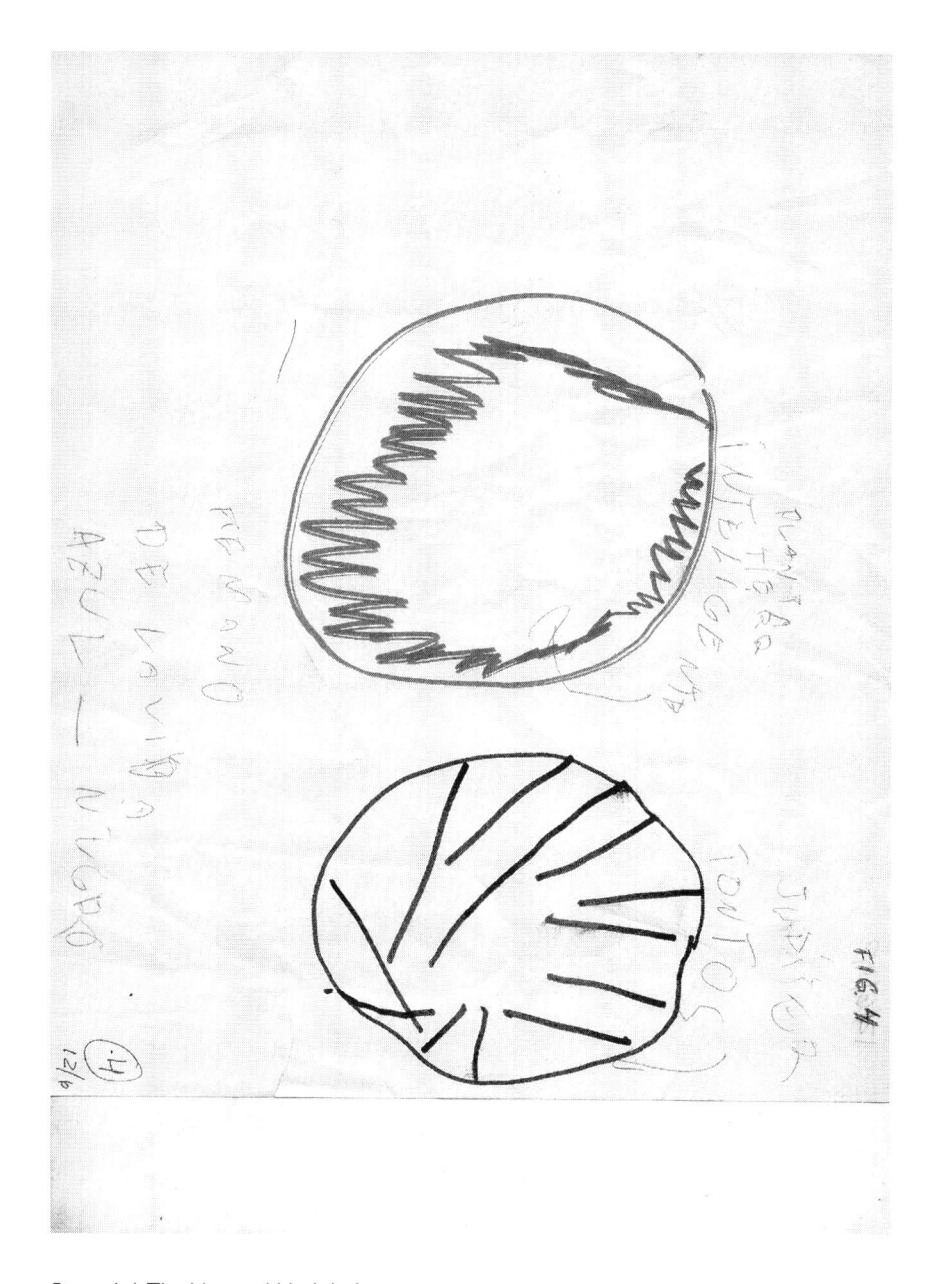

Figure 6.4 The blue and black holes

the pirate ship at the amusement park because riding on it tickled his balls). Then, 'No, I've had enough of the amusement park, let's learn the mouth', emphasizing the 'b' for *boca* ('mouth' in Spanish). He drew a mouth with all the teeth, cut it out and asked, 'What fruit does it look like? A banana', and then sang, in an effeminate way, something like, 'Little banana of Paris' and, giving me a look of complicity, he laughed, allowing, 'Norma Beatriz came'. I said that the banana reminded him of his willy, and that it scared him so much that he 'made believe' he was Norma Beatriz. Placing the cut-out mouth in front of his own, he asked, 'Does it look like a hippopotamus's mouth?'. He laughed quite manically, making me hold it up in front of my mouth many times. Then he made a hole in the mouth of the cut-out (Figure 6.5), placed it against his mouth and made me put my finger through the hole, assuring me that he was not going to bite it. I said of this that the finger through the hole was like the willy in the hole: he laughed in a quieter way.

This sequence of the 'canoe-mouth'/'finger-penis' shows a crucial enactment in the working through of anxiety, differentiating the oral-sadistic universe and the sadistic sexual relation on one hand, and the habitable universe of the blue vagina on the other.

At mid-year, his tantrums had not yet been manifested in sessions. One day his sister brought him, and he came into the consulting room furious because he had not been able to get her to take his backpack. He swept everything on the desk to the floor. Turning, he said 'So you can see what I'm like when I get mad'. Then, resuming his play, he turned off a light; night was falling – then turned off another – now it was night and we had to sleep. He turned them back on and said that we had to change everything round and rearrange the furniture so that the place would be different. He threw himself onto his stomach on the couch (now it was a mat), saying, 'C'mon, be a sport'. I remarked that it was like the rides at the amusement park. He said it looked like the mad bus, that 'when he goes back towards it tickles your balls'; something she liked a lot. 'You can't be like this, you've got to be a bit more game', he continued, unbuckling the last fastener of my belt. I said, 'When you feel the tickle in your balls you touch me. It seems that you want to know what women are like'. (Here, his masculinity kicked in without any castration anxiety surfacing, for when he challenges me to be more game, I am the one who isn't a sport.) He turned off a light, then another, saying that it was time to go to sleep, under the desk, together. Then, for a week, he played in a rather agitated way at very effeminate games, creating scenarios, moving the furniture, sometimes throwing himself on the couch, crying, 'Good-bye, cruel world! Good-bye, cruel world!'. On one occasion, he bit into a felt-tip pen until he destroyed it, then yelled, 'I destroyed it', somewhere between excited and sorry, and I said that he was afraid his willy would be ruined and destroyed like the

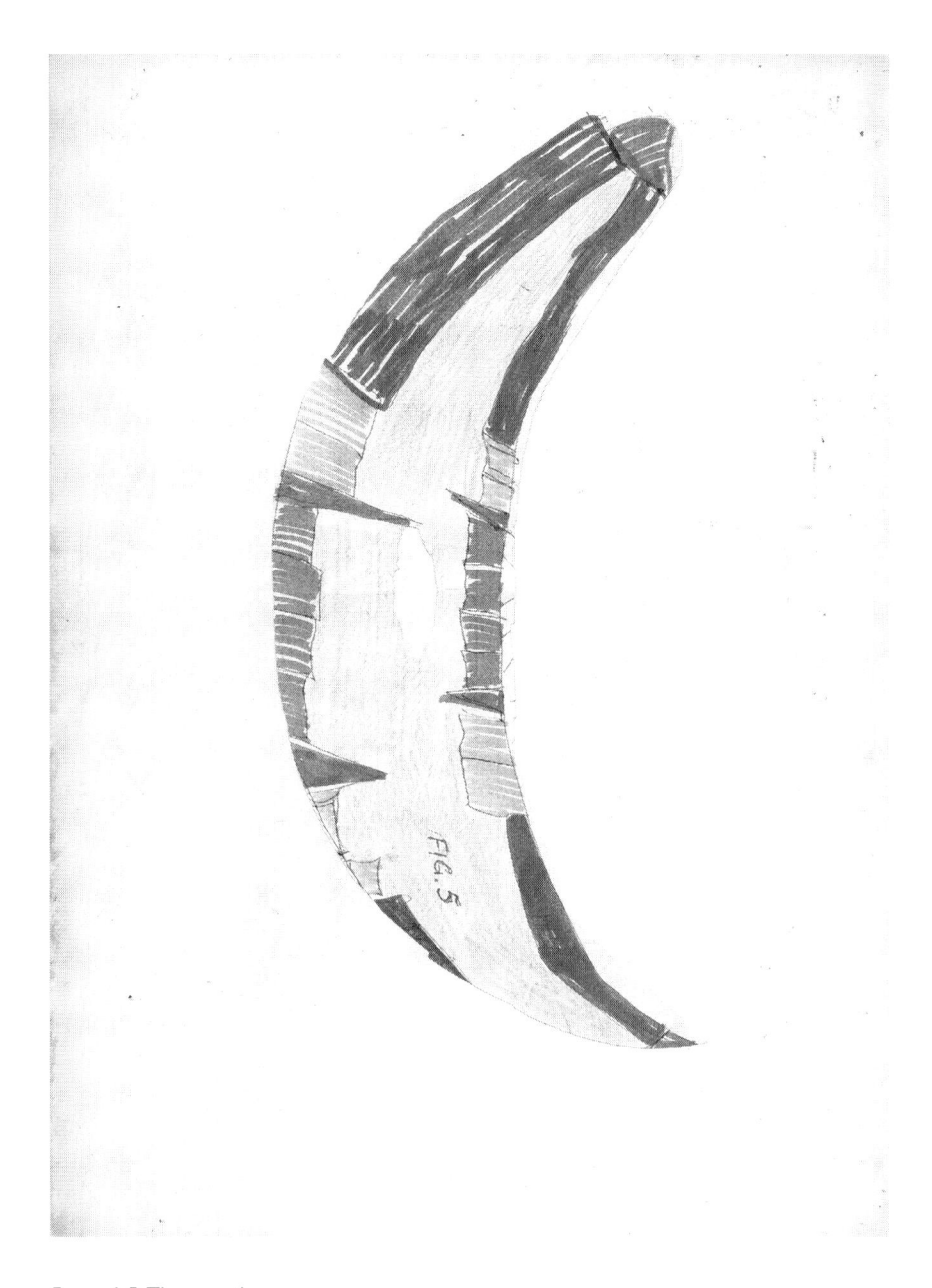

Figure 6.5 The mouth

felt-tip pen. He gave me an astounded look and answered, 'Yes'. Looking for another pen, he ran into Barbie and said with regret that her hair never did grow back. I said that it was hard for him to accept that what he expected did not happen. He took up the ruined felt-tip pen to paint her hair: 'This way she looks better', and 'D'you remember when I made fashion shows? Last year I think she walked in a show one time only . . . she's in Poquea . . . looking very lovely . . . there too were Norma Beatriz, María del Carmen, Yolanda, but Barbie is the loveliest!'. When he left he turned off the lights. I said that he didn't want me to see other children. He wanted me to close up the consulting room when he left.

During the winter holidays, he was annoyed at the sessions because he had thought he wouldn't have to come. He opened the box, found Barbie, took her out, caressed her, stroked her hair and got hold of a felt-tip pen with which to paint it. He also found a *Titanic* that he had finished with plasticine and tape. He said 'Wow! The *Titanic* . . . Barbie is going to visit the remains of the *Titanic*'. He threw it under the couch and had Barbie ask how much it would cost to visit the remains under the couch. He answered, 'Thirty thousand pesos'. She would pay, so he asked me to turn off the light because in the ocean depths everything is dark. I turned off one light and he said, 'No, no, don't turn off the other one, I get really frightened down there in the dark'. I remembered the black hole. He made Barbie descend under the couch to rescue the remains of the *Titanic*. I said, 'Down there in the depths, it is all dark and there are the remains of something to be rescued'. He answered, 'Yes, we're going to fix it'. I think he was speaking about himself, about those remains that must be fixed, revolving around the fear for the *Titanic* in the black hole and also his fear of depending too much on the analyst.

He lined a new *Titanic* with tape but made a mess of it and got angry, swearing and exclaiming, 'The *concha* of the monkey'. When I asked him what he meant, he explained, 'This is Barbie's *concha*. There are two kinds of *concha*: one is this one (he came out from behind the desk and touched his genitals) – well, of women, obviously – and the other is the marine shell'.

He repaired the *Titanic* with tape, and when it looked ready he placed it over the Barbie. 'It's small for her. It looks like a piece broke off in front, she and a lot up top, well . . .'. He threw it all back in the box, 'Barbie's off to Poquea. They're flying. I thought they were swimming . . . fly to Poquea and she gets down because she becomes nauseous'. Then he made me sit on the couch, saying 'It's got to be properly fixed up. Don't you see it looks like a mess?'. He arranged the couch and two chairs, saying that it was a hotel. Barbie acted and asked how much the hotel cost. He said, 'I'm a manager for Barbie. This is a very good hotel: they give you this for your breasts', taping a bodice onto Barbie and saying, 'I'm going to put tape and the waist and some more on the *concha*. No, better not'. He dressed her after taking off the bodice, saying that the hotel would give it to her – that it was discardable – showing more acceptance of feminine breasts and genitals.

After the winter vacations, there was a football tournament. In August, he moved the furniture of the consulting room to make the couch and desk into goalposts and create room for kicking. He was playing well, with precision and strength, and getting many shots by me. When it was my turn to shoot, he made quite an effort to stop the ball, throwing himself onto the floor and generally winning fairly, though if I ever got close he would change the rules so that he could win. I noted this, saying that he did not like to lose, but that we should have good rules and abide by them. We played: he taught me how to improve my technique, how to trick the goalie by kicking with the upper part of the foot and not the tip. After one weekend, he told me that he had played a lot with his father and brother, and that was why he was now playing and kicking better.

In September, when I called him 'Jaime' instead of the usual 'you', telling him that he was playing and practicing a lot and that was why he was beating me, he answered, 'Thing is, Norma Beatriz isn't coming anymore'. When I tried to ask him about this, he explained, 'Well, you remember the black hole: the one with the teeth, not the blue one? It ate her up. Okay, go on, shoot'.

I did not insist. He said that he played a lot and that his football team was the school's champion. He organised championships, and we also played tic-tac-toe and hangman: he played using the names of countries. In November, a hanged man he had chosen turned out to be called Maria Norma. He surprised himself when he read out the name, and noted, 'I was muddled: it was Norma Beatriz or perhaps Maria Norma. It was so long ago!' He laughed. 'Ever since the black hole swallowed her up, I never remembered again'. He did not want to continue with this topic.

In the penultimate session of the year, he said, 'I was thinking that after this I won't come until March'. He brought out the ball, threw it against the wall and then put it away. He said he was going to do something different with the *Titanic*, as it would be in March: 'We're going to reinforce it'. He found a model in the box and asked me to help him strengthen it with tape: 'We've got to reinforce it'. I said that the holidays frightened him and that, since we were not going to see each other for some time, both of us had to be strong. He agreed and became pensive, then said, 'Okay, the time we have left, let's play the game of the million (a TV game). He made me choose a million and a motorcycle and he chose a million and a wheelchair. When I questioned this, he replied, 'Because I need it'. I said that he felt he was going to need help until he returned in March.

After the holidays, he played football, brought raises from school and told me about his weekends: he was spending more time with his father and seemed much more connected. Towards the end of March he came up with an idea: since the year 2000 would begin at the year's end, we would make envelopes to keep things in until then. For the first envelope, he drew a factory, using a pencil as the ruler. I remarked that he was like an engineer making a blueprint, and he answered, 'Yes, my dad's an engineer, did you know?'. He made smoke come out of the smokestack, then cut the whole thing out, but when he tried to place it into the envelope, the 'smoke' would not fit. He wondered whether to cut off the smoke or fold it, then said, laughing, 'It's like a factory's willy, the smoke, isn't it? Finally, he put the factory into a larger envelope, smoke and all. After a weekend in the country, he made a very good drawing of the house he had stayed at and provided detailed explanations.

The return of the *Titanic*

In the fifth year of analysis, Jaime asked whether I remembered the *Titanic*; he said he was going to make one. He drew the windows and pasted on the smokestacks. He said there was third, second and first class, four stacks and windows in the holds. He didn't like how the prow had turned out but said he couldn't make a better one. He said that he had searched under 'Titanic' in the computer's encyclopedia but did not find much, and that there was nothing for 'sunken Titanic'. He was happy with what he had made. 'It's better than the other ones; d'you remember? It's much bigger'. He made it sail from the table (London) and, after going round the consulting room, he went to New York. He asked me to hold up the stern because it was drooping. Then, saying, 'But this is a very short little trip; there's no space for the crash with the iceberg', he asked to use the entrance and passageway, where the bluish-grey tiled floor 'looks like water'. He placed me at the far end, with two cushions from the couch representing the iceberg. Turning the lights on and off, he simulated daybreak and nightfall. He then turned them all off: 'Like this it's perfect, it's night-time, it's all dark'. He became frightened, turned on one light and said, 'We'll pretend it's daybreak'. He advanced up the passageway carrying the ship in both hands, got close and yelled, 'Iceberg ahoy! Full speed and turn!'. He grazed the cushion and told me to wait because he had forgotten something, then took the scissors, repeated the scene and, after grazing the iceberg, cut the *Titanic* in half. 'A great hole was made in "third class", the stacks fall, the prow sinks (it falls to the floor), the stern is now sinking like this (the stern slowly rises), it fills with water . . .'. Then the stern fell to the floor as well. It was a dramatic moment; we were experiencing the sinking of the ship – the murky water, the water-coloured floor, the greyish-blue cushions.

He said, 'It's all destroyed at the bottom of the sea'. He remained in silence for a moment, sighed, brought the pieces together and said, 'C'mon, let's make another one', and taped up three sheets of paper. I said that just as a boat that big and strong sank, there are also babies that feel big and strong, but when they don't have their mother, they feel they are sinking. He did not answer but listened attentively.

At the following session he brought the boat out again and continued to make it with tape and adhesives contentedly. 'It's really good. It has four storeys: the first is the biggest . . . Okay, go and set up the iceberg'. He asked me to stretch out my arms and arranged the three cushions, taking care to have a point jut out. I was to stand at the end of the passageway like the previous time. He advanced with the ship, yelling 'Icebergs ahoy!', and the boat grazed past, suffering no damage. He turned and executed another pass, now making the noises of a crash. The air was murky; drama was high. The finale was slow. He pulled off the stacks 'so that they may sink very deep'. The next bit of the ship proved hard to break off: 'I think it's pretty well made: it will hardly break'. Finally, he broke it up. The pieces fell into the deep; the stern gyrated slowly and sank. I remarked again that this powerful but fragile ship that broke up and sunk reminded me of a baby – also fragile – that, when his mother is absent or is busy elsewhere, feels he sinks; that nobody holds him up; that he is going to pieces down there on the floor. He dropped the last piece and said, 'Now a submarine will come to investigate the pieces that are left'. I remarked that the submarine was like the two of us, investigating what might have happened to Jaime when he was a baby. He replied that the submarine was inspecting what happened – what conditions the pieces were in afterwards. He took a sheet of paper and folded it – it was the submarine 'navigating' over the pieces of the *Titanic*. He said, 'C'mon, let's draw the *Titanics*' – him one, me another. 'Now the submarine has made a reconnaissance, we know what it was like. We can draw it. This one is not going to break anymore because we'll keep it in my envelope. It's smaller but it will not sink anymore. It's also like a remembrance'. He drew the ocean, saying 'This is very deep, very deep, but when it floats you don't care, it goes along on top and steams on'.

Before the winter holidays, he said he was going to make a small *Titanic* that would not sink. While he made the stern, he remarked that 'it was the saddest part when this sank'. He appeared to fall slowly into intense sadness. I told him that, again, I believed that at some time when he was a baby he must have felt like that. He answered, 'Yes, mom told me that once she went off to Mar del Plata when I was still just a baby, to the house of a cousin'. Then, about the *Titanic* that he was making, he said, 'Okay, here we have to stick on the upper part. We'll tape it and paste it – both things – that way it'll be stronger, that way it won't sink, this one'. Then he reinforced the prow and cut out the smokestacks: 'These too must be strong and hard; that's the way they have to be'. He stood the boat up on the table: 'Like this, so they'll stand straight; if they are limp they won't stick up properly'. I said that what stood out – making the difference between men and women – had to be well reinforced, and that the stacks were like the boat's willies. He replied, 'Yes, like mine that gets hard and stands straight . . . like that they're really okay. We've got to make the windows; the special ones are for first-class'. It was time.

At the following session he continued making windows and, asking me to make the last rows, said, 'It's not really a *Titanic*, it's a remembrance. That's why it's not going to sink'. I said, 'Like the things that happened to you when you were a baby, when Mummy went on a trip. Now you don't go to pieces or sink; now they are remembrances'. He was happy with how it had turned out. He continued, 'The smokestacks and the point (prow) shouldn't be hidden; they have to stick out properly'. I said, 'You want the point to be really visible; that which makes women and men different – the willy – should be visible. These are important things of this *Titanic*, like willies are for boys and fathers'. He put it away, saying that he believed this stage had ended. He said, 'It's in the folder and we can get it and take it out'. I said, 'Like the memories you keep in your head, it can also be found and taken out'.

After the winter holidays, he spoke quite naturally of his activities with cousins or at school, and we played card games. After August, he came alone to his sessions. He talked about the computer and its programs, including the new encyclopedia, and about seeing an eclipse. When I asked whether he remembered how he used to draw the solar system, he answered, 'Yes, I used to make the Earth and the planets, and something else . . . what was it? Black holes? Those – I didn't see them in the computer'. I said, 'The ones you drew up here swallowed things up'. 'Yes!', he exclaimed. 'Norma Beatriz! The fool wanted to go to Jupiter and passed very close and it swallowed her up'. I asked if he remembered who Norma Beatriz was, and he replied, 'One who was here (he pointed to the centre of his head) but who wasn't me'. He threw himself on the couch and, after a silence, said 'I once made up a map of my brain . . . if I made one now it would be different . . . *Chiquititas* (a TV series for girls that he used to enjoy) wouldn't be there . . . what else was there? Norma Beatriz was here in the middle, in the centre (he touched his head). Yes, then I think I sent her to China, or the black hole ate her up, d'you remember? I imagine the black hole like a whirlwind that turns and turns and catches everything close to it. Pity I threw out the map of the brain, to see how different it was'. He drew his 'new map of the brain' and put it away in an envelope.

We made envelopes. He proposed drawings that we would open after the new millennium. In November, he asked me to help him draw the Casa Rosada

(Argentine presidential palace), the Pyramid in Plaza de Mayo and the Obelisk: he drew them better than I and ended up doing them on his own. He spoke more and more about his father: they played tennis and football together, and he accompanied his father on rounds; they kept up with the elections and other external events. Towards the end of the year, he spoke about the generations in his extended family. When he opened the envelopes in April, he remembered what he had made originally. At that time, his mother spoke about the need to end the analysis because he seemed very well and a sister required treatment. We agreed to terminate in July. He said that ever since he could remember, he had come to the consulting room, and that he would be quite sad not to come anymore. He asked whether he could ring me up, and I answered that he could. Following the idea that he wanted to contact me internally as a good object that he could count on, I told him that, confronted with missing me, he wanted to be certain that there were conditions for me to be available, even if just inside his head. He told me, quite happily – as an achievement because this frightened him somewhat – that his school had moved somewhat further away, and that he was going to school and coming home with a friend. He was doing very well at school, and they considered him to be responsible, as was the case at home, except for occasional upsets. During his last appearances, in sessions tinged with nostalgia, he collected the materials from the preceding term, especially in the envelopes. On the last day, his mother came to collect him. When he went, he was somewhere between ashamed and sad and, for the first time, said goodbye with a kiss. As for his things, he asked me to keep them for him.

Conceptual ideas on the clinical material

The classical conceptualisation of transvestism, based on adult patients, centres on phallic monism, a late Oedipus complex and the central role played by castration anxiety. What this clinical material suggests to me is restitution for the psychic catastrophe the patient experienced at the end of the first year of life, which generated secondary autism with predominant confusion (Tustin 1981). Transvestism – the point of maximal ego-syntonic vitality – established a fusion-type identity with the mother as a delusional restitution in view of an emptied-out psychic universe: in the Freudian terms, we might say that here the dependency situation was reverted, with the infant being the object instead of having the object. The restitutive structure of transvestism reappeared and was expressed in play in the analytic process through feminine personifications as a defense against anxiety: first, because of the analytic dependency and, later, because of genital-phallic impulses that exacerbated his fear of oral sadism, projected onto the maternal 'mouth-vagina'.

His 'stages' worked through, on different levels, the oral trauma of the first year of life, making it possible for him to establish the 'penis-as-link' in the framework of the analytic relation.

Jaime had no identifiable transitional object, although his mother's and sisters' hair may well have been such an object. Winnicott (1971) noted that when hope is absent, the transitional object becomes a fetish and forms the nucleus of a perversion. While I agree with Greenson (1966) that to imitate the mother is the equivalent of becoming her, it is clear that to conceive of dressing up as a woman as a transitional activity undervalues the differences – notorious for Winnicott – between fetish object and transitional object, and ignores the role of the quasi-delusional reversions of the situation of oral dependency, as well as the role of sadism in the child's internal world, both essential factors in the evolution of sexual integrity.

As to reversion in the situation of dependency of 'being the object', the dynamics of which make it possible to understand the different 'stages', I have relied on Ahumada (1980, 1990) regarding the transposition of self and object. Thus, the role of Señorita Norma Beatriz, the teacher, dramatised in a delusional way the reversion of dependency and the sexual reversion linked to 'being the object', alternating with moments marked by confusion and manic feelings. Jones' (1933) fundamental contribution is that the voracity of the maternal vagina is a projection of the infant's oral sadism, and that from there stems excessive castration anxiety (the 'mouth-genitals' equation is usually observed directly in small girls who provide nourishment to their genitals). This needs to be amplified by Bion's (1962) notion about the 'need for a breast/bad breast', because the areas of oral need that are not tolerated are, for the infant, indistinguishable from sadism. Because of this, until the quasi-delusional reversions and the indiscrimination evolve in the process, it is not right to directly interpret sadism as such, but to separate out, in each situation, that which, based on his projected sadism, the child feels that the object is doing to him. When this complex dynamic is understood, it is respected and contained in a receptive way in play and enactment in sessions, and only comes to be interpreted as appropriate; then the phallic-genital impulses emerge as a fundamental factor in strengthening and integrating the ego, connected to the re-establishment of the internal link with the mother, making possible the working through of the trauma.

The vicissitudes of the emptied-out and emptying oral-traumatic psychic universe – with the corresponding unfolding, working through and resolution being central in structural psychic change – interacted with sexual confusion in the different 'stages' of the process: as we saw for Jaime at the beginning, relations with other children and assertive masculine attitudes were absent, except possibly in tantrums. In the process of resolving his reversion, he gradually made distinctions between what is masculine and what is feminine, placing himself on one or the other side: these even included his name ('Lulú'). At certain moments, especially before analytic separations, the traumatic threat of a congealed universe would surface. A part of the aggressive-masculine impulse appeared directly – that is, in a non-reverted way – at the beginning, in the form of the sadistic cutting of Barbie's hair; then, in a mitigated form, the impulse was displaced to the hole in the consulting room's ceiling fan, into which Jaime tried to insert his felt-tip pen; and finally it was manifested in an even more direct form in the sexualised relation with the analyst.

The fourth year of analysis opened the fifth 'stage', where traumatic zones – annihilating, gelid and vitality-draining – gave way to greater psychic representability, with the iceberg and the black hole taking on form and definition, and with more initiative from the boy in assuming an active masculine role. This, in turn, opened the way to the resolution of the early trauma in clear experiences of mourning.

Let us revisit his stages: after the 'out of contact' phase of the first month, the analytic process became established through reverted situations where he predominantly assumed the role of the primary object, projecting the dependent infantile self onto the analyst. In the first stage of the '*cacas*', Jaime made 'little sausages', which, if they were faeces, were also babies, since they died – this in a gelid and chaotic universe where the sun is cold, in the psychic situation that, after Clifford Scott (1948), Marion Milner called 'catastrophic chaos' (1955). In this stage of the *cacas* – illustrating the identification with the mother within an anal-sadistic theory of pregnancy and childbirth – Jaime reverted the oral roles, for it is he who fed the analyst. The primary scene appeared in his 'secret' games with Ken and Barbie; along with these, we saw the sadistic fetishism of the haircuts, culminating when he tore her apart.

In the second 'stage', that of the 'little tablecloths' he gradually differentiated masculine from feminine but without being able to separate them, for he drew them on opposite sides of the same sheet of paper and he was on both sides, even including his name. If at times, especially before separations, the congealed universe reappeared, at other times, and in the case of the hole in the ceiling fan, phallic impulses were a point of confluence for reconnecting, regaining vitality and integrating the ego – in the manner of the life-giving penis (Munro 1955).

The third 'stage', that of 'Señorita Norma Beatriz', the teacher, illustrated sexual reversion and especially reversion of oral dependency in an oscillation that included confused/manic moments. As shown by the first map he drew of his brain, he established distinctions, rescuing himself from confusion.

At the beginning of the fourth year of analysis, the invitation to the analyst to travel to Uruguay in little boats opened the fourth 'stage', the stage of the

Titanic. Here, as in the following 'stage' of 'interplanetary voyages' and in his final return to the theme of the *Titanic*, there was more co-operation and we became closer (travelled together): here, too, phallic-genital impulses surfaced in a more direct way; the iceberg's and the black hole's traumatic, annihilating, gelid and vitality-draining properties were clearly represented, and there was more initiative in the active masculine role. My role there included, besides interpreting, co-operation in building a more robust masculine organ – a factor in the construction and subsequent collision of each *Titanic*. I also had to receive and contain his phallic-genital impulses in session, where he asked me to be more 'game' as he dramatised the primary scene and oscillated between assuming a more masculine role and sudden flights into sexual reversion. In receiving and interpreting that mutual enactment (Tuckett 1997), representability was achieved. The enactment, as it unfolded in the session's 'zone of illusion' – that is, in the transference as playground (Freud 1914a) – made it possible to then arrive at a representable discrimination between an annihilating oral vagina with teeth, equated to the black hole, and a blue vagina – the good vagina inherited from the 'good breast/good mouth' – where he could enter and emerge without being annihilated. The enactment of the oral-genital conflict in the movement to achieve the 'penis-as-link' (Birksted-Breen 1996) generated extreme anxiety for him at times, leading him to revert, though increasingly as parody, to the role of Norma Beatriz, where the *in crescendo* conflict of the unfolding of the phallic-genital impulses and the underlying terror were volatilised through sexual reversion.

Jaime's attempts to penetrate and see through the confusion of the oral and phallic-genital anxieties that permeate the material and gain some discernment culminated in the sequence, expressed in his drawings and played out with the analyst, of the 'mouth-vagina/finger-penis', where he separated, on one hand, the oral sadistic universe and the sadistic sexual relation from, on the other, the blue vagina, establishing the 'penis-as-link'. In the decisive interaction that occurred in the scene of the 'finger-banana-penis/mouth-vagina', he kept to the reverted (feminine) role of the 'mouth/vagina *dentata*', and from that role received the therapist's finger, which represented his own penis and his father's penis in the primal scene. While it is evident that he was inoculating his own fear into the analyst when he told her he was about to bite her, this dramatisation did imply a delimitation and a crucial renunciation of his sadism. By separating out, in this enactment, the role of the good receptive object – the mouth/blue vagina – he rescued 'a firm island of sanity in a sea of chaos' (Money-Kyrle 1969), an island that functioned as a 'base' (Money-Kyrle 1968) and re-established at another level – the genital level – the sane (that is, non-reverted) link with the mother. This made it possible for Jaime to give up what he called the 'upside-down' world of perversion. Thus, as Freud anticipated in *Three essays on the theory of sexuality*, 'the finding of an object is in fact a refinding of it' (1905, p. 222).

Once the confusions of his sexual identity were deciphered, we witnessed a descent into the blue depths, which took place after the dramatic double crash of the *Titanic* with the iceberg in the consulting room's passageway, putting into play the traumatic situation of the first year of life, where everything ended up 'destroyed at the bottom of the sea'. Here we encounter the limits of the discernible, for we do not know whether the depths of the ocean are an evolution of the structure of the black hole in the dire action of the blue hole, or if these remains represent him or, perhaps, the dead (aborted) infant brother from his first year of life. But we do know that renouncing omnipotence, with its deep sadness, and then working at the submarine level to explore and integrate, all made it possible for Jaime to become buoyant (J.-M. Quinodoz 1994); in the work of mourning, trauma was transformed into memories that could be kept in his head, found and pulled out.

Jaime's masculine identity was forged in analysis with a woman therapist; thus, there is no explaining it as identification with the masculinity of the analyst. Rather, it is explicable as a function of analytic receptivity inside a 'zone of illusion' created on the basis of his sexual unfolding in sessions. With regard to the classic figure of the phallic mother, she hardly appeared in the material at all, and when she did, it was clearly as a defense against the 'mother-witch': 'I don't want to become a woman: they are all witches. . . . You, you're going to be a man'.

The reader will have noted how few references to countertransference there have been, which is a difference from what could be expected in any analysis of a neurotic patient – we find the same in Tustin's work. The question would be whether, at properly autistic levels, the processes of projective identification and counteridentification become activated or not. Faced with the hypersensitivity of these children, Tustin (1981) emphasised that we must avoid premature interpretation, granting priority to finding an optimal 'fit' with the children's need for contact. Such fit, which must be kept at a distance from mothering, implies adjusting to and complementing the different games and interactions. If the process manages to contain the anxiety, and representability is achieved at deep levels, then the moment arrives when interpretations become rather obvious, as is the case of most of the ones that I have recounted here.

Even though, when working at the autistic level, the connection will take place in the 'fit' of play, coexisting with a measure of 'countertransferential autism' regarding one's own experience, at more integrated levels I could better discern my own emotional involvement, as was the case when Jaime, assuming a masculine role, told me to be more 'game', or in the pathetic scenes of the *Titanic*'s final sinking.

The evolution of this case in a framework based on two sessions per week demonstrates the potential of the analytic method even in cases where the setting is restricted. This is important, for in the present cultural context and because of issues beyond our scope, the pathologies of autism and bisexuality – and for their part the restrictions in the setting – are on the rise. I emphasise that child analysis is a privileged terrain for treating and preventing pathologies of bisexuality. The fluid and generous nature of these treatments stands in contrast to the extreme difficulty encountered in treating adults for perversion, transvestism and transsexuality, as Danielle Quinodoz (1998) illustrated with striking clarity in her analysis of a transsexual patient.

To summarise, this clinical presentation has described the therapeutic process of a male child beginning at 5 years and 10 months old presenting as a main symptom quasi-delusional feminine enactments starting at an early age, which persisted for most of his five-year treatment. This symptom was understood in terms of an attempt at restitution, the result of being confronted with an autistic structure stemming from a series of dramatic incidents during the oral phase: his mother's pregnancy, abortion, depression and subsequent three-month absence at the end of his first year of life. The clinical material, drawings included, has illustrated the interplay of oral, anal and phallic levels, with enactment predominant in sessions. The oral traumatic situation initially led to anal-manic play, then to quasi-delusional female personifications in sessions, later surfacing as an annihilating 'black hole'. All the above issued into a broad enacted phallic-genital unfolding that dramatised an oral-genital primal scene, in the course of which he managed to structure his male identity and then, near the end of the analytic process, the analysand reworked the 'stages' of the link to the analyst.

Chapter 7

Conceptual remarks on early mind

Having gone through our clinical material, the time has come to comment on our evolving ideas on early mind as deployed in our work. As stated in the Foreword, we have strived to keep to Freud's basic methodological advice, that psychoanalysis "keeps close to the facts in its field of study, seeks to solve the immediate problems of observation" (1923a, p. 253). On entering the conjectural terrain of 'theory' we must say that, as happened when child analysis brought far-reaching conceptual applications, attention to autistic spectrum disorders stirs up conflictive conceptual issues.

In psychoanalytic theory-making, historical order has often gained canonical status, later concepts becoming subordinate to antecedent notions. That in Karl Abraham's (1924) classical description of the libidinal stages the biologically driven libidinal phases succeeded each other on their own push while being implicitly granted akin weight, has off-put change in core psychoanalytic concepts. It fell upon Ronald Fairbairn in the early 1940s to sustain the oral basis of hysteria, the oral phase being put at the base of psychopathology: the next phases – anal-expulsive, anal-retentive, phallic and genital – involved diverse techniques whereby the issues of absolute dependency issuing from the oral phase were handled in later development (Fairbairn 1952).

That the earlier libidinal stages permeate later ones is validated by Freud's avowal that the importance of the penis "can appeal to the fact that that organ is a guarantee to its owner that he can be once more united to his mother – i.e. to a substitute for her – in the act of copulation. Being deprived of it amounts to a renewed separation from her" (1926, p. 139). Previous findings overtaking later ones is exemplified by mimetic dynamics, first described by Freud as a mode of *imitative identification* in schoolgirls that "leaves entirely out of account any object-relation to the person who is being copied" (1921, p. 107); that is, that does not acknowledge the singularity of that person as an individual.

Imitative identification functioning on a *pars pro toto* basis was assimilated into the concept of hysteria, which is an Oedipal, developmentally later pathology. This notion came into ampler sense in Helene Deutsch's concept of mimetic identification signing "as if" personalities, which, she says, are outside of neuroses but too well adapted to reality to be deemed psychotic: there "the individual's whole relationship to life has something about it which is lacking in genuineness and yet outwardly runs along 'as if' it were complete. . . . Outwardly the individual is normal" (1942, p. 302). Their relationships are devoid of any trace of warmth, and they do not register any difference between their empty forms and what others actually experience. As she puts it, what goes on is not an act of repression but a real loss of object cathexis; they function upon a child's imitativeness in a mimicry leading to good adaptation to the world of reality despite the absence of object cathexis. While completely passive, they display a highly plastic readiness to pick up signals from the outer world and to mold themselves accordingly: any object will do as a bridge for identification, and at the first opportunity this former object is exchanged for a new one and the process is repeated. Their group attachments, in order to give content and reality to their inner emptiness, establish their validity by an automaton-like identification. Their masked aggression lends them an aura of amiability which, however, is readily convertible to evil. Such type of identificatory mimesis preannounces the superficiality and provisionality of emotional links in autistoid pathologies.

We consider mimetic interchanges as a basic modality of human contact, readily demonstrated in the first weeks of life, if not in utero, as basic constituents of the baby–mother primal dialogue, which much antedate self-object discrimination; they involve an initial, pre-Oedipal, emotion-laden primal thinking signing the early stages of self-object indifferentiation but which, as is clinically illustrated, are liable in unfavourable cases to detain further evolution of thought.

In the field of autistic spectrum disorders, precedence accorded to historically previous descriptions is noticeable as concerns the dynamics of the anal stage and of obsessional neurosis, which were described in the early decades of psychoanalysis. Later authors, Meltzer et al. (1975) being the most prominent, model the early psychic dynamics of the autistic spectrum disorders upon the developmentally later anal stage and the obsessional dynamics, encompassing the themes of control surging from the earliest stages on under the rubric of obsessionality.

A related, unfortunate issue is that access to primitive dynamics was first obtained in the treatment of adult psychotic patients: as is well known, in his pioneering study of the libido, Karl Abraham (1924) put the dividing line between psychoses and neuroses in the gap between the first and second anal phases, the anal-expulsive and the anal-retentive. Offhand equivalence of 'psychotic' with 'primal' came to dominate the field, as evidenced by a 1954 Winnicott letter:

> I would like to say what I mean by psychotic. I mean that the child's neurotic defenses are either insufficient or the child never reached a stage of emotional development at which neurotic defenses could be brought effectively into play. This means to say that the child has been under threat of such conditions as disintegration or lack of contact with reality or depersonalization.
>
> (Winnicott 1987, pp. 80–81)

Obviously, to affirm that the baby is immature and lacks a well-established sense of reality, and that she/he has come under threat of disintegration, lack of contact or depersonalisation, should not be the same as deeming her/him psychotic. Equivalence of 'primal' and 'psychotic' would lead to considering babyhood and infanthood prior to the establishment of neurotic defences to be psychotic states, and to considering Spitz's primal dialogue between baby and mother to be a psychotic dialogue! This would be counterproductive indeed, so one must distinguish a restricted sense of the term *psychotic*, denoting clinical child psychoses, and an extended use where it is synonymous with *primal*, that is, with what precedes the emergence of neurotic dynamics and of an adult-like sense of reality. We strive to keep use of the term *psychotic* to its restricted sense, as was forcefully asked for by André Green (1980) 35 years ago, arguing that overall extension of the concept of psychosis to non-neurotic structures was a false solution to a real problem.

Child autistic spectrum dynamics are primal in the sense of being antecedent to neurotic dynamics, but they in no way need be clinically psychotic, as is best evidenced by our child patient Sophia (Ch. 4). Additionally, the conflation of what is "psychotic" and what is "primal" fosters deeming clinical findings in psychotic adult or adolescent patients as being "primal", and then building upon the findings in such adolescent or adult patients a theory of psychic origins, as happens with Ogden's (1989) autistic-contiguous position (see Addendum 2).

Concerning organ-language, which drove much early psychoanalytic theorisation in the work of Freud, Abraham and Klein, likely the time has come in which its outright primacy obstructs understanding. As shall now be explored, caution in using organ language is an ongoing trend in post-Kleinian thinking, as noted by Spillius (1988, 2007).

Some notes on the evolution of post-Kleinian thought on early mind

Writing in 1988, a noted Kleinian scholar, Elizabeth Spillius, highlighted that one of the most striking features of Klein's work was her concentration on anatomical part-objects in the thinking and play of small children, assuming that the breast was the focus of the infant's first experiences of the mother and in a sense *is* the mother and is used virtually as a representation of her. She noticed in post-Kleinian analysts a shift from structure to functions, being more cautious when formulating interpretations about using the language of anatomical part-objects (1988, pp. 4–5). Spillius further noted that "Klein's followers have made very little change in her basic conceptions of the paranoid-schizoid and depressive positions" (1988, p. 195), adding that as they continued to explore psychoses, narcissism, borderline states, addiction, sexual perversion and perverse character disorders, they developed the concept of 'pathological organizations' standing somewhere between the paranoid-schizoid and the depressive positions. Two decades later, she again recalled that according to Klein the infant "has innate unconscious knowledge, however hazy, of objects – breast, mother, penis, intercourse, birth, babies" (Spillius 2007, p. 28), that there exists in the unconscious a fear of annihilation of life (p. 34) – a point on which most analysts agree – and that to Klein from birth on infants can distinguish between self and object, between me and not-me (p. 36). According to Hinz (2012, p. 193), an *ab initio* experience of separateness rather than non-separateness or merger is a prerequisite of Kleinian developmental theory; in such context, projective identification becomes the decisive communicative bridge between inside and outside, between infant and caring person (p. 195).

This quite controversial Kleinian assumption, that there is from birth on a stable awareness of separateness on the side of the baby, guided the work of her disciples Bion and Meltzer: inasmuch as self-object differentiation is assumed to be there from the very start, it disappears as an issue. Thus Bion's theory of thinking does not take into account issues of self-object discrimination. Initial differentiation of baby from mother being taken as a premise, the dynamics of projective identification (and of adhesive identification in Meltzer's case) provide the link between two assumedly separate psychic entities, baby and mother. Contrarily in our stance, in the wake of Ferenczi, Alice and Michael Balint, Mahler, Winnicott and Tustin, issues of attaining self-object distinction and their disturbance gain prime clinical relevance.

Importantly, Spillius allowed that there has been a gradual though largely tacit admission among Kleinian analysts that an essential aspect of the shift to the depressive position "is the individual's increasingly realistic perception of the 'otherness' and 'separateness' of his objects, together with the recognition of his own identity as separate from but related to his objects" (2007, p. 201). This has incorporated into post-Kleinian thinking an explicit concern with the issues of self-object differentiation that, despite her Budapest initial training, had found no place in Melanie Klein's pioneering investigations. That Birksted-Breen (1989) placed fusional impulses and anxieties at the centre of the dynamics of anorexia nervosa, while Spillius avowed in a 2002 paper that "the return to maternal fusion is a threat to individuation" (p. 407), evinces that our conceptual outlook, putting grasp of fusional impulses and anxieties on a par with that of separation anxieties, is not far removed from ongoing post-Kleinian thinking.

Growing post-Kleinian openness to the issues of self-object discrimination does not apply to authors approaching the field of autism from Kleinian-Bionian stances such as Meltzer, Ogden and Grotstein. As shall be detailed later, this leads to a conceptual and technical gap between their predominantly sensation-centred metapsychology of the initial mind and Winnicott's and Tustin's predominantly baby-mother-relationship-centred notions.

Winnicott vis-à-vis Klein

It fell upon a pediatrician turned psychoanalyst who long supervised with Klein and acknowledged her as his foremost teacher, Donald Winnicott, to vouch from the 1950s onward that an earlier psychic dynamics anteceded Klein's paranoid-schizoid object-relational dynamics. His paper, "A personal view of the Kleinian contribution" (1962a), evinces that their conceptual differences did not detract from his gratitude. As we see it, while Kleinians and Winnicottians evolved into competing psychoanalytic 'schools', Winnicott's contributions do not involve a dismissal of Klein's work but can usefully be taken as complementary in addressing different areas and levels of mind.

Winnicott, who all along his career kept a practice as a pediatric consultant, built his contribution on the attention given to good-enough mothering in the initial stages, whereby he concluded that "it is not possible to describe an infant without describing the mother whom the infant has not yet become able to separate from a self" (1962a, p. 177). As he puts it, much infant pathology is pre-Oedipal, and so it happens that "many infants never in fact arrived at so healthy a thing as an Oedipus complex at toddler age" (p. 175). He did object to Klein's use of the life and death instincts as core explanatory concepts, as well as to primary envy, and differs from her in considering that "the capacity for concern and to feel guilty is an achievement, and it is this rather than depression that characterizes arrival at the depressive position" (p. 176): which, he says, does not come about before the seventh month of life. A core clinical and technical issue that our clinical materials illustrate once and again appears in his statement that

> A good object is no good to the infant unless created by the infant. Shall I say, created out of the need? Yet the object must be found in order to be created. This has to be accepted as a paradox, and not solved by a restatement that, by its cleverness, seems to eliminate the paradox.
>
> (1963, p. 181)

Having sustained that the dynamics of insight involves traversing pragmatic paradoxes (Ahumada 1991), we take this statement about accepting the paradox as meaning that it must be respected by an analyst, who allows it mostly to be solved by ongoing discriminations and evolving working-through on the child's side – often helped along by interpretations when the time comes that these are understood and tolerated.

On mimetic identicity

Respecting the paradox is part of ongoing healthy everyday life: let us introduce a recent homely personal example (Ahumada 2015). Our daughter and two grandchildren living in New York flew in for a visit; I (JLA) had not seen them for some eight months. At the airport the older boy, aged 4, came running from afar on seeing me, shouting 'Abu, Abu' (*Abuelo*, grandfather). We embraced profusely, I threw him up in the air, and embraced him again and again. On approaching, the younger boy, Tim, aged 21 months, sitting in his stroller looked at me perplexed, with quite mixed feelings: on the one hand, I was a stranger, but on the other hand he clearly felt that the affectionate expansions his admired and much imitated older brother had sought and enjoyed must pertain to him too. Perceiving both horns of his affective dilemma, that is, that he would feel ignored and excluded in case I did not respond adequately enough, and that he could easily feel himself intruded by too vigorous an affectionate display on my side, I embraced and kissed him tenderly with some care, and he responded embracing me tenderly, though with some reticence. Later in the day, when we were already at home, he came walking over to me and brought, putting them briefly in my hands, his most precious possessions: his two woven pieces of cloth, his two pacifiers and his water bottle – evidencing that he had 'adopted' me affectionately, that is, that his link to me had managed to traverse the initial paradox.

Perplexity is a sophisticated psychic affair, as it involves tolerance to a contact with antinomical feelings. We can here appreciate that thought derives, early on, from affective-instinctual impulses leading to an emotional thinking. The scene, though intensely significant, did not include verbal expressions on his side or on my side, that is, it corresponded to the level of the Freudian thing-presentations. Significance at an enacted level – that is, at the level of an emotional pragmatics – antecedes semantics, such as Freud sustained on saying that "in the beginning was the Deed" (1913, p. 161); at such level I had to take care of my attitude in front of the two horns of the ongoing affective dilemma, any of which could presumably lead to an 'emotional frenzy', which would be traumatic for Tim and *a fortiori* for his link to me.

Following upon Matte-Blanco (1988, p. 142), the counterpoised issues building up Tim's perplexity would be expressed as follows: on the one hand "someone (Tim), someone else, and the relation of 'strangeness'", and on the other hand "someone (Tim), someone else (the older brother) and the relation of loving familiarity (of the older brother) with that someone up to then felt as 'stranger'". Thus the felt context propelling the enacted emotional dilemma leading Tim into a problem (Tim, and me also) derived from a level of mimetic identity in which for Tim his older brother and himself *are one and the same*. To sustain that at the level of Tim's psychic reality his adored elder brother is at a time himself, puts into play here a psychic dynamic similar to the one Freud attributed to the baby's relation to the breast, that in the beginning the baby *is* the breast, only later possesses it as something different from himself: "'The breast is a part of me, I am the breast'. Only later: 'I have it' – that is, 'I am not the breast'" (Freud 1941, p. 299).

This allows mimetic identicity ample place in psychic dynamics that in Kleinian thinking belong to projective identification. As we understand it, mimetic identicity provides a conceptual hinge going far beyond simple imitation, being from early on, perhaps from the beginning, at the root of emotional thinking. Emotional thinking in our example is in itself contextual: it includes as its motive, often centrally, the feelings of others, in this case those of his elder brother toward his *Abu*. Such evolutions carry, as we had the chance to observe, a strong emotional load, and when everything goes well, they gradually allow to resolve the inevitable paradoxes that do emerge, as happened successfully for Tim on meeting me: this success is evidenced by his 'gift', evincing the role of emotional reciprocity as a dimension of the situational pragmatics. Mimetic identification can thus be placed as part of the working-through process in the road toward discrimination and through it to its ultimate stage, genuine introjective identification.

The point we want to make is that mimesis is many-pronged, that it becomes from its origin part of context-thinking, and that as it evolves it can and does involve intensely felt affective participation, being an initial step in the processes of symbolisation.

On the roots of our conceptual bearings

While as said the main schools of child analysis – Anna Freudian, Kleinian and Winnicottian – make conceptual place for neuroses and psychoses but not for autistic spectrum disorders, in our view *mimetic-autistic dynamics form a conceptual tripod with neurotic and psychotic dynamics, on an even keel with them*, and have the potential to modify in depth the conceptual structure of psychoanalysis. This idea was firmly put forward almost 20 years ago by

André Green (1997) in a jacket note for the memorial book in tribute to Frances Tustin edited by Theodore and Judith Mitrani, *Encounters with Autistic States*, holding that "Tustin influenced not only those interested in the specific problems of autistic states but also those who shared an intuition that autism could play the role of a new paradigm for the study of the mind".

Regarding our conceptual outlook, as mentioned in the Introduction, our psychoanalytic upbringing was Freudian-Kleinian with a Racker-Bion-Meltzer bent. Contact, half a century ago, with Harold F. Searles' Mahler-inspired outlook on the symbiotisation-desymbiotisation processes in the therapy of schizophrenic patients left a lasting imprint on one of us (JLA): seen in this light, Klein's avowal of an initial baby–mother psychic separateness appeared as a premise convenient for her work, rather than something pertaining to babies. Later on, such notions gained force in dealing with the clinical challenges posed by autistic spectrum disorders. As said, contact with, and study of, mimetic, autistic and autistoid dynamics prompted us to a conceptual shift from our Kleinian-Bionian-Meltzerian outlook. It must be highlighted though that although Klein did not directly address self-object differentiation, her description of the depressive position (Klein 1935) shines as an essential step in such evolution; Joan Riviere's (1936) firm grasp of the depressive position as itself potentially traumatic seems to apply fully to mimetic-autistic levels. As is best noticeable in the case of Jaime (Chapter 6), the Kleinian outlook, and the use of organ language, finds its place in advanced stages of treatment.

Our effort at expanding our conceptual framework, clinically prompted as it is, draws on descriptions and concepts coined by Ferenczi, whose notions of baby–mother initial psychic symbiosis and of autotomy in the face of trauma merit pride of place in a psychoanalytic pre-history of autism, while in the realm of infantile autism we draw our bearings from Kanner, Bettelheim, Mahler and Tustin. Beyond such pioneering authors, our work with autistic children led us to give central place to some closely interrelated concepts, Winnicott's going-on-being (1949, p. 189) as well as mirroring (1967a), and Spitz's (1964) primal dialogue, the mutually-mirroring, affect-driven action-dialogue between baby and mother, starting before birth and long antedating verbal dialogue. A way of expressing this interrelation is to say that the infant's psychic going-on-being is nourished and sustained by the mutually mirroring primal dialogue with the mother.[1]

Conceptual expansion of psychoanalytic theory from its origins as a theory of neuroses (and later of adult and child psychoses) into a theory making place for the upsurge of autistic spectrum disorders and their 'autistoid' offshoots – in Bernd Nissen's (2008) apt term – in postmodern patients requires to give pride of place to the issues of self-object differentiation and the handling and working-through of primal loss.

The Freudian grounding of our concepts

As our conceptual reworking retakes Freud's ideas and findings, it needs to widen his notions on the instinctual drives because, while amounting in relevant instances to processes of discharge, instinctual drives are to be understood as being from the very start of life both *inter-psychical* and also *interpretative* in the widest sense. We use the term inter-psychical rather than the currently more fashionable term inter-subjective which, inasmuch as it implies two subjectivities having already attained a me/not-me distinction accords the primordial stages of mind a development of the self that ill fits them. Freud's admonishment in "The unconscious", that "It is a very remarkable thing that the *Ucs.* of one human being can react upon that of another, without passing through the *Cs.*" (1915, p. 194) is at the core of the primal dialogue and fully applies to the infant–mother duet from the start: intersubjectivity is a gradual accomplishment, which is absent or interrupted in autistic dynamics.

Our conceptual reshuffling follows Freudian lines of clinical thinking that did not come into his theorisation: its most accomplished form, Freud's tripartite Id-Ego-Superego model corresponds to a post-Oedipal, already differentiated and constituted psyche. The psychic terrain we explore pertains in Freudian terms to the initial stages of development of the primal Id-Ego: there Freud's purified pleasure ego can in its boundlessness, which Mahler (1968) noted, be deemed an antecedent to Alice Balint's (1939) notions of a dual-unity and of archaic egotistic love. It is a moot point that not all of Freud's clinical concepts found a place in his metapsychology: unavoidably, in the attempt to systematise complex multileveled phenomena, one gains something at the cost of losing something.

As early as 1910, in his *Leonardo* paper, Freud stated that nursing at the breast the baby obtains *the highest erotic bliss*, which is never again attained, and that the trauma of rupture in primal loss upon weaning and maternal loss brought as its result an alteration of the ego in a basic dimension, its sexual character, leading to Leonardo's homosexuality.[2] In *The ego and the id* (1923b) he avowed that "At the very beginning, in the individual's primitive oral phase, object-cathexis and identification are no doubt indistinguishable from each other" (p. 29). Again, in *Civilization and its Discontents*, Freud sustained (much in the line held by Ferenczi) that

> originally the ego includes everything, later it separates off an external world from itself. Our present ego-feeling is, therefore, only a shrunken residue of a much more inclusive – indeed an all-embracing – feeling which corresponded to a more intimate bond between the ego and the world about it.
>
> (1930, p. 68)

The original intimate bond to 'the world about it' being with mother and mother's breast. As mentioned, in *Findings, Ideas, Problems* Freud is explicit on an initial merger of ego and breast: "Example: the breast. 'The breast is part of me'. Only later: 'I have it' – that is, 'I am not it' . . . " (1941, p. 299). We amplified such dynamics in the above-stated instance of 21-month-old infant Tim.

Having tracked the Freudian roots of a merger conception of early mind, let us recall that Michael Balint (1968) evinced three distinct theories of psychic origins in Freud's work: primary auto-eroticism, primary narcissism and primary object relation. The above-cited statements allows adding a fourth distinct Freudian theory of psychic origins: primary self-object merger, in which object-cathexis and identification are not yet discernible.

The Freudian definition of affects in terms of processes of discharge, though relevant in many instances, needs to be amplified. In so doing we have ample company: as is expounded in detail by Rayner (1990), akin postures have characterised most British Independents for some decades.

Conceptualisation of instincts and affects is the site for a clash between two of Freud's background ideational schemes: the Cartesian and the Darwinian frames. That instinctual drives, and affects as their expression, are thought out as being processes of discharge largely derives from the notions of neuronal discharge issuing from Freud's neuroanatomical and neurophysiological background, as is apparent in the *Project* (1895). The neurophysiological model of affects as discharge fueling mechanistic ambitions, such as quantification in the economic models, is part of the Cartesian influence early imprinted upon Freud by his neurophysiological training under the influence of Helmholz's and Brücke's physicalistic 'scientific medicine'; this goes against his oft-stated Darwinian coordinates that shine in his final avowal that the psychic apparatus's id-ego-superego tripartite psychic structure "may be supposed to apply as well to the higher animals that resemble man mentally" (Freud 1940, p. 147). Given that Freud claimed that instinctual drives are "at once the most important and the most obscure element of psychological research" (1920, p. 34), we trust he would be hardly surprised by the extensions that follow.

In a Darwinian frame of thinking, instincts are grasped from the very start of life as being both *inter-psychical* and *interpretative* in the sense of evolving by a cognitive component (Money-Kyrle 1968). Quite distinctly from the Cartesian ambition to grasp in material, mechanistic terms instincts and affects, drastically set apart by Descartes from cogitative reason and deliberate will held to be immaterial and privative to man, Darwin (1879) claimed in *The Descent of Man* that all along the evolution of living beings it is far from easy to distinguish between instinct and reason, and that this can only be judged by the circumstances. Whereby the distinction between the instinctual drives and the processes of thinking, instead of being clear-cut, must be pondered situationally in each individual instance. To Darwin there was no hard-and-fast Cartesian divide between instincts and affects on the one hand and thought on the other hand. On stating that the ego is a differentiation of the Id (that is, of the instinctual drives) under the influence of perception – or, as we would put it, by way of experiences – the later Freud explicitly joins Darwin in precluding a sharp distinction between drives and thinking. Often enough, unbeknownst inmixions of Cartesian ambitions occlude understanding instead of enhancing it.

That instincts and affects are at least as much processes of contact as they are processes of discharge is relevant from the initial stages of life: the link with the mother is at the core of both survival and psychic continuity and growth. On similar grounds we must take distance, as being too restrictive, from Melanie Klein's notion that the foremost task of the primordial mind is to deflect the death instinct, a notion giving no proper place to the healthy baby's going-on-being and to the psychically essential joys and mutual mirroring in relating to mother in the primal dialogue.

Freud sustains in *An Autobiographical Study* that higher-level conceptualisations in terms of agencies or systems "are part of a speculative superstructure of psycho-analysis, any portion of which can be abandoned or changed without loss or regret the moment its inadequacy has been proved" (1925, p. 32–33). Concerning early mind, the structural theory in terms of id-ego-superego, schematizing an evolved post-Oedipal psyche, was highly modified by child analysts such as Melanie Klein and Winnicott.

Contact with autistic dynamics require us to emphasise the core Freudian distinction between a psychic level of thing-presentations constituting the unconscious and on which meanings ultimately reside, on the one hand, and word-presentations on the other hand. To us, thing-presentations are not set apart from thought, which to Freud was from early on initially unconscious: in Susanne Langer's (1957) terms, they fit at the level of presentational symbolism. Thing-presentations are the building blocks of experience emerging in the primal dialogue in a pragmatics prior to, and much later concomitant with, the realm of verbal semantics for which it sets the grounds. A relational pragmatics of thing-presentations – of presentational symbolism – goes on in the primal dialogue in and out of the session, as is best noticeable in the treatment of Lila, where attainment of verbal language clearly depended on building an affective relational socle where verbalisation found a place to root.

What, in inspired words, Melanie Klein (1957, p. 180n1) called "memories in feelings" illuminates the psychic level of the thing-presentations from which, Freud held once and again, meaning derives. That 'memories in feelings' happen from the earliest stages on is precisely illustrated by Salomonsson

(2012) in his work with nursing baby–mother duets. His 3-month-old baby Frida evinced how she and her mother were "involved in an intercourse that is sexual, in the psychoanalytic sense of the term" (p. 643). Quoting Freud on that "the child has its sexual instincts and activities from the first; it comes into the world with them" (Freud 1910, p. 42), he clinically details how the emotional incidents and experiences of the nursing baby–mother link are incorporated as 'memories in feelings' of the relationship, and shape up the ongoing nursing conflicts. Melanie Klein (1936, p. 301) also sustained that sexual instincts are active from birth onwards.

Notes

1 Massive ethological evidence supports the quite vital psychic dependency on mother's presence (the primal dialogue) in our next-of-kin, the already weaned infant chimpanzee: children aged 6–7, who feed fully by themselves, usually die in case their mother dies. This occurs despite the fact that adolescent and adult sisters range around to support the child (Goodall 1986).
2 This Freudian conceptual unfolding is explored in detail in Ahumada (1990).

Chapter 8

A roaming view of the Autistoid Age

Addressing mimetic-autistoid dynamics in the larger society, as well as in current adolescents and adults, unmasks an epochal change in society at large. In good measure we no longer inhabit the Age of Neurosis in which psychoanalysis came to be. This was implicitly argued by René Spitz half a century ago, speaking of the impact of the derailment of dialogue in present-day culture, from infancy on:

> Looking back over my own lifetime, it seems to me that there has been a rapid increase in juvenile delinquency, ever more sadistic; widespread and at the same time socially ostracized homosexuality; severe neurosis and psychosis; strange forms of social groupings with, to say the least, peculiar mores; ever more inappropriate child rearing practices.
>
> (1964, p. 762)

To which an increase in the use of drugs, promoted as 'recreational', and an ever-present autistoid disconnection onto the electronic media must be added. Globally, as noted in the Foreword, the world-wide impact of autistic disorders prompted the United Nations General Assembly to declare April 2 as World Autism Awareness Day. Locally, there is consensus among teachers that children have become ever harder to educate, and according to the president of the Argentine Academy of Literature, the vocabulary of teens has currently collapsed to some 200 words!

For motives of space and opportunity, this being a clinical book on child autism, we refer the reader to previous contributions on the changes in the psychopathologies (Ahumada 1997b, 1999, 2001, 2004, 2006, 2011, 2014; Ahumada and Carneiro 2006; Etchegoyen and Ahumada 2002). For our roaming purposes here, we start with the cultural changes involved upon the philosopher of history and art Roger Collingwood's warning in 1937 that the dominance of amusement in everyday life bifurcated experience into a "real" part and a "make-believe" part: daily affairs and daily work turned tedious and irritating, while boredom became a recurrent state of mind, to be dispelled by means of drugs, or by risky or criminal activities. The Age of Media came to wide public perception with Marshall McLuhan (1964): that *the medium is the message* meant that the media impose their assumptions on the unwary, altering their patterns of perception, steadily and without any resistance. Narcissus means narcosis or numbness: that men are fascinated by extensions of themselves in any material marks the bias signing our narcotic culture.

As was summarised in the Postscript of *Insight. Essays on Psychoanalytic Knowing* (Ahumada 2011), in "The culture of narcissism", Christopher Lasch (1979) held that the narcissist sees the world as a mirror of himself and has no interest in external events except as they throw back a reflection of his own image, whereby much of modern life takes the character of an enormous echo chamber, a hall of mirrors. Upon an extreme competitiveness jointly with a narcissistic preoccupation about oneself, the concept of personal identity turns problematic. Behind a relaxed, tolerant façade, the "new narcissist", says Lasch, is fiercely competitive in his demand for approval and acclaim, demanding immediate gratification while living in a state of restless, perpetually unsatisfied desire. Lacking a sense of historical time, for him the world is a mirror where despite his illusions of omnipotence he cannot live without an admiring audience. In the context of the mechanical reproduction of culture, the proliferation of the visual and auditory in a "society of the spectacle", much of modern life takes the character of an enormous echo chamber, where what is taken as mental health is the overthrow of inhibitions and the immediate gratification of every impulse: the voyage to the interior, holds Lasch, discloses only a blank while the world, even in its emptiness, is but a mirror of himself. In the perpetual present, personal links provide no assurance of continuity, while a *flight from feeling* erodes the chances for lasting intimacy; under such conditions more and more people seek emotional detachment, pursuing sex only inasmuch as they can define and limit their involvement in the relationship: which makes deep and lasting friendships, love affairs and marriages increasingly difficult to achieve. The "liberated" personality of our times is signed by its charm, its pseudo-insight, its protective shallowness, its promiscuous pansexuality, its avoidance of dependence, its inability to mourn, its dread and loathing of aging and death, its inability to feel oneself part of a historical stream, its fear of binding commitments, its desire to keep one's options open and its incapacity for loyalty and gratitude. The omnipresence of mediatic images and the overexposure to manufactured illusions lead to an indifference to reality, if not to the collapse of the very idea of reality – confirming Collingwood's concerns. In a later book, *The Minimal Self: Psychic Survival in Troubled Times* (1984), he noted that from the 1950s on the notion of identity lost its connotations of sameness, definiteness and continuity, and it came to refer to a proteic, fluid and problematical self defined by the roles performed, by the groups one belongs to, or by the deliberate management of its 'presentation', all of which blurs the limits between self and others. This reflects on the wider sociocultural milieu in such a way that protagonism and action displace reflection and argument.

As mentioned in the Foreword, the changes in adolescent and adult psychopathologies in the Age of Media shape up an Autistoid Age where, upon the current impact of the 'epidemic of autism', mimetic-autistic dynamics require being put on an equal level with neurotic, narcissistic and psychotic dynamics. The liveable psychic space, in everyday life and in session, tends to oscillate between two equally unsustainable poles: on the one hand, a fusional ecstasy easily leading to entrapment and terror, and on the other hand, felt separateness that leads to primal depression also equated to annihilation. Present-day patients, and this is most noticeable as concerns adolescents, oscillate, often brusquely, from euphoria and ecstasy to despair, flight into themselves and depression: in the frame of present-day psychiatry they are often diagnosed as bipolar and medicated as such. They reject high-frequency psychoanalytic settings, and in any setting are intolerant of progress to the point of skirting the negative therapeutic reaction.

As noted elsewhere (Ahumada 1990), Freud initially introduced narcissism in 1910, – first in a footnote added to the *Three Essays* (1905, p. 145n.1) and then in the *Leonardo* paper (1910) – as an early traumatic alteration of the ego, and only four years later, in *On narcissism: an introduction* (1914b) constructed the classic developmental theory of narcissism. Advancing that early autistic disturbances are at the core of later narcissistic disorders, Symington (1991) implicitly retook Freud's initial concept on a traumatic genesis of narcissism: thus no hard and fast line can be traced between mimetic-autistoid disorders and narcissistic states. Some patients show a dominance of autistic dynamics, as shall be exemplified by our patient Tom (Ahumada 1997a, 2011, 2014; see below); others will show diverse admixtures of mimetic-autistoid with narcissistic or neurotic dynamics, as shown by Florence, a nomadic girl in her early twenties (Ahumada 2010; see below). That we choose to speak of mimetic-autistic (or mimetic-autistoid) dynamics evinces some degree of clinical priority accorded to mimesis over autistic retraction, which can be likely envisaged as resulting from failed mimesis.

The boy – let's call him Tom – was brought to analysis by his parents at age 15 when their idea that – despite his deftness in handling quite complex mechanical objects – he was intellectually subnormal was shaken by the finding of an IQ of 131 in a test prompted by his pediatrician. He had no relationships outside his family except for a sole, disturbed friend he contacted occasionally, and he lived in the main in what to his parents was a state of distraction, truly of mindlessness. He did not pay attention at school and was able to read just a few lines at a time; he fell asleep in class as soon as the teacher started speaking. At school he was two years behind his age level, and this he attained because his mother would read volumes to him as examinations approached, which, when he managed to pay attention, he remembered phonographically. Unconscious terror made itself obvious only in relation to the maternal grandparent, of whom he was in dread; his inhibition of play and aggression lifted only in a peculiar context: he was an excellent marksman and an enthusiastic hunter. The analytic process was painfully slow and consisted mostly of silence, which demanded the utmost patience on my part. It took him years in a four-times-a-week analysis to contact, and then acknowledge, feelings of anger or rivalry.

We came gradually to grasp a basic split in his universe: on one side the world of Adults, the annihilating 'Big Ones' he avoided or submitted to, the place of excitements he cannot 'think'; on the other side his own place, the no-place of the submitting-child-subject-to-annihilation, a place allowing neither pleasure nor any success. This became strikingly clear in case he gained a very good grade at school, which happened occasionally: he would panic, and the following day he managed to get the lowest grade, which calmed him immediately. The world of Adults he felt as a combined-parental-couple locus, and it was a major relief, which he expressed, when he came to feel mother and dad as persons distinct from each other, which allowed him to handle his relationship to each parent in distinct ways. This capacity was acquired after years in analysis, having gained some social life outside his family and having mostly emerged out of his post-autistic state. By that time he had gained private spaces for himself where he did not feel intruded upon by adults. This had begun, or was reflected by, his sailing alone in a small boat for hours on end in a relaxed, vital mood. After a time he started taking his small brother or his cousins for a sail as passengers, enjoying it as long as it was clear that he and no one other than he was the captain on board.

An incident while hunting throws light on the quite covert rivalry and violence underlining his basic split of the universe. Targeting his telescopic sights on a big buck deer, he was suddenly very emotionally struck by the thought that the buck was unaware of what was happening. When he mentioned this in session, I told him – but this had already become clear to him on narrating the event – that what had struck him so much was coming in touch with the fact that this was the way *he* usually felt, both in life and in the session: as the one being targeted on the wrong side of the gun. This certainly happened whenever he approached the possibility of contact with pleasure or sexuality.

It is relevant in the present context that as happens with post-autistic patients (or as I prefer now to call them, extending Bernd Nissen's (2008) term, 'autistoid' ones), as distinct from neurotic cases, Tom brought no dreams and no daydreams, and in fact denied having any fantasies at all; early memories were non-existent and continued to be so throughout treatment. It was thus a momentous time when, several years into treatment, he did bring in a daydream, the only one that ever came into his analysis, but one, he said, he had entertained in many variants: he was the sole man in the universe, the only partner to the only girl, and the only possessor of a gun, car, boat or plane in which his girl and he unendingly went on and on at his whim. By way of a highly ideal contrast, the analysis of this daydream provided him with some intellectual grasp of his intolerance to rivals but produced no substantive change. It must be noted here that changes eventually leading to a broadening of an area of privacy in his mind started in quite a remote place, removed from adults, the analyst included, in his sailing by himself where no rivals disputed his being captain: it often took weeks or months before such progressions found their way to being mentioned in session. In fact, a capacity on my side to interpret without in so doing being equated with or experienced as an intruding annihilating Adult from whom Tom must immediately become disconnected, was requisite to sustain an ongoing analytic process.

Now to our second case. A post-adolescent woman in her early twenties, Florence (Ahumada 2010) was sent by an esteemed colleague who asked me (JLA) to do whatever I could in the short time span available, as she was soon to resettle abroad. Though she fitted as "thin-skinned" narcissistic in H. Rosenfeld's (1987) terms, we shall depict the psychic dynamics drawing and amplifying on Gaddini's (1984) contributions on mimesis and on Symington's (1991) notion that autistic disturbances are at the root of narcissistic ones.

Florence came in quite late to the first interview; she was overweight and childish in appearance with an air of perplexity; she spoke enthusiastically but confusedly, interrupting or correcting herself as soon as she started a phrase. From the start on, she sort of "spilled" herself over me, seeking that I somehow grasp what she had obvious difficulties to understand. She had no idea why she came, insisting that anyhow she would be coming for just a few months, because then she would leave the country. In fact, she had gone abroad the three previous summers, working in menial tasks. She felt that her posh life with her family in the suburbs was oppressive if not unbearable.

She often felt she did not exist, and had for certain that nobody loved her. In case she met affection she took it to be false, which she admitted as bizarre and due to her oft-mentioned hypersensitivity; this, though, did not help her deal with her loneliness and despair. She felt good for nothing, unable to go ahead: her university studies had soon flopped, as she fell into paralysis and abandoned in front of examinations; seeking relevant work seemed to her impossible. Family contact was non-existent, especially as concerns her father, and living with them she felt as an entrapment, at a time gelid and potentially explosive. She kept to her room for weeks in a row, chatting on the Internet or looking at TV, sunk in the mindlessness of media-mimesis. She had had suicidal ideas and had scratched her arms, but did not think she could commit suicide. Things had always been like this, and insomnia had been a problem from infancy on; in fact, her early life evinced its share of discontinuities. She was sure she would die before age 27: thinking of herself beyond such age was inconceivable. Contact in session was overly friendly and fluid, smiling while narrating her plight; at times she came close to tearing, which she felt as a weakness and strived to suppress. That she firmly stuck to coming just once weekly and for a short time shows that her spilling onto me in session triggered strong anxieties of loss-of-self.

Things had gone differently in her summers abroad, where she related in a friendly way to her working peers; also, she would approach a boy who paid her no attention, have a sexual relationship with him, and dump him as soon as he grew interested in her, a pattern repeating itself several times. This had changed in her last stay abroad when she got involved with a married man: opposite to her casual relationships, she felt she loved him dearly, which put her in a bind, because the felt damage to his wife and children turned him radically unavailable. She spent nights awake waiting for his phone call, feeling horribly bad if he didn't call, but when he hinted he would take a plane to visit her, she panicked and dissuaded him: she would not know what to do with him should he come and would fall to pieces on his departing. Awareness of such paradox did nothing but heighten her despair. She got some relief when I pointed out to her that the fleetingness of her casual relationships and the impossibilities of her relating to a man felt as radically unavailable served her to handle the affects she felt as unmanageable, a sort of erotic-affective tsunami she dreaded to be swamped by; this, I added, fitted in well with her allowing herself no relationship at all – social, affective or sexual – with boys from her own milieu.

Despite claiming that nobody cared for her, she kept a group of girlfriends from school. Here again a pattern was discernible: she became close with some girl only to find she was not up to her expectations, or else the girl retracted, throwing her into black despair. Something akin happened with her mother and upon mother's attention to a sister. Florence came to agree on that she was unable to keep viable psychic distance in her affects, getting too close, which turned unbearable, or too far, in which case she fell into despair. We also grasped that a rigid restriction of contact ruled her future plans, namely to work on whatever it be for weeks or months, and then move in perpetual errancy; whereby, despite her glowing tone, her plans enacted a nomadic road with no roots or links, a guide for psychic survival with no emotional ties. A memory then emerged: at age 12 she felt attracted to a schoolmate, and when this boy was accompanying her home, she took notice that a brother of hers followed them; from then on, and till many years later when she started her summer trips to Europe, she had avoided all contacts, even social, with boys.

As weeks went on, her perplexity lessened. She grasped what I told her but insisted it was of no use: to be helped, in or out of treatment, threatened to increase her fusional dependency. The moment came in which, desperate in the context of her relationship with her married beau, she asked for a second session, but she immediately withdrew saying that at that time she had to go to a rock concert. In fact, her best moments happened in rock concerts, allowing a euphoric group mimesis where unbridled anonymity precluded the anxieties of loss-of-self. She managed to get an office job and although she was much ambivalent about it, she felt for the first time that working was possible. Then, on the relief of being able to put an end to her link with her married beau, she came to briefly acknowledge the benefits of treatment and to question her future plans. Upon the understandings gained in this all-too-restricted setting, Florence came to sustain work tasks pleasurably for the first time; such advance, though, did not stop her nomadic route. Weeks before the time set for departure, she brought up with tears in her eyes, on going out of session, that she found emotional contact more and more painful and so, given that we must stop, it was better that we stopped then.

As mentioned before, in *The Culture of Narcissism* (1979), the social historian Christopher Lasch described in postmodern media society a *flight from feeling*, which we deem to grasp in terms of mimetic-autistoid dynamics. Thus seen, liveable psychic space, in daily life as in session, dangles between two equally unliveable poles: an affective *fusional pole* leading to the terrors of ecstasy and entrapment and a *pole of separateness* conducting to annihilating despair on the model of primal depression. (A third pole, dominant in thick-skinned narcissism (Rosenfeld 1987) is that of *psychic hardenings*, risky behaviours included.) Mimetic dynamics, as manifested in seriality, forego (or splits-off) otherness and individuality: this is illustrated by Florence's fleeting sexual enactments and her unending media mindlessnesses in Internet chat and looking at TV; her nomadic future sought to warrant a seriality of links and places. No major "window of opportunity" in such mini-treatment, as has happened with our child patients: just an attempt at belated damage repair.

As Tustin insisted (and as Bettelheim was well aware of, voicing that autistic children do not bear using the "I" or the "yes"), some stable sense of "me-ness" is requisite for the emergence of a genuine tolerance of the "not-me", that is, to a tolerance of singularity in the link to others, of their individuality and otherness. When Florence attempted to emerge from seriality into individuating her love-object and herself in relating to her married beau – that is, attempted to attain the Oedipal level – the situation veered to the catastrophes of loss-of-self, inasmuch as emotional dependence on an individuated person turned unbearable; something akin happened in session.

Blunting one's and the others' singularity, mimetic dynamics draw an autistoid limit to emotional contact, and thus a limit to learning from experience, evading the work of psychic two-ness, which is at the core of the depressive position. Evasion of in-depth emotional experience and of the ensuing insights is propelled, from early age on, by the omnipresent virtualities of the Age of Media.

Can autistic disconnection – i.e., the repudiation of a capacity for affective contact with human objects – as it is found in different ways in autistoid, mimetic-autistic and narcissistic states be considered a form of splitting? If so, we must assume that such splitting is primarily a split of the early ego rather than of the object, and that at the limit –that is, in autism proper – it sweeps away all affective contact with the primal object. It would then be at a quite different level from, and must be thought of as being developmentally previous to, the sort of splitting into a good object and a bad object signing Klein's paranoid-schizoid position. In our view a psychic level of pre-paranoid-schizoid, dual-unit fusional dynamics with no achieved distinction between self and object continues throughout life. As mentioned, Spillius recently allowed that gradually and largely tacitly, Kleinian analysts admit as essential to the depressive position "the individual's increasingly realistic perception of the 'otherness' and 'separateness' of his objects, together with the recognition of his own identity as separate from but related to his objects" (Spillius 2007, p. 201).

At the psychic levels of dual-unit fusional dynamics with no achieved distinction between self and object, contacts with the depressive position bring up a threat of loss-of-self, as was masterly argued by Joan Riviere in 1936. In those cases, that in the Age of Media become ever more usual society-wide, and of which Florence's mimetic-autistoid, nomadic dynamics offer a fair enough example, psychic developments seeking to approach the depressive position, indispensable to the work of two-ness and to personal maturation, are felt to be unbearable inasmuch as they bring up the anguishes of loss-of-self, threatening to reinstate a psychic catastrophe that is unconsciously felt as having already occurred.

About these patients' 'minimal self', Winnicott was clairvoyant a half-century ago saying that: "Our patients, more and more, turn out to be needing to feel real, and if they don't then understanding is of extremely secondary importance" (1989, p. 582). What on the survival value of autistic dynamics Bettelheim had highlighted in his child patients: "if 'I' do not really exist, then neither can 'I' really be destroyed" (1967, p. 429) seems definitory for current mimetic-autistoid patients. That coming to exist is thus equivalent to being destroyed is an ongoing dilemma at each step of psychic maturations, in and out of treatment: contacts with the depressive position and the renouncement of omnipotence become a threat to their going-on-being, and the negative therapeutic reaction is around the corner.

As is likely best shown by the case of Tom, in 'autistoid' patients the severity of the attentional impairment blocks the access not only to memories but also to experiences felt as real, in and out of session. Coming to feel real through the gathering of real experiences requires a protracted work of affective mirroring in session, by which the patient's massive attentional disconnection from affect is repaired in the person-to-person link to the analyst, whose interpretative work is part of the requisite holding.

Rounding these comments on the psychic impact of the Age of Media, let us mention a disheartening early case brought to consultation (LBA) just before the last vacation, a toddler of 2 years old, Ben (see Ahumada 2016). He was sent by his pediatrician because of unending shrieking: when not given his mother's smartphone to play with, he went into a furious, unbearable cry, which lasted some two or three hours, and he would throw himself violently backwards heedless of pain. At age 6 months the mother gave him her smartphone to entertain himself with, and found that 'he was happy'. We felt he was hardly treatable; his early handling of the screen had fed his feelings of omnipotence in ways that a teddy bear or a rattle would not have. As we understand it, we met the dynamic of empowerment disclosed by Leo Kanner (1943) in the autistic spinning of objects. Ben connected to his smartphone screen, and just to it: his omnipotent 'ego' was an 'I and my smartphone screen', while his threatening, furiously rejected 'not-me' included his mother and the rest of the universe. This case strikingly illuminates how early access to screen technology breeds autistic pathology.

Addendum I

Bion's theory of thinking and autistic-mimetic dynamics: a dialogue with Antonino Ferro

Sophia's clinical narrative had an eventful journey, meeting different psychoanalytic outlooks and cultures. What follows is a second look at topics raised by our paper "From mimesis to agency. Steps in the development of psychic two-ness" (Ch. 4), dealing with the first 18 months of treatment of Sophia's mimetic autism. We take special heed of Antonino Ferro's (2007) comments on its Spanish version, opening a dialogue with a Bionian, and partly Meltzerian, conceptual frame. Our most general point is that, working with adult psychotic patients, Bion developed a theory of thinking but not a theory of self-object differentiation and the evolution of the self. We hope to mark the gap between the Tustinian conceptual frame to which we keep and the Bionian and especially the Meltzerian frame.

Generously, Ferro deemed Sophia's case important on several accounts: (1) because it puts to the fore the issue of the psychoanalytic approach to autism at a time when it is being widely contested; (2) because it shows an analyst that does not evade the profoundest level of psychic suffering, managing to conduct Sophia towards a level of psychic normalcy in a relatively brief time span; and (3) because it engages in an exquisitely psychoanalytic manner the deepest level of psychic life: autism and stupidity as a defense, whereby its value reaches beyond child analysis into the deep functioning of adult analyses. At a conceptual level, Ferro offers considering, on the side of our model which he finds coherent, agreeable and rich in results, another model or perhaps another language, inspired by Bion's (and Meltzer's) ideas.

The state of indistinct sensoriality, Ferro argues, includes proto-emotive states that need to find the *reverie* of a receptive mind so that, passing from reception to transformation, it allows progressive alpha-betisation of sensoriality. By this process, *beta-elements* (sensoriality – proto-emotions) are transformed into *alpha-elements*, that is, into emotive pictograms giving place to the development of wakeful dream-thoughts, which is at the base of a capacity for thinking, feeling and dreaming. In the absence of such process, or due to a negative or reversed *reverie*, the most diverse defences come up, the most extreme of them being autism, which empties itself not only of alpha-elements but also of the apparatus to produce them; that is, it empties itself of *alpha-function*, with ensuing bi-dimensionalisation of the mind. Stupidity and flattening are extreme defences erected to avoid that all be destroyed by the tsunami of beta-elements.

In bi-dimensionality, he says, we find a sort of undifferentiated fog where everything turns indistinguishable and having no emotional thickness, a kind of dyslexia of the emotions, if not an alexia, that does not allow them to be perceived nor discriminated due to a lack of the transforming reception of maternal *alpha-function*.

If things go well, he holds, we are on the road from the clouds of sensoriality to the emotive pictograms. We find then that it is possible to discern the different emotional states, and thereby to give a name to and to contain the emotions, that is, to gain access to consciousness (Sophia), which in the first place is being conscious of oneself and our internal world. In the absence of such road, we will find "-Sophia" (-K), leading to an unknowing of oneself and to any possibility of deciphering the internal world (impoverished by emptying or evacuation) and the external world (invaded by projective identifications). Through her analyst, argues Ferro, Sophia meets for the first time a capacity for positive reverie, someone that can psychically perceive her, that can be on the same wavelength (*at-one*), that is able to receive her communicational fragments and complete them (alpha-betisation processes), but, especially, someone who is not afraid of proto-emotive states: her analyst can accept to be dirtied by emotive stains because she is aware of having a way for removing such stains (that is, to receive, contain and transform proto-emotive states). Dirtiness (the mass of *beta-elements* that do not scare the analyst), the same as the tiger, the furies, can be accepted because the analyst has the instruments to accept and transform them. Also, the analyst is sensitive to the emotional voltage that Sophia is able to tolerate (the personified game, Lola), so that such personifications allow for the transit from emotional indifferentiation to a capacity to individualise the diverse emotional states. We assist, holds Ferro, to the feminine development through the analyst's ability to be receptive and let herself be penetrated by the girl's emotions: the analyst knows that she has to attain *alpha-function* (lavabo function) so that trust can be established. At the end of the alpha-betisation process, the child can read her name as well as numbers from 1 to 10. Also, the child now has a separate identity. The analyst is unafraid of emotional violences, knowing their importance for psychic evolution, and is able to contain and transform them, which allows her to provide to the child the method to contain and "cook" her emotions with no need to fall into terror or camouflage herself in indifferentiation or stupidity.

We have quoted at length Dr. Ferro's exquisitely thoughtful comment in order to build the background for our response; we have no doubt that despite the differences in our conceptual languages, an analyst deploying such sensitivity would be quite able to proceed on the framework he poses, but this might well not be valid for less endowed therapists. We thank him for providing the stimulus for an examination of Bion's theory of thinking from the standpoint of Sophia's clinical narrative: in other words, for a comparison between the conceptual model Bion built upon his clinical work with adult schizophrenic patients, and what emerged from the clinical process of childhood mimetic autism.

We coincide in that stupidity and emotional flattening attempt to hold off what is felt to be an emotional tsunami, but not on the need to introduce Meltzer's term "bi-dimensionality": in our view, nothing in Sofia's material supports such skin-anchored assumption. That we as therapists find ourselves initially in front of "a sort of undifferentiated fog where everything turns indistinguishable and lacks emotional thickness" can be better grasped in our view by what Ferenczi (1932, p. 220) called *autotomy*, emotional dematerialisation ensuing as a consequence of cumulative trauma.

Let's start our discussion with the Bionian term "alpha-betisation". The term alpha-function was introduced by Bion in 1962 as an "empty" function, in order to pinpoint and delimit an area of ignorance that he cautions against filling prematurely with meanings. In our view, the human communicational tool is certainly not in the beginnings, nor often fundamentally, verbal language: as Freud aptly put it quoting Goethe's *Faust*, "in the beginning was the Deed" (Freud 1913, p. 161). Emotionally relevant deeds take place within a relationship, so this may be paraphrased, using Batesonian terms, as: "in the beginning is the relationship". In Ferenczian terms we might state that achieving a verbal language suitable for valid communication with others will be possible for the autistic child only inasmuch as the emotions that had been dematerialised by a lack of adequate responses along his development (in Ferro's Bionian terms, by negative reverie) come to be "re-materialised" in the session.

Conceptually, Ferro places as the initial elements of the mind, corresponding to what he forwards as "the state of indistinct sensoriality", the "*beta-elements* (sensoriality, proto-emotions)", which are to be transformed into alpha-elements. To us, these different terms, beta-elements, sensoriality and proto-emotions, cover quite diverse psychic items: we find no use in drawing a sharp distinction between the proto-emotive and the emotive, and to us beta-elements are on a quite different footing from both sensoriality and proto-emotions. Instead of thinking about beta-elements as part of an initial socle of the mind (as being, let's say, part of Freud's wider notion of an unrepressed unconscious), we think of them in terms of Bion's beta-screen, that is, as restitutionally defensive rather than as primordial; if we were to use them in Sophia's narrative (which we chose not to), we would place them at the level of the many ways, nonverbal as well as verbal, in which she provided her persistent "I don't know". Perhaps the most striking differences in our respective conceptual schemes come upon the term "sensoriality" as used in such phrases as "progressive alpha-betisation of sensoriality" or, later on, "from the clouds of sensoriality to the emotive pictogram", where the term "sensoriality" gets primordial status.

We all have only conjectures about the baby's primordial mind: use of the term "sensoriality" evades our ignorance. This is also true for the term alpha-function, which as said Bion introduced in 1962 to pinpoint an area of ignorance that he cautioned against being filled out prematurely with meaning. We prefer to think of such area of ignorance as something to be helped and inquired on in each case, this being basically an evolution by the patient rather than something that can be purveyed: that is, as something that eventually evolves, framed by the analyst's capacity for emotional contact while bearing a nearly unbearable ignorance. Besides, the term alpha-function seems too abstract to nominate what is emotionally involved.

We coincide in that the road to emotional maturation often involves traversing strong emotional turbulence, which in Sophia's clinical material tends to take the form of the crisis of two-ness. Bion's term "alpha-betisation", with its pull toward verbal language, would cover only the late stages of these emotional evolutions in session, as happens when Sophia comes to read her name and count from one to 10. What comes to scene in previous stages is a series of emotional deeds, "moments of contact" only marginally linked to verbal language.

Autistic patients, as Kanner noted, do not distinguish between a "me" and a "not-me", nor between an "I" and a "you": attaining such distinctions is not covered by Bion's idea of reverie, but it is essential to the ongoing task. We must achieve on the one hand a function of emotional *contact* and *holding* (the *at-one*), and on the other hand a function of *delimitation*, which is indispensable in order to arrive to a tolerance of the discrimination of the analyst as part of a bearable "not-me". Also, in the long run, it does not suffice to sustain the paradox, as Winnicott puts it, because in case the I-you discrimination is not achieved, the analyst would continue to be indefinitely co-opted as internal to what the child deems to be "me": it happens though in our clinical narrative that, on nearing discrimination of the analyst as part of a "not-me", we approach the violences of the crisis of two-ness.

Delimitation requires some measure of confrontational slant of the analyst's actions and/or verbalisations when issues of me–you distinction come to the fore, which is notorious in the dramatic scene during the fifth month of treatment, where the girl mirrors in a strictly mimetic manner the analyst's posture and the analyst decides to keep such posture. As a result, Sophia manages to take conscious contact with the bodily mimesis that emotionally sustains her, bringing in a process of insight that leads such mimesis towards fracture. We thus witness a transformational cycle in the passage from *mimetic mirroring* to the emergence of *a self-interpretive space* as concerns relationship, a process that was initially mute: following her collapse and after three or four minutes, the girl looked at the analyst, the analyst smiled at her but did not speak, the girl's gaze examined the analyst's face and hands, the analyst pointed out that thinking by herself seems to scare her, and then, in front of a question the analyst poses her, after seeking a puppet and speaking "from" the puppet, the child for the first time offered a proper name, "Lola" – the name of her mimetic partner at the kindergarten.

Some tolerance to a discrimination of the "me" and the "not-me", that is, of self and object as two distinct terms in the relationship, comes up in this sequence, as a requisite first step in the way to an acknowledgment of individuals and their nomination. At such late stage, Bion's term "alpha-betisation" might apply properly.

The most difficult technical issue to conceptualise clinically – again not conveyed by the term "reverie" – is the relation between the functions of contact and holding in the *at-one*, and those of delimitation and insight: these depend on each other inasmuch as only in the context of the *at-one* comes to be built a tolerance for psychic pain and for the emotional turbulence accompanying "me"–"not-me" discrimination. The dependence on the *at-one* togetherness of "me"–"not-me" for attaining delimitation, and the resultant opening up to genuine symbol-formation happen in the sequence just described and in other sequences, too: such as, and perhaps foremostly, in the scene of intrauterine communion after the first vacation, which is followed by crucial progress inasmuch as Sophia arrives to realise, and to verbally express, that she does not want to think. This dependence on the communion of the *at-one* might be due to the issue that fusional "wholes" are felt to be torn apart by the processes of thought, which impinges negatively on the receptivity to verbal interpretations. In any case, the clinical material presented shows that moments of ego integration and symbol-formation in turn lead to emotional turbulence, as notably happens at 14 months of treatment, on realising that for the first time she has written "So-phi-a": awareness of such momentous progress precipitates the full-blown furies of the crisis of two-ness.

A further comment on the term "sensoriality", a term having blunt mechanistic Cartesian overtones, which Bion takes as the socle of his theory of thinking: in using it, Bion unwittingly takes leave from the Darwinian outlook, which was Freud's and also his own. To again recall Freud's famous statement in *The Ego and the Id* (1923b, p. 26), "The ego is first and foremost a bodily ego": it comes about in perceptual interplay, as a differentiation of the id. Freud adds later on that the ego "is continued inwards, *without any sharp delimitation*, into an unconscious mental entity which we designate as the id and for which it serves as a kind of façade" (1930, p. 66, italics added). He argues soon after that "the ego is in its very essence a subject" (1933, p. 58). So for the later Freud the socle of the mind, the Id, is in his words "an unconscious mental entity", whereby *the body is a psychically endowed body*, it is an integral level of mind instead of being opposed to mind, as Cartesianisms would envisage. Alternatively, it could be said that to Freud *the mind is first and foremost an embodied mind*. This bodily rooting of the unconscious and the subject is not an isolated statement of the Viennese master: bodily unconscious psychism is for him the socle to meaning. In so thinking, Freud is consistent with his Darwinian framework: as was earlier mentioned, Darwin had claimed in *The Descent of Man* (1879, p. 96–97) – to Freud one of the 10 most important books in the history of humanity – that instinct and reason cannot be clearly put apart, and this can only be judged in each case by the circumstances. The unconscious's basic components, the *Triebe*, that is, the instincts or drives, are bodily both on their arising from erogenous zones and on their object, the other's body or eventually one's own body. The bodily nature of psychism in Freud's conception is valid for the unconscious 'thing-presentations', traces of early life experiences invested by libido from each erogenous zone (Valls 1995). From these traces of experiences derives, says Freud, the meaning of conscious verbal terms and ultimately all meaning. Freud precisely holds that verbal meanings depend on the thing-presentation (that is, on the invested unconscious experiences) that words link to. This is why we do not follow Ferro in putting together the terms "sensoriality (beta-elements, proto-emotions)". To us – and we think this is also Tustin's position, in that her use of the term *sensation* mostly retains a link to embodied mind – *the term* sensory *finds a place at the psychic level only inasmuch as it is thought of as "sensuous"*. Primitive mind, as it comes to be experienced and to evolve in the primal dialogue, would to Bion pertain to the proto-emotions, which to us cannot be equated to beta-elements, at which level there is no "experience".

As said, the counterpoising of the terms "sensoriality" and "psyche", like those of "body" and "mind", derives from philosophy, mainly from Descartes, who ontically (that is, absolutely) opposed psychism as what is properly human – the reasoning mind (*cogitatio*) and conscious will – to a purely mechanical sensoriality belonging, the same as affects, to what being merely animal in man is fully mechanical. Descartes' impact, though most noticeable in French psychoanalysis, has weighted widely: a foremost Cartesian scholar,

John Cottingham, reminds us that philosophers on both sides of the Channel "bear the unmistakable imprint of Descartes' thought concerning the structure of human knowledge, the nature of the mind and the relationship between mind and matter" (1986, p. xxxvii). In the philosophy of consciousness derived from Descartes – which means in most philosophies – sensoriality opposes the properly psychic.

How could an assumedly non-psychic, purely mechanical "sensoriality" be distinguished clinically from what pertains to the primordial psyche, that is, from what Bion calls the proto-emotive and the proto-mental? In our clinical material, we are witness to Sophia's self-differentiation from the analyst as it evolves in the very same fifth-month session through different perceptual modalities – at the level of the gaze and soon after at a tactile level with the piece of Scotch tape. What is relevant there is not the "sensoriality" involved in such experiences but the psychic evolutions transcurring thereby. So we leave aside the term "sensoriality" as a philosophical and psycho-physiological abstraction. The situation is different, and can be pinpointed clinically well enough, for concepts such as auto-sensuousness in Tustin's description of "hard" and "soft" autistic objects (1986, p. 59) or at more advanced levels in the mimetic identity with another not acknowledgeable as such: both are at the service of the obviating of contact with the "not-me", that from Kanner on rules of autistic dynamics. To Tustin the term *sensation* is not counterpoised to nor does it evacuate psychic content, except as part of the dynamics of encapsulated autism.

At the level of the primordial psychic stages, the terms "relationship" and "indifferentiation" do not oppose each other, which can again be exemplified by the scene at the fifth month of treatment, where the girl's mimetic mirroring sustained itself in her "hanging" from the analyst's gaze. This shows that mimetic identity and relationship go well hand-in-hand, insight on mimesis being, if all goes well, a main step on the road toward self-object discrimination. Also, that we hold that a capacity for a "me"–"not-me" distinction is not to be found at the level of primordial psychism – what Matte-Blanco (1975, 1988) calls the 'homogeneous mode' – in no way precludes the activity of an initial ego, given that from the start the baby undergoes affects and anxieties, and builds his experiences upon them. Lacking a sustained awareness of itself, such primordial ego only vaguely amounts to an initial self.

In our view the clinical material presented and, more amply, experience with the treatment of children in the autistic spectrum range, require an extension of the theory of thinking Bion built upon the treatment of adult psychotics, in order to make a relevant place for the issues of self-primal object differentiation with their attending pain and turbulence. This is to say, it needs to be extended to include the primordial, pre-schizo-paranoid levels of mind that come into play in the primal dialogue, with no acknowledged distinction between baby and mother at the level of psychic reality. Phenomena of self-primal object differentiation are explicit in the clinical course of the unfolding of Sophia's mimetic autism, but we gather – and here again we agree with Ferro – that they apply in some manner or other to other clinical pictures and to adult patients.

Such multilevel model of early mind, at a time fusional *and* schizo-paranoid from a certain point in development on, throws additional light on, or provides an alternative to, such controversial concepts as primary envy. As elsewhere stated (Ahumada 2004), acknowledgement of the goodness of the object *as* goodness pertaining *to* the object entails a surrender of fusional identity, and thus is apt to bring up the agonies and furies of self-loss.

Addendum 2

On Tustin's revised edition, a response to Angela Joyce, and an excursus on Ogden's autistic-contiguous position

As mentioned, our outlook on early mind keeps a Ferenczi-Winnicott-Mahler-Tustin line: Mahler's first paper acknowledged drawing from Ferenczi her basic concept of 'primary mother-infant symbiotic unit' (1952, p. 288), and it picked up Winnicott's notion of 'primary maternal preoccupation'. Today, many, if not most, Winnicottians fail to acknowledge and to accept his 'merger' stance on early mind; similarly, Tustin's akin stance is minimised. While, as quoted, Winnicott was quite aware of 'a discrepancy between what is observed and what is being experienced by the baby' (Winnicott 1971, p. 130), under the impact of child developmental studies, authors shy away from the 'merger' model of early mind.

Most authors working on autism emphasise the corporeal – sensoriality taken up as 'physical' in the sense of non-psychical – at the expense of the *ab initio* psychical, pursuing a long tradition in psychoanalysis starting from Freud's (1905) hypothesis of an anobjectal autoeroticism as the initial form of instinctual satisfaction. Margaret Mahler adopted such a Freudian notion of a normal, objectless initial primary autistic stage, which Tustin joined only to firmly reject it later.

Now, if upon Darwinian grounds it is accepted that we humans are primates, then the survival status of the baby–mother primal dialogue and the need for the baby's attunement to mother's states of mind become moot points: primate babies from birth on are closely attuned to and bound to *interpret* mother's states of mind, as they must cling for dear life to mother's hairy breast should her anxiety rise because of predators. The infant's survival depends on mother's survival: a primate mother vying to escape from predators dangling from branch to branch can hardly spare a hand to hold her baby. The primate baby's survival equipment requires his attunement, psychically and thereby bodily, to mother's psychic states: in the forest, in terms of a viable survival unit, the Winnicottian dictum that there is no such thing as a baby applies direly! It should be a moot point then that, as happens with every primate, the human baby is born phylogenetically primed for attunement to mother's mind: as mentioned in Chapter 2, "mind-reading" is, from birth on, a basic ability of higher mammals.

We shall now comment on some misunderstandings issuing from Tustin's (1992) revised edition of her 1981 book *Autistic States in Children*.

Tustin's 1992 revised edition

In the revised edition of *Autistic States in Children* (1992), Tustin partly shifted her conceptual stance from a mother-centred to a body- and sensation-centred stance. As stated by Maiello (1997, p. 7), "she tried more and more, as her life came to an end, to bridge gaps rather than to exacerbate differences", drawing closer to the Bick and Meltzer views held by most of her disciples such as Haag, Houzel, Maiello and Mitrani and paying homage to her analyst Bion's concepts of alpha-function and container.

Turning in the revised edition to wider use of organ-language and sensation-language, as well as introducing a notional split between the bodily and the psychical, she argued that

> nipple-tongue is 'hardness' and mouth-breast is 'softness'. In a satisfactory suckling experience sensations of 'softness' and 'hardness' work together to promote a state of 'well-being', which is a psychological as well as a bodily experience. Thus, bodily sensations have been transformed into *psychological* experience through reciprocal and rhythmical activity between mother and infant. The stage is set for percept and concept formation. But this is a mysterious process.
>
> (1992, p. 101)

A few pages later, she holds of shell-type children:

> the child has experienced 'two-ness' too harshly, too suddenly *for him*. In early infancy, comfortable 'softness' is the prime consideration. To preserve this, the hard 'not-me' is felt to be outside. But then this hard 'not-me' is threatening. . . . It seems possible that these 'not-me' threats combine with the atavistic fear of predators from our animal ancestry to which ethologists have drawn our attention. Certainly, these 'nameless dreads' often become focused upon 'creatures'.
>
> (1992, p. 105)

Discussing the states of ecstasy that "result from a sublime sense of 'oneness' between mother and infant" (p. 106), as well as the tantrums that she considers to be intense "bodily-cum-psychological discharges" (p. 107), she discusses such 'overflow' states, quite surprisingly to us, under the rubric of pre-animate states, as follows:

> Bion's term 'container' seems very apt for the concretised functioning in terms of the inanimate objects which are under discussion. The early states of differentiation between 'hardness' and 'softness' take place before the important distinctions between 'animate' and 'inanimate'. . . are made or before they have become securely established. These early differentiations are the bedrock of human personality before the 'humanness' of psychological functioning has emerged. They are physiological integrations with incipient psychological overtones which are extremely important in giving the personality its basic 'set'.
> (1992, pp. 108–109)

Tustin's conclusions in seeking support in the infant observation studies of Trevarthen and others are open to the caveat raised by Freud in the *Three Essays*, that direct observation of children has the disadvantage of working upon data which are easily misunderstandable (1905, p. 201): this is the more so in such elusive subject as self-object differentiation, which as argued by Mahler and McDevitt (1982) reveals itself by its pathology much more readily than by its normal variations. Crucially, infant experiments unavoidably convey a behaviourist bias: thus, we find much to differ from in the proceeding paragraph. To us, as for Mahler with her acknowledging protodiakrisis as an initial postnatal finding, to which as quoted primatologists concur with their notion of "mind-reading", the 'humanness' of psychological findings is there from the beginning, and such humanness is ruptured in autism where, as stated by Kanner (1951), children treat the animate, mother included, as inanimate. So we coincide with a close Tustin associate, Maria Rhode (2008), in that "very early imitation has a quality which comes over as instinctive as well as being in the service of relationship" (p. 149). It makes no psychoanalytic sense to postulate anteceding physiological integrations, to which the clinical method provides no access; we rather surmise that, as Mahler had drawn from ethologists, "perceptions exist only in so far as they are part of a wider totality of action in which object and inner experience exist as a syncretic indivisible unit" (1968, p. 87). It is from an initial syncretic indivisible unit that differentiations gradually advene through experience.

As we understand it, in her attempt to integrate quite diverse approaches going from observational experiments in infants to the ethologic, as well as notions from her teachers Bick and Meltzer and those of disciples and friends, Tustin forsook her usual policy: keeping close to her clinical material in an "honesty of ignorance", as her friend Isaacs Elmshirst (1997) touchingly put it. Seeking to integrate such unlike approaches, she backpedaled into a Cartesian trap, severing mind from body as well as giving quite unwarranted epistemic and chronological precedence to the inanimate and the physiological over the psychological. This led her into an untenable pseudo-problem: how to grasp the 'mysterious' jump from the inanimate and purely physiological to the psychic-animate. Such a trap was alien to Freud, for whom mind was first and foremost embodied mind and knew well that what goes on is originally felt as animate. Discrimination of the inanimate results from evolved cogitations: the pervasiveness of animism in children and in primitive people signals according to Freud (1913) the psychic precedence of the animate.

Her disciples and associates, such as Haag (1997), whose thinking has kept in the main to Bick-Meltzer lines, amplify Tustin's conceptual shift, building up a 'Meltzerian' Tustin who purportedly no longer supported the initial baby–mother merger as a basic notion. But Tustin's final papers do not avail such a thesis. Two years after publishing the revised edition, she summarised her position thus:

> I began to realize that in seeing this perpetuated state of unified 'at-oneness' with the mother as a *normal* situation in early infancy, we had been extrapolating from a *pathological* situation and mistakenly seeing it as a normal one. This was an error we must be careful not to repeat. I now realize that the infantile state that was being re-evoked in the clinical situation was an *abnormal* one. I have come to see that autism is a protective reaction that develops to deal with the stress associated with a traumatic disruption of an abnormal perpetuated state of adhesive unity with the other – autism being a reaction as is specific to trauma. It is a two-stage illness. First, there is a perpetuation of dual unity, and then the traumatic disruption of this and the stress that it arouses.
>
> (1994a, p. 14)

In such a statement, which closely echoes Mahler's stance, Tustin deems abnormal a *perpetuated* state of unified 'at-oneness' with the mother. The core role of psychic merger with mother in the initial stages comes out in diverse final statements, such as her avowal that "[t]he psychotic child's early pathological fusion with the mothering person means that awareness of bodily separateness is not experienced in slow and manageable degrees, as is the case in normal development; it comes suddenly and traumatically" (1992, p. 35). Importantly, she additionally states that she found to her surprise that "such 'broken-away' phenomenon, experienced as a hole or wound (usually in relation to the mouth) and the associated devious sensuousness, was also an invariable feature in the analysis of neurotic children" (1992, p. 225). The ever-presence of an initial baby–mother merger and its ensuing rupture shines in the concluding remarks of the revised edition, that such 'broken-away' phenomenon is part and parcel of our becoming a person:

> work with psychogenic autistic children brings home to us how we become a person in our own right. Such children have *missed the first essential step in this process, that is, the toleration of the awareness of their bodily separateness and difference from their mothering person,* as the first representative of the outside world.
>
> (1992, p. 239, italics added)

This, she sustained, to some measure happens also in neurotic children who are phobic or have psychosomatic disorders, because

> a segment of their personality has gone in an autistic direction due to their having achieved psychological birth only partially. In an enclave of their awareness such children have felt that they have remained fused with the mother's body. In this part of their awareness they have never tolerated their bodily separateness and difference from her. This constitutes a block to their psychological development and to psychoanalytic work with them. The study of the almost *total* block in psychogenic autistic children helps us to understand this *partial* block in neurotic children. To a more limited extent, this block to achieving psychological birth as a separate individual is present even in relatively normal people.
>
> (1992, p. 239)

So what Tustin considers pathological is the *perpetuation* of merger in the dual unity. As quoted, she holds that in normal development awareness of bodily separateness is experienced in slow and manageable degrees (1992, p. 35), that the 'broken-away' phenomenon experienced as a hole or wound is "an invariable feature in the analysis of neurotic children" (1992, p. 225), and furthermore, that such 'broken-away' phenomenon is an essential first step in our becoming a person (1992, p. 239). Additionally, it can be argued that the omnipresence of the temper tantrum, the 'crisis of two-ness', occurring regularly in childhood (and adolescence) as well as in close affective links at all ages, foremostly in the conflicts of married couples, is an everyday witness to the pertinacity of merger at unconscious levels of mind.

As Tustin again and again fits autistic disorders into the psychoses, we must underline her statement that

> psychogenic autism is a defense against the confusion and entanglement of psychosis, rather than psychosis itself. It seems more accurate to see it as a gross arrest of mental and emotional development. When the autism is lifted, a vulnerable, clinging, confused, helpless child is revealed who may become psychotic unless we realize his need for safety and protection, and can provide it for him by our understanding.
>
> (1986, pp. 45–46)

This, jointly with her granting that a partial block to achieving psychological birth as an individual distinct from mother is found in neurotics and even in relatively normal people, attains what we consider the right conceptual relation between autistic dynamics and properly psychotic ones.

Response to Angela Joyce's comment

As mentioned in the Foreword, our version of Sophia's case responding to Antonino Ferro's Bionian/Meltzerian commentary in turn met a Winnicottian response by Angela Joyce (2010), allowing us to compare our respective conceptual frameworks. Joyce avows that "As the treatment gets going Sophia re-presents with the analyst her silent early life", and continues:

> her only existence is as *an echo; devoid of a self* and the spontaneity that would indicate its existence, she functions in an imitative way, mechanically repeating behaviours of 'care' with the doll figures. This seems to be the limit of psychic representation: the play lacks imaginative elaboration and seems to be simply a repetition of events to which she has been subjected. There is no aggression. We have the sense that the analyst allows this to unfold, not pre-empting or forcing premature understanding.
>
> (p. 177, italics added)

Conceptual language fit for autism, it being mainly asymbolic, differs from the language fit for neuroses. To us, the term "represents" is too evolved for the ongoing mimetic-autistic level: the terms "presents" or "enacts" fit better a child that Joyce acknowledges is an echo devoid of a self and of spontaneity. Similarly, we prefer the term "serially" to describe Sophia's handling of her dolls instead of the term "mechanically": this last term does not discriminate such handling, which however poorly attends to the 'human' character of the dolls though erasing their individualities, from the autosensuousness-generating mechanical character of the autistic spinning of objects. Due to her subsuming autistic-mimetic dynamics into higher-level neurotic dynamics, our accounts diverge in conceptualizing the psychic ongoings. Joyce continues:

> As the analytic setting is established where the analyst is receptive to Sophia's psycho-somatic states, particularly her 'constantly seeking the analyst's eyes for approval', Sophia can risk 'her first fit of rage' against the puppet (old man/witch) which does not look at her. Not being seen by her 'subjective object' (Winnicott 1962b, p. 57) Sophia's archaic self is imbued with the affective sense of non-existence, just as her object also does not exist, which is the stuff of the autistic mimetic bubble she inhabits. This play suggests that Sophia is already beginning to move from the imitative form, indicative of Ogden's (1992, p. 30) 'autistic-contiguous position' where sensory-based experience not yet psychically represented predominates, towards a space where the transitional object as a primitive symbol is 'both a memorial to the lost unity with the object and an attempt to re-instate it *in effigia*' (Wright 1991, p. 104).
>
> (p. 177)

Does it help to call Sophia's utter reliance on the analyst's gaze a "psychosomatic state"? Of course, the ego being a bodily ego, all psychic states can be deemed psychosomatic in the widest sense. Psychosomatic states proper tend to be devoid of overt anxiety, which is not the case here. Also, while our term "approval" for the sought-for response from the analyst is valid at neurotic levels, it here involves sheer psychic survival: it would fit better to say that on being "held" by the analyst's gaze, Sophia comes to exist psychically (concomitantly feeling an object to exist) to the point that she can get angry at the non-recognizing 'old man-witch'. Again, the term "play" is too bland a term to describe the intense pathos of her interaction with the 'old manwitch'. (Joyce's reference to Ogden's 'autistic-contiguous position' will merit an excursus at the end of this chapter.)

Appeal to more evolved states of mind than Sophia is able to muster comes up again in the quotation Joyce takes from Wright's book, *Vision and Separation* (1991). To us, Sophia was as yet far from a mentation able to install "both a memorial to the lost unity with the object and an attempt to re-instate it *in effigia*" (Wright 1991, p. 104), a level of mentation that in Kleinian terms would imply rather advanced steps into the depressive position. We would gladly substitute for it Winnicott's mention that the autistic child *"carries around the (lost) memory of unthinkable anxiety"* (1967b, p. 221, italics original), which is valid also at mimetic levels. It is true that, as exemplified by Tustin's key patient John (and by our child patient Jaime), in late stages of treatment some patients are able to recover and comment on what they went through at the height of their autistic ongoings, but Sophia was then in an initial stage of her treatment.

Concerning the scene during the fifth month of treatment where Sophia mimics the analyst's posture, this is taken up by Joyce as expressing a false self that Sophia has defensively constructed to deal with her falling forever/annihilation feelings, and that she now has to relinquish. On a wide enough definition, *all* autistic dynamics would fit under the rubric "false self" vis-à-vis a yet-to-be-engendered true self. We ask: is it pertinent to take recourse at these fleeting psychic levels to such a purportedly fairly organised, stable psychic organisation as a 'false self'? We find no indication that Winnicott would apply the term "false self" at the autistic levels which he clearly put apart from neurotic ones. Nor would Tustin:

> I have come to realize that I was incorrect in attributing to psychogenic autistic children a "false self" as described by Winnicott (1960). . . . The psychogenic autistic child, and neurotic patients in an autistic state, avoid human relationships. Thus they are empty of a sense of self, and cannot be said to have a "false self" or to be narcissistic.
>
> (1986, p. 44)

We reserve the term *false self* for more evolved and structured psychic stages.

Turning to the *Conceptual discussion* of our paper, Joyce mentions a long history within psychoanalytic developmental theory of a split between those proposing a primary unit of infant and mother and those that took an albeit primitive separateness as present from the beginning of life; now, she holds, there is a greater contemporary consensus, partly prompted by findings in developmental psychology, on the multilayered complexity of inter-psychic and intra-psychic contributions to development. To this, we must counter that the systematic observations of the developmental psychologists introduce an experimentalist bias by pre-delimiting and pre-defining the universe of findings: this is to say, they circumscribe what they will take into account and what they will not. When they are granted epistemic primacy on the basis of their purported "objectivity", the wider universe of what goes on clinically is impoverished by its becoming reduced to what developmentalists can observe and systematise. This is notable for Daniel Stern in his widely influential book "The interpersonal world of the infant" (1985): though he freely admits that he deals with dimensions of the self readily observed in daily social interactions, rather than with unconscious, potentially pathogenic psychic reality dynamics (p. 20), he proceeds to abrogate not just the Winnicottian and Mahlerian merger concept of early mind but also the usual child psychoanalytic conceptual fare, such as unconscious conflict and wish-fulfilling phantasies, while work upon transference is throughout replaced by attunement. Unswerving demise of the psychoanalytic clinical framework is explicit in Stern's sweeping statement a quarter of a century later: "the dynamic unconscious of classical psychoanalysis, that which is under repression, gets relegated to a very small part of everything that is not consciously available" (2008, p. 184). To us, this shows that although the systematic, experimental approach is a good servant, it is a quite poor master. Once clinical findings are filtered through the meshes of whatever the pre-programmed rules of systematic observation are set out to catch, little remains. Indeed, the richness of the clinical method relies on opening the widest possible observational setup for emerging psychic facts: observations arising from free association for the analysand and evenly suspended attention for the analyst in the case of the neuroses, free clinical observations of the children's fleeting spontaneities in the case of autistic spectrum disorders. Besides, there was no need to wait for the developmental psychologists in order to be aware that psychoanalysis is multilayered: it was multilayered right from its start.

Joyce's avowal that as a result of the impact of the developmental psychologists Mahler and Tustin (1991) came "to alter their own theorizing" (2010, p. 179) easily misleads. What Mahler and Tustin rejected was the Freudian assumption of an initial anobjectal autistic stage as a stage of normal development, which had led to autistic disorders being misunderstood as regressions (Tustin 1994b, p. 1307). To her, and to us too, psychogenic autism is a traumatic disturbance of affective contact, not a regression to a non-existent initial autistic stage.

Asking "is there a primary separateness or not at the beginning of life?", Joyce responds that her reading of the clinical case has used "a primarily Winnicottian frame which espouses a subtle view of early life where merger and separateness are paradoxically both present" (p. 179). However, such multilayered evolving process evinces no logical paradox, which is an antinomy that cannot be resolved (Rescher 2001); it is an evolving process that is difficult to inquire on: as was discussed in our response to Ferro, we accord the ongoing resolution of pragmatic paradoxes a core place in the early processes of symbolisation, which take place in the main at the level of thing-presentations, of what Susanne Langer (1957) called 'presentational symbolism'. In Joyce's reading, the concept of "subjective object" is supposed to go against – in our view, mistakenly – those of infant–mother merger, fusional impulses and anxieties, and the ruptures of such merger.

As Joyce assumes to provide a Winnicottian posture, it is pertinent to examine Winnicott's statements on the primordial psyche. In 1953 he stated: "Psychologically the infant takes from a breast that is part of the infant, and the mother gives milk to an infant that is part of herself. In psychology, the idea of interchange is based on an illusion" (p. 239), and next he argued that "it is not possible to describe an infant without describing the mother whom the infant has not yet become able to separate from a self" (1962, p. 177). Years later he stated:

> The infant, of course, is at this first and earliest stage in a state of mergence, not yet having separated out mother and 'not-me' objects from the 'me', so that what is adaptive or 'good' in the environment is building up in the infant's storehouse of experience as a self quality, indistinguishable at first (by the infant) from the infant's own healthy functioning.
> (1963a, p. 97)

A time later, he again mentions: "Baby and object are merged in with one another" (1971, p. 47). Even more relevant in its inmixing of object-loss and early ego-loss is his considering, apposite to reactive depression, a psychotic depression or schizoid depression involving loss of self, in which:

> the loss might be that of certain aspects of the mouth which disappear from the infant's point of view along with the mother and the breast when there is a separation at a date earlier than that at which the infant had reached a stage of emotional development which would provide the infant with the equipment for dealing with loss. The same loss of the mother a few months later would be a loss of object but without this added element of a loss of part of the subject.
> (1963b, p. 222)

That Tustin repeatedly quotes (1972, p. 5, 1981, pp. 71–72, 1988, p. 41) this paragraph illustrates Winnicott's influence on her conceptions. Such 'loss of a part of the subject' retakes Ferenczi's 1932 notion of autotomy.

Half a dozen years later, Winnicott's conceptual scheme on the initial stages of the psyche again closely parallels Ferenczi's classic paper "Stages in the development of the sense of reality" (1913), taking as its start baby–mother 'primary merged state'. In his book *Playing and Reality*, which being published months after his death can be deemed a final statement, he crucially sustains: "It is not the object, of course, that is transitional. The object represents the infant's transition from a state of being merged with the mother to a state of being in relation to the mother as something outside and separate" (1971, pp. 14–15). There he defines *potential space* as "the hypothetical area that exists (but cannot exist) between the baby and the object (mother or part of mother) during the phase of the repudiation of the object as not-me, that is, at the end of being merged in with the object" (1971, p. 107). About the condition that assumedly exists at the beginning of the individual's life, he manifests himself thus:

> the object is not yet separated out from the subject. . . . From the observer's point of view there may seem to be object-relating in the primary merged state, but it has to be remembered that at the beginning the object is a 'subjective object'. I have used this term subjective object to allow a discrepancy between what is observed and what is being experienced by the baby.
> (Winnicott 1971, p. 130)

Winnicott was well aware of the gap between purportedly objective behavioural observation and the baby's experiences, and on the question of whether there is a primary separateness between baby and mother at the beginning of life, he holds once and again to the notion of a 'primary merged state': his concepts of 'subjective object' and 'potential space' are evolving derivatives out of an initial 'primary merged state', rather than arguments against it. He rejected the term *symbiosis* as too biological, but this does not detract from his avowing for a 'primary merged state' in which "the object is still an aspect of the baby" (1970, pp. 254–255).

Was Winnicott conceptually closer to Ferenczi than he knew himself to be? To his disciples and editors Ray Shepherd and Madeleine Davis (Winnicott 1989, p. xiii), it was a vexed issue that Winnicott was often notoriously unable to trace what had influenced him, and concerning Ferenczi he explicitly recognised this: "I never know what I've got out of glancing at Ferenczi, for instance, or glancing at a footnote to Freud" (Winnicott 1989, p. 579). As above quoted, his conceptual scheme on the initial psyche closely parallels that of Ferenczi (1913), taking as its point of departure a baby–mother 'primary merged state'. While André Green (2002, p. 419) arrived to consider Winnicott's work as continuing that of Ferenczi, such fusional stance in Winnicott's position on early mind is something that many, if not most, Winnicottians refuse to acknowledge.

On whether there is a primary separateness or not at the beginning of life, Tustin had raised in 1971 the possibility of "flickering moments of awareness" of separateness from early on. The important point is that these would in no way detract from the operativeness of a merger level of psychic oneness exposed to traumatic ruptures, leading to primal depression or autistic withdrawal, as Winnicott and Tustin had envisioned.

A Bion analysand, James Grotstein (1983), in a book review of Tustin's book *Autistic States in Children* (1981), had proposed a "dual track" hypothesis with "two simultaneous and continuing sides of normal infantile experience, separateness and non-separateness" (p. 492). The shadow of Descartes falls though upon Grotstein when he asks: "When does the new-born infant become mental?" and then goes on:

> We generally take for granted that thinking and feeling occur in a mind that is already differentiated from the body, but how does one 'think' when one's body and mind are still undifferentiated, are one and the same, and the 'thinking' apparatus comprises only raw sensations, not even yet feelings, let alone thoughts?"
>
> (p. 493)

The Cartesian skew is blatant in his assuming that the newborn infant is not mental, his 'thinking' apparatus being reduced to (unfeeling) raw sensations. Conceiving mind as disembodied leads Grotstein to the typical Cartesian pseudo-problem: how to deal with the 'mysterious' leap from body to mind. Privileging "separateness" over "non-separateness", he keeps to the Kleinian assumption of an initial psychic separateness of baby from mother: we assume development goes otherwise, from merger to differentiation and separateness.

How could "the beginning of life" be fixed? One could set the start in the intrauterine period, as explored by Piontelli (1992), or at birth, or maybe at the time shortly thereafter when on his own impulse the baby connects, putting his mouth to the breast and anchoring his gaze to mother's gaze, in a connection at once instinctual and relational. Our clinical material cannot throw light on such matters.

Joyce emphasises Sophia's "relinquishing her primary aggression that alternatively could have been harnessed in the service of the integration of her ego and the 'destruction of the object' in omnipotent fantasy, allowing her to find this object as a separate external reality". But we ask: does the term 'alternatively' fit this context? The term 'alternatively' implies a choice, and this level of mimetic-autistic dynamics offers no choice in any usual sense of this term. Winnicott's (1969, p. 93) concept of the 'destruction of the object' means that relinquishing the omnipotence of one's own aggression requires that it be displayed and the object survives, as happened in the aftermath of Sophia's 'crisis of two-ness'. Such development, purveying "the unconscious background for love of a real object" (p. 94) presupposes long-standing, successful affective containment and is not an 'alternative' at such stage. Again Joyce presupposes a properly symbolic neurotic level that is yet to be attained.

Concerning the dynamics of the gaze, Joyce avows (quoting Wright, not Winnicott) that "the significance of the gaze is linked to the gradual move towards separateness both in its somatic nature (a gaze is held across the distance between two bodies) but also in its expressive potentiality" (Wright 1991, p. 181). Optically and anatomically, the gaze is indeed a distance receptor; at the level of affect, quite contrarily, *avoidance of the gaze* marks emotional distancing.[1] It would be disingenuous indeed to sustain that at the start of nursing, when on hearing mother's voice the newborn baby at the breast seeks and then fixes his gaze on mother's eyes, the baby is seeking an emotional distance from her! Psychically, the gaze plays first and foremost a fusion-contact function, as is shown by Sophia's outright rejection of the old man/witch puppet that does not look at her. So we join Geneviève Haag in that in autistic children "restoration of the feeling of 'flowing-over-at-oneness' may be experienced in the very primitive tactile reestablishment of eye contact" (1997, p. 376), the gaze being an organ of contact, indeed a powerful one. Seducers of both sexes have, from time immemorial, been aware of this! As will soon be shown by our everyday Second Scene on a baby aged 3 months, abrupt interruption of the excited, blissful mutual 'orgy' with its gleaming gaze contact brought about not just an emotional distancing but outright rupture with enduring, if minor, sequels, temporary as this rupture was. This issue, the contact function of the gaze, is crucial to grasp the mimetic-fusional dynamics unchained by the screen effects of our Age of Media, the effects of which are glaring in the cases of Juan's predominantly mimetic autism and of Lila's encapsulated autism.

About the scene at the fifth month of treatment, Joyce argues that

> The analyst holds Sophia's gaze, seeing in it meaning about Sophia's need of her; her approval is sought indicating that she matters to Sophia. Indeed we see just how sensitive and receptive the analyst is to Sophia's states, and particularly to Sophia's use of play as the arena for the emergence of her re-presented history. The difference is now that the object (analyst) is available to her young patient, mindfully elaborating meaning with her. The analyst's timely de-adaption where Sophia's imitation of her posture so eerily tests whether this autistic world of non-existent objects is to prevail, succeeds because it coincides with Sophia's readiness to relinquish her distorted infantile omnipotence and instead find both her self and the separateness of the other in her analyst.
>
> (pp. 181–182)

We are thankful for the clinical compliment but, again, such account would fit were Sophia a neurotic child. Sophia did not seek commonplace approval in her analyst's gaze: as mentioned in the clinical account, she depended for her existence on being kept alive by the analyst's gaze; her very vitality, or conversely her crumbling down, hung on the analyst's response or non-response in contact at the level of the gaze. Similarly, when Joyce speaks of "Sophia's use of play as the arena for the emergence of her re-presented history", we must counter that the scene involved no proper "play", just stark agony, and that she was not re-presenting, just presenting: her use of the gaze at this scene is akin to an anguished baby's fusional seeking of mother's eyes. This, as well as our Scene Two, is at the level of Tronick et al.'s (1978) 'visual violation' experiment in which the infant's gaze anxiously seeks contact, not distancing.

Granted that by the time she engaged in such scene, Sophia's tolerance to separateness had evolved in treatment and was much better than that found in the encapsulated autistic child, who sharply avoids the gaze (she never was a proper encapsulated autist). But she did not seek her analyst's approval in any usual sense of this term: she hung for dear life to her analyst's gaze, as at this psychic level awareness of separateness equaled loss-of-self.

As comes out of this discussion, and as was highlighted in the Introduction, basic conceptual reshuffling needs to be done in order to incorporate autistic spectrum disorders into the psychoanalytic conceptual corpus; contrarily, in Joyce's re-reading, autistic disturbances are pressed into schemes that are valid for childhood neuroses. It seems clear to us that Winnicott sharply put apart the pathos of autism from that of the neuroses.

The most conclusive evidence that autistic dynamics stand apart from neurotic ones is that severe childhood autism hits a "window of opportunity", full accessibility to treatment being restricted to the earliest years of life; fortunately, this does not happen in child neuroses. For useful work to be accomplished in child autism, it is far from enough that, as Joyce put it, the analyst holds the setting. There is a dire need for sustaining his patient, initially almost in a void, putting to work the capacity for emotional immediacy that Tustin calls the 'quality of attention'. The analyst must (as Winnicott highlights) be ready to bear psychic wear and tear much beyond that required in treating neurotic cases, so much so that to Tustin (1994a, p. 104) older children are well-nigh untreatable because of the emotional ravage involved. This need not be taken too literally: in milder cases much improvement can be gained (see Tom's case in Chapter 8). It stands though that in the treatment of autistic spectrum disorders, the 'window of opportunity' is not easily expanded.

We insist that our effort to discern autistic spectrum dynamics from neurotic ones is not of purely theoretical relevance: as mentioned in the Foreword, Tustin (1988a, p. 35) had warned that psychoanalysts working on child autistic patients with the classical technique devised for the neuroses had failed in the 1950s to fulfill their task.

An excursus on Ogden's autistic-contiguous position

Appeal to Ogden's autistic-contiguous position, which Joyce takes for granted, requires an excursus because such terms have come into common parlance in the field of autistic spectrum disorders. As stated in his 1989 paper "On the concept of an autistic-contiguous position", it was on the basis of the clinical and theoretical work developed by Esther Bick, Donald Meltzer and Frances Tustin with autistic children that Ogden developed as a synthesis, interpretation and extension of their work the idea of a theretofore insufficiently understood dimension, more primitive than the paranoid-schizoid position, which he calls the autistic-contiguous position and which he posits as integral to normal development, having equal organizing significance to the paranoid-schizoid and depressive positions (1989, p. 127).

Ogden associates the autistic-contiguous organisation with a specific mode of attributing meaning to experience in which "raw sensory data are ordered by means of forming pre-symbolic connections between sensory impressions that come to constitute bounded surfaces. It is on these surfaces that experience of self has its origins" (1989, p. 128). He states that he retains the word *autistic* for this most primitive psychological organisation despite its association with a pathological entity because he believes that such entity involves hypertrophy of the types of defense, forms of attribution of meaning to experience and mode of object relatedness characterizing the normal autistic-contiguous organisation.

In the autistic-contiguous mode, argues Ogden, experiences of sensation, particularly at the skin surface, are the principal media for the creation of psychological meaning and the rudiments of the experience of the self, sensory-contiguity of skin surface and rhythmicity being basic. The organisation of a rudimentary sense of 'I-ness' is seen to arise from relationships of sensory contiguity (i.e., *touching*) that over time generate the sense of a bounded sensory surface on which one's experience occurs ('a place where one lives') (1989, p. 129). After such considerations on the origins of 'I-ness', in line with Bick's and Meltzer's ideas of sensoriality, he invokes Tustin's autistic shapes and autistic objects as part of the vicissitudes of sensoriality, and he illustrates with therapeutic work on a congenitally blind schizophrenic adolescent who started treatment at age 19. To Ogden, experience at the skin surface is critically important in that it constitutes an arena where there is a convergence of the infant's idiosyncratic, pre-symbolic world of sensory impressions and the interpersonal world made of objects (which an outside observer would view as) having an existence separate from the infant and outside his omnipotent control.

We have summarised Ogden's concepts in order to respond to Joyce on why we do not use the concept of autistic-contiguous position: nothing in Sophia's case (nor in our other cases) approaches Ogden's descriptions of raw sensory data or of bounded skin surfaces as the beginning of the self. To us, the experience of self has its origins in the primal dialogue.

Years later, Ogden conceded that these are speculative metaphors he finds useful in the consulting room (2008). But speculative metaphors, as conjectures generally, must keep close to the factual contexts from which they are drawn and cannot be transposed freely from the adult psychotic to the healthy baby. Our objections to the use of the term "sensory impressions" for the socle of the psyche, as above exposed in relation to Bion's theory of thinking, fully apply here.

To us, the terms "sensation" and "sensory impressions" apply to autistic phenomena just as part of auto-sensuousness, because at crossgrain to the dominant philosophical tradition going back to Descartes, to us the term *sensation* has no merit as the initial socle of mind. Ogden's conviction that the earliest stages of normal infantile experience are of a "sensation-based sort" (2008, p. 233) must derive from his work with severely sick adult and adolescent patients. But his being a master clinician as well as a consummate and sensitive writer does not authorise his clinical findings in highly disturbed adolescent and adult patients to be transposed to infancy as early stages of mind, less than to raise such findings to the status of a "position" on a par with Klein's paranoid-schizoid and depressive positions. Salomonsson (2012) has eloquently objected to transporting to early infancy reconstructions arising from findings in adult analyses, highlighting that Freud took up whatever opportunities he had for direct infant observation – the most famous one being on his grandson's 'game of the bobbin' (1920), in which the infant worked through his mother's absence. Quite pertinently for the present discussion, Salomonsson had earlier argued that in psychoanalysis we investigate mental phenomena that are unknown, not that are unknowable or unsignified, and that in concretizing a psychic event as a "sense impression", we place it outside of psychoanalytic investigation (2007, p. 1212).

Ogden describes the use of bodily odour by his key patient, a blind schizophrenic adolescent who used unsupportable body smell as a core identity aspect and as a way to keep others at bay: to us, this is restitutive rather than primordial. That we know of, babies do not use their odour to keep others at bay; rather, it helps their sense of going-on-being, being felt as self-soothing just as mother's odour is. Even in the case of the smell of the soft transitional object, the piece of cloth that mothers and nannies know well should much preferably not be washed, demand for such odour can on occasion be obviated by the baby, as shown by the following example. A usually tranquil 13-month-old infant was fussy and sleepless on a long overnight flight, and despite his mother's usually effective consolations, he continued to be restless on arrival: then, on learning that the well-worn knit cloth he used as his transitional object had been left home, the grandmother provided an identical, new one that despite its lack of smell the baby adopted on-the-fly, falling soundly asleep. Thus, the infant easily bypassed a sensory channel such as smell when what remained helped him retake the sought-for sense of on-going continuity. Upgrading smell to the status of an elemental "raw" sensation, that is, as Cartesianly 'primary' stuff, likely led Ogden to translocate it from his blind adolescent patient's restitutive pathology to the dawn of early mind.

Most notably, on the overall idea that the unpredictability of affective contact makes it unsupportable to the healthy baby, he considers use of autistic hard objects and autistic shapes as a core part of normal development: they are used, as he put it, "as a form of buffer against the continual strain of being alive in the world of human beings" (1997, p. 189). Ogden's conjectural baby is to our eyes a disturbed unhappy baby, not a healthy going-on-being one. We agree that healthy babies often take support in the use of equivalents of autistic shapes – the pacifier and thumb, and later on the caressing and smelling of a soft transitional object – but in voicing that ample use of hard and soft autistic objects (which Tustin firmly deemed obstructive of psychic growth) is at the core of healthy development, Ogden transposes to the healthy baby the inability to bear affective contact that his highly disturbed patients displayed. The central task of the primordial mind, he postulates – to keep off basically unpredictable affects – is *inverse* to Winnicott's and Tustin's focus on the enjoyment of the continuities in the baby's affective experiential going-on-being. That by systematic use of hard and soft autistic objects the basic task of the healthy baby's mind is to keep off emotional contacts that are in principle unbearable, turns playful going-on-being into an anomaly. In such intellectual context to speak of healthy emotional contact becomes an oxymoron.

Four everyday infant scenes

The yes/no question about ab initio differentiation of self and object put forward by Dr. Angela Joyce in her comment on Sophia requires us to underline a basic distinction between *perceptual awareness* on the one hand, and *self-object affective discrimination* on the other hand, two issues that pertain to quite different levels of mind and run quite different courses, in infancy and in variable measure throughout life. To hold that perceptual reality equals psychic reality would amount to a comeback to the Cartesian psychology of consciousness, throwing overboard all that psychoanalysis has learned. So let us bring to bear, for a balance, some everyday observations from healthy going-on-being infants.

A lively baby turning 3 months of age much enjoyed being paid attention to, gleefully engaging in interchanges: smiling, crackling with laughter, 'verbalizing' gurgling sounds with his mother and the immediate family (his father, his 3-year-old brother, both sets of grandparents); in those gleeful interchanges his gaze was firmly locked to his interlocutor's gaze. By that time he visually contemplated his hands, played with these and explored sucking them in various ways.

Our First Scene, shortly before 3 months of age, concerns his 'discovery' of his right foot: calmly bending his trunk, he thrusted both hands forward until he found the foot, which brought an upsurge of joy, an act which he repeated. At these times he was, so to say, very much with himself, though readily available to connect with those around. Such 'discovery' with its accompanying glee evidences his capacity for, and his joy at, attaining *perceptual* bodily distinctions at quite an early age (discovering his left foot took weeks longer). We cannot know what role, if any, mother had at those moments in the baby's mind, though we might surmise that she was present in the background as mother-as-environment; but we can be confident that during these enterprises of joyful corporeal 'eureka' discovery, he evinced no sign of the anguishes of "spilling over" or "falling into a void" that Esther Bick had assumed happened in a hypothetical early fluctuating stage of the ego limits. His enterprise of bodily self-discovery – his gleeful expansion of his bodily ego limits – was an enjoyable part of his going-on-being. We might here witness, at 3 months of age, the inklings of a context of play.

Our Second Scene took place the following week, after he turned 3 months. Sitting in his stroller he was immersed in an intensely joyful smiling and laughing and kicking orgy with his maternal grandmother, his gleaming gaze firmly anchored to hers: then, calamitously, Grandma's cell phone rang, and for some five minutes she took the call, disconnecting herself. On turning again to the baby, things had changed drastically: angry and despondent, he avoided her gaze, turning his head away whenever she tried to approach and to re-connect visually; he kept up, though, a lively connection with other members of the family, his mother included. It took a half day for the baby to 'pardon' the grandmother for her withdrawal of attention, after which she was readmitted to his affection. Again, we here find, observationally, evidence of separateness, in this instance not just perceptual on the baby's side as it included a violent emotive enacted response, apparent in his withdrawing from the inattentive grandmother's efforts to contact him. The peak of ecstatic emotional 'fusion' with the love-object, his euphoric merging, his joyful "flowing over at one-ness" (Tustin's terms) to his [grand]mother exposed him to the hardships of rupture. Nothing akin took place when attention was withdrawn from the baby in usual, calmer circumstances, either by the mother or by others. Ecstatic merging states, which we regard as sexual inasmuch as they are blatantly erotic (we used the term 'orgy' advisedly, to highlight its sexual character) involve risky contacts, potentially leading to mini-remakes of a ruptural trauma. If we follow Tustin in that "autistic reactions are an exaggeration of an inbuilt repertoire of elemental reactions which are part of the lot of all human beings" (1988a, p. 44), then this scene likely provides a mini-model of the sort of elemental threat of ruptural loss of a sense of existence that could eventually lead to autistic spectrum disorders.

We join Salomonsson (2012) on that sexuality is undervalued and mostly forsaken in present-day psychoanalytic infant theorisation, being displaced by attachment theory. As illustrated by the scene just described, baby–mother sexuality does not necessarily involve organ contact: in fact, nothing akin happened when our baby fed at the breast. That in this scene the love-object was the grandmother rather than the mother should not surprise those who are acquainted with Matte-Blanco's (1975, 1988) overall dictum that the unconscious does not recognise individuals.

A Third Scene came up days later: the baby, who up to then had been breast-fed except for occasional bottle feedings of mother's milk on short absences, was suddenly withdrawn from the breast due to his mother's ingestion of a toxic antibiotic. For the first time, the mother fed him formula for a week and then resumed breast-feeding. Relevantly for the discussion, the baby showed disgust, mildly protesting when bottle-fed the formula, but abrupt withholding of the nipple/breast and of maternal milk did not evince an adversive withdrawal from his mother akin to the rupture shown upon Grandma's brusque inattention during their ecstatic glee.

The issue, then, of what the psychoanalytic literature conveniently refers to in organ language as 'the breast' admits no simple answer. Somewhere, Bion wryly commented that were he asked what he meant by the breast, he would respond that he means what he assumes the baby means by the breast! As concerns Winnicott, in a letter to Betty Joseph written in 1954, he speaks about

> the idea of a bad environment, or in your sort of language, a bad breast. . . . I am trying to draw attention to the very early stages, quite apart from the fantasy. . . . I find it very difficult to get people to leave for a moment the infant's fantasy of a bad breast and to go to stage further back to the effect

of a bad mothering technique, such as for instance rigidity (mother's defense against hate) or muddle (expression of mother's chaotic state).

(Winnicott 1987, p. 59)

Beyond mothering technique as such, Winnicott here speaks loudly about the baby's dire contact, for better *and* for worse, with mother's affective states.

Sometime later, when the baby was 6 months in age, he was weaned from the breast and put to the bottle with no untoward reaction. But, whenever his mother, while bottle-feeding him, took a phone call withdrawing her gaze and her attention, the baby evinced an angry adversive ruptural withdrawal, similar to the one displayed with his grandmother at age 3 months. As previously mentioned, Melanie Klein's (1957, p. 180n1) "memories in feelings" fit the psychic level of the thing-presentations from which to Freud meaning derives, as is illustrated by Salomonsson's (2012) work with nursing baby–mother duets. In the present case, these ruptural experiences are, in Winnicott's remarkable phrase, "the (lost) memory of unthinkable anxiety" (1967b, p. 221).

From these examples it might be surmised that what our 3-month-old baby meant by 'the breast' relates as much to the emotional psychic link to mother's mind (eventually to a grandmother located in mother's emotional place) as to the breast (or its milk) as feeding organ. Already close to the beginnings, and presumably from the beginnings on, *instinct is inter-psychical* and centrally involves cognitive dimensions.

Perceptual awareness might conjecturally be admitted to exist from the start, from the moment when the newborn baby seeks the nipple and, on hearing mother's voice, seeks her gaze. Such perceptual awareness from the beginning is a valid lesson to be extracted from infant observations. But the point is that *perceptual awareness* does not by itself entail a tolerance for *self-object emotional distinction*: this belongs to evolutions of unconscious levels of mind, comes about much later, must be gained hardily and is never fully accomplished.

To illustrate later vicissitudes of this long-drawn process, we might take a Fourth Scene of a toddler nearly 2 years old where the boy, playing quietly with some toy cars while in another room his mother was chatting with a friend, at some moment stepped on a toy car, fell on his face and got up angry and crying, ran straight to where mother was, and hit her furiously. Obviously enough, at the *perceptual level* separateness between them had been fully attained; at the *emotional unconscious level* that Freud would deem his *psychic reality*, it would appear that despite quietly playing by himself, the boy inhabited some sort of affective *mother-space* whereby mother, present or not, was felt as being in charge of his well-being and was responded to on such basis.

So our response to the question, "Is there a primary separateness or not at the beginning of life?" is that in order to be fruitful, the issues of me/not-me separateness, as most issues in the realm of mind, must be posed in terms of psychic levels. Our Four Scenes illustrate the level of what Freud obscurely called 'thing-presentations', of which the unconscious is built and where meaning is generated; perceptual separateness belongs at the preconscious-conscious levels, dim and incipient as these might be in the early stages.

Note

1 This is valid not only for human beings but also for primates like our next of kin the bonobo, the so-called pygmy chimpanzee. Bonobos, which have nearly 30% of their coituses in ventro-ventral position (Kano 1986, p. 141), attend during coitus carefully to their respective facial expressions while fixing their gaze on each other's eyes; if either male or female avoids the other's gaze, the usual response of the partner is to interrupt sex and withdraw (de Waal and Lanting 1997, p. 105).

References

Abraham, K. (1924). A short study of the development of the libido, viewed in the light of mental disorders. In *Selected Papers on Psychoanalysis*. London, Hogarth.

Ahumada, J. L. (1980). On the transposition of self and object. In *The Logics of the Mind: A Clinical View* (pp. 51–64). London, Karnac, 2001.

—— (1984). The analyst as "base". In *The Logics of the Mind: A Clinical View* (pp. 37–50). London, Karnac, 2001.

—— (1990). On narcissistic identification and the shadow of the object. *International Review of Psychoanalysis* 17: 177–187 (Also in *The Logics of the Mind: A Clinical View* (pp. 95–113). London, Karnac, 2001).

—— (1991). Logical types and ostensive insight. *International Journal of Psychoanalysis* 72: 683–691. (Also in *Insight. Essays on Psychoanalytic Knowing* (pp. 19–30). London, Routledge, 2011).

—— (1997a). Counterinduction in psychoanalytic practice: Epistemic and technical aspects. In *Insight: Essays on Psychoanalytic Knowing* (pp. 133–153). London, Routledge, 2011.

—— (1997b). The crisis of culture and the crisis of psychoanalysis. In *The Logics of the Mind: A Clinical View* (pp. 1–13). London, Karnac, 2001.

—— (1999). The academy of the spectacle. *Journal of the American Psychoanalytic Association* 47: 585–593.

—— (2001). On e-growth, education and e-sanity. *Journal of the American Psychoanalytic Association* 49: 1035–1040.

—— (2004). On intolerance to the object's goodness. Response to Dr. Symington. *International Journal of Psychoanalysis* 85: 1005–1007.

—— (2005). The double work on the clinical evidences, and the nature and limits of symbolization. In *Insight: Essays on Psychoanalytic Knowing* (pp. 163–180). London, Routledge, 2011.

—— (2006). La dynamique mimesis-autisme dans les psychopathologies d'aujourd'hui. In Green, A. (ed.) *Les voies nouvelles de la thérapeutique psychanalytique* (pp. 661–694). Paris, Presses Universitaires de France.

—— (2010). La dinámica mimético-autística y la reacción terapéutica negativa en los pacientes de hoy. *Revista de Psicoanálisis* 67: 275–287.

—— (2011). *Insight. Essays on Psychoanalytic Knowing*. London, Routledge.

—— (2011). Postscript. 'What hath God wrought?'. A plea for insight in media society. In *Insight: Essays on Psychoanalytic Knowing* (pp. 201–207). London, Routledge, 2011.

—— (2014). The waning of screen memories: From the Age of Neuroses to an Autistoid Age. In Reed, G. S. and Levine, H. (eds.) *On Freud's Screen Memories* (pp. 104–117). London, IPA-Karnac.

—— (2015). Ignacio Matte-Blanco: interrogantes y desafíos. *Calibán, Revista Latinoamericana de Psicoanálisis* 13:212–219.

—— (2016). Rejoinder to Robert A. Paul's response. *International Journal of Psychoanalysis* 97: 873–874.

Ahumada, J. L. and Busch de Ahumada, L. C. (2010). Further comments on Sophia's mimetic autism, with special reference to Bion's theory of thinking. In Leuzinger-Bohleber, M., Canestri, J. and Target, M. (eds.) *Early Development and Its Disturbances* (pp. 153–173). London, Karnac.

Alvarez, A. (1992). *Live Company*. London, Routledge.

—— (1995). Verbal rituals in autism: The concept of autistic object and the countertransference. In Mitrani, T. and Mitrani, J. L. (eds.) *Encounters with Autistic States* (pp. 231–256). Northvale, NJ, Aronson.

—— (2010). Levels of analytic work and levels of pathology: The work of calibration. *International Journal of Psychoanalysis* 91: 859–878.

—— (2012). *The Thinking Heart: Three Levels of Psychoanalytic Therapy with Disturbed Children*. London, Routledge.

Asperger, H. (1944). Die 'Autistischen Psychopathen' im Kindersalter. *Archiv für Psychiatrie und Nervenkrankheiten* 117: 76–136.

Balint, A. (1939). Love for the mother and mother-love. *International Journal of Psychoanalysis* 30: 251–259.

Balint, M. (1968). *The Basic Fault: Therapeutic Aspects of Regression*. London, Tavistock Publications.

Barrows, K. (ed.) (2008). *Autism in Childhood and Autistic Features in Adults*. London, Karnac.

Bettelheim, B. (1967). *The Empty Fortress: Infantile Autism and the Birth of the Self*. New York, The Free Press.

Bhaskar, R. (1978). *A Realist Theory of Science*. Brighton, Harvester.

Bick, E. (1966). Infant observation in psychoanalytic training. *International Journal of Psychoanalysis* 45: 558–566.

—— (1968). The experience of the skin in early object-relations. *International Journal of Psychoanalysis* 49: 484–486.

Bion, W. R. (1962). *Learning from Experience*. New York, Basic Books.

—— (1965). *Transformations: From Learning to Growth*. London, Heinemann.

Birksted-Breen, D. (1989). Working with an anorexic patient. *International Journal of Psychoanalysis* 70: 29–40.

—— (1996). Phallus, penis and mental space. *International Journal of Psychoanalysis* 77: 649–657.

Bisagni, F. (2012). Delusional development in childhood autism at the onset of puberty: Vicissitudes of psychic dimensionality between disintegration and development. *International Journal of Psychoanalysis* 93: 667–692.

Bleger, J. (1967). *Simbiosis y ambigüedad*. Buenos Aires, Paidós.

Britton, R. (1999). 'Primal grief' and 'petrified rage': An exploration of Rilke's Duino Elegies. In Bell, D. (ed.) *Psychoanalysis and Culture: A Kleinian Perspective* (pp. 27–47). London, Karnac.

Busch de Ahumada, L. C. (2003). Clinical notes on a case of transvestism in a child. *International Journal of Psychoanalysis* 84: 291–313.
Busch de Ahumada, L. C. and Ahumada, J. L. (2005). From mimesis to agency: Clinical steps in the work of psychic two-ness. *International Journal of Psychoanalysis* 86: 721–736.
—— (2009). Autische Mimesis im Medienzeitalter: Eine Fallgeschichte. In Nissen, B. (ed.) *Die Entstehung des Seelischen: Psychoanalytischer Perspective* (pp. 141–163). Giessen, Psychosozial-Verlag.
—— (2012). Formen autistische und autistoid Dynamic: Das Zeitfenster für eine günstige Wendung (the window of opportunity). In Reiser-Mumme, U. et al. (eds.) *Spaltung. Entwicklung und Stillstand* (pp. 342–356). Deutsche Psychoanalytische Vereinigung Frühjahrstagung.
Call, J. D. (1964). Newborn approach behavior and early ego development. *International Journal of Psychoanalysis* 45: 286–294.
—— (1968). Lap and finger play in infancy, implications for ego development. *International Journal of Psychoanalysis* 49: 375–378.
—— (1980). Some prelinguistic aspects of ego development. *Journal of the American Psychoanalytic Association* 28: 259–289.
CDC (2013). 1 in 10 US kids diagnosed with ADHD. adhd/news/20130401/
Cecchi, V. (1990). Analysis of a little girl with an autistic syndrome. *International Journal of Psychoanalysis* 71: 403–410. (Reprinted in Barrows, K. (ed.) *Autism in Childhood and Autistic Features in Adults* (pp. 81–94). London, Karnac, 2008).
Christakis, D. A., Zimmerman, F. J., DiGiuseppe, D. L. and McCarthy, C. A. (2004). Early television exposure and subsequent attentional problems in children. *Pediatrics* 113: 708–713.
Collingwood, R. G. (1937). *The Principles of Art*. London, Oxford University Press, 1958.
Cottingham, J. (1986). General introduction: The meditations and cartesian philosophy. In Descartes, R. and Cottingham, J. (eds.) *Meditations on First Philosophy*. Cambridge, Cambridge University Press, 1997.
Dale, F. M. J. (1997). The absent self. In Mitrani, T. and Mitrani, J. (eds.) *Encounters with Autistic States: A Memorial Tribute to Frances Tustin* (pp. 305–325). Northvale, NJ, Jason Aronson.
Darwin, C. (1879). *The Descent of Man, and Selection in Relation to Sex* (2nd ed.). London, Penguin, 2004.
Deutsch, H. (1942). Some forms of emotional disturbance and their relationship to schizophrenia. *Psychoanalytic Quarterly* 11: 301–321.
De Waal, F. and Lanting, F. (1997). *Bonobo: The Forgotten Ape*. Berkeley, CA, University of California Press.
Etchegoyen, R. H. and Ahumada, J. L. (2002). Que faire? Le rôle de la psychanalyse dans la postmodernité. In Botella, C. (ed.) *Penser les limites. Essais en l'honneur d'André Green* (pp. 418–423). Paris, Delachaux & Niestlé.
Fairbairn, R. (1952). *Psychoanalytic Studies of the Personality*. London, Tavistock.
Fenichel, O. (1930). The psychology of transvestism. *International Journal of Psychoanalysis* 11: 211–226.
—— (1946). *The Psychoanalytic Theory of Neurosis*. London, Routledge and Kegan Paul, 1963.

References

Ferenczi, S. (1909). Introjection and transference. In *First Contributions to Psychoanalysis*. London, Karnac, 1980.
—— (1913). Stages in the development of the sense of reality. In *First Contributions to Psychoanalysis* (pp. 183–201). London, Karnac, 1980.
—— (1932). Notes and fragments. In Balint, M. (ed.) *Final Contributions to the Problems and Methods of Psychoanalysis* (pp. 216–279). London, Karnac, 1994.
Ferraro, F. (2001). Vicissitudes of bisexuality: Crucial points and clinical implications. *International Journal of Psychoanalysis* 82: 485–499.
Ferro, A. (2007). El largo camino de Sofía. Comentario al trabajo de Luisa C. Busch de Ahumada y Jorge L. Ahumada: De la mimesis a la espontaneidad. Pasos en el camino de la separatidad psíquica. *Revista de Psicoanálisis* 64: 849–851.
Firth, U. (1991). Asperger and his syndrome. In Firth, U. (ed.) *Autism and Asperger Syndrome* (pp. 1–36). Cambridge, Cambridge University Press.
Folch Mateu, P. (2001). Book review of: Descubrimientos y refutaciones. La lógica de la indagación psicoanalítica, by Jorge L. Ahumada. *International Journal of Psychoanalysis* 82: 183–189.
Freud, A. (1936). *The Ego and the Mechanisms of Defense*. London, Karnac, 1993.
Freud, S. (1893). On the psychical mechanism of hysterical phenomena: A lecture. *S.E.*, 3.
—— (1905). Three essays on the theory of sexuality. *S.E.*, 7.
—— (1910). Leonardo da Vinci and a memory of his childhood. *S.E.*, 11.
—— (1913). Totem and taboo. *S.E.*, 13.
—— (1914a). Remembering, repeating and working through. *S.E.*, 12.
—— (1914b). On narcissism: An introduction. *S.E.*, 14.
—— (1915). The unconscious. *S.E.*, 14.
—— (1920). Beyond the pleasure principle. *S.E.*, 18.
—— (1921). Group psychology and the analysis of the ego. *S.E.*, 18.
—— (1923a). Two encyclopaedia articles: (A) Psycho-analysis. *S.E.*, 18.
—— (1923b). The ego and the id. *S.E.*, 19.
—— (1925). An autobiographical study. *S.E.*, 20.
—— (1926). Inhibitions, symptoms and anxiety. *S.E.*, 20.
—— (1930). Civilization and its discontents. *S.E.*, 21.
—— (1933). New introductory lectures on psychoanalysis. *S.E.*, 23.
—— (1940). An outline of psychoanalysis. *S.E.*, 23.
—— (1941). Reflections, ideas, problems. *S.E.*, 23.
Gaddini, E. (1969). On imitation. *International Journal of Psychoanalysis* 50: 475–484.
—— (1984). Changes in psychoanalytic patients up to the present day. In Wallerstein, R. (ed.) *A Psychoanalytic Theory of Infant Experience* (pp. 186–203). London, Brunner-Routledge, 1992.
Gaddini, R. (1995). From fear of change to mourning. In Mitrani, T. and Mitrani, J. L. (eds.) *Encounters with Autistic States* (pp. 213–230). Northvale, NJ & London, Jason Aronson.
Gilmore, K. (2000). A psychoanalytic perspective on attention deficit/hyperactivity disorder. *Journal of the American Psychoanalytic Association* 48: 1259–1293.
Goodall, J. (1986). *The Chimpanzees of Gombe*. Boston, MA, Belknap/Harvard University Press.
Green, A. (1980). Passions and their vicissitudes: On the relation between madness and psychosis. In *On Private Madness* (pp. 214–253). Madison, CT, International Universities Press, 1986.

—— (1992). Transcriçao da origem desconhecida. A escrita do psicanálise: critica do fundamento. *Revista Brasileira de Psicanálise* 26: 151–190.

Green, A. (1997). Jacket note in Mitrani, T. and Mitrani, J. L. *Encounters with autistic states. A memorial tribute to Frances Tustin.* Northvale, NJ, Jason Aronson.

—— (2002). ¿De qué se trata?. *Revista de Psicoanálisis* 59: 411–430.

Greenson, R. R. (1966). A transvestite boy and a hypothesis. *International Journal of Psychoanalysis* 47: 396–403.

Griffin, D. R. (1992). *Animal Minds*. Chicago, IL, University of Chicago Press.

Grotstein, J. S. (1983). Book review of: Autistic states in children by Frances Tustin. *International Review of Psychoanalysis* 10: 491–498.

—— (1997). One pilgrim's progress: Notes on Frances Tustin's contribution to the psychoanalytic conception of autism. In Mitrani, T. and Mitrani, J. (eds.) *Encounters with Autistic States: A Memorial Tribute to Frances Tustin* (pp. 257–290). Northvale, NJ, Jason Aronson.

Haag, G. (1993). Fear of fusion and projective identification in autistic children. *Psychoanalytic Inquiry* 13: 63–84.

—— (1997). Encounter with Frances Tustin. In Mitrani, T. and Mitrani, J. L. (eds.) *Encounters with Autistic States: A Memorial Tribute to Frances Tustin* (pp. 355–396). Northvale, NJ, Aronson.

Hinz, H. (2012). Projective identification: The fate of the concept in Germany. In Spillius, E. and O'Shaughnessy, E. (eds.) *Projective Identification: The Fate of a Concept* (pp. 186–203). London, Routledge.

Houzel, D. (1999). The creation of psychic space, the 'nest of babies' fantasy and the emergence of the Oedipus complex. In Barrows, K. (ed.) *Autism in Childhood and Autistic Features in Adults* (pp. 119–145). London, Karnac, 2008.

—— (2004). The psychoanalysis of infantile autism. *Journal of Child Psychotherapy* 30: 225–237.

Jones, E. (1933). The phallic phase. *International Journal of Psychoanalysis* 14: 1–33.

Joseph, B. (1971). A clinical contribution to the analysis of a perversion. *International Journal of Psychoanalysis* 52: 51–66.

Joyce, A. (2010). Discussion of Jorge L. Ahumada and Luisa C. Busch de Ahumada's paper. In Leuzinger-Bohleber, M., Canestri, J. and Target, M. (eds.) *Early Development and Its Disturbances* (pp. 175–183). London, Karnac.

Kanner, L. (1943). Autistic disturbances of affective contact. *The Nervous Child* 2: 217–250.

—— (1951). The conception of wholes and parts in early infantile autism. *American Journal of Psychiatry* 108: 23–26.

—— (1953). Round table discussion: Problems in child psychiatry. *Pediatrics* 11: 393–404.

Kano, T. (1986). *The Last Ape: Pygmy Chimpanzee Behavior and Ecology*. Stanford, CA, Stanford University Press, 1992.

Klein, M. (1930). The importance of symbol-formation in the development of the ego. In Money-Kyrle, R. et al. (eds.) *Love, Guilt and Reparation and Other Works 1921–1945: The Writings of Melanie Klein Vol. 1* (pp. 219–232). London, Hogarth Press, 1975.

—— (1935). A contribution to the psychogenesis of manic-depressive states. In Money-Kyrle, R. et al. (eds.) *Love, Guilt and Reparation and Other Works 1921–1945: The Writings of Melanie Klein Vol. 1* (pp. 262–289). London, Hogarth Press, 1975.

―― (1936). Weaning. In Money-Kyrle, R. et al. (eds.) *Love, Guilt and Reparation and Other Works 1921–1945: The Writings of Melanie Klein Vol. 1* (pp. 290–305). London, Hogarth Press, 1975.

―― (1952). Some theoretical conclusions regarding the emotional life of the infant. In Money-Kyrle, R. et al. (eds.) *Envy and Gratitude and Other Works 1946–1963: The Writings of Melanie Klen Vol. III* (pp. 61–93). London, Hogarth Press, 1975.

―― (1957). Envy and gratitude. In Money-Kyrle, R. et al. (eds.) *Envy and Gratitude and Other Works 1946–1963: The Writings of Melanie Klein Vol. III* (pp. 176–235). London, Hogarth Press, 1975.

Klein, S. (1980). Autistic phenomena in neurotic patients. *International Journal of Psychoanalysis* 61: 395–401.

Kohut, H. (1971). *The Analysis of the Self*. New York, International Universities Press.

Korbivscher, C. S. (2013). Bion and Tustin: The autistic phenomena. *International Journal of Psychoanalysis* 94: 645–665.

Landhuis, C. E., Poulton, R., Welch, D. and Cox, R. (2007). Does childhood television viewing lead to attention problems in adolescence? Results from a prospective longitudinal study. *Pediatrics* 120: 532–537.

Langer, S. (1957). *Philosophy in a New Key*. Cambridge, MA, Harvard University Press, 1973.

Lasch, C. (1979). *The Culture of Narcissism*. New York, NY, Norton, 1991.

―― (1984). *The Minimal Self: Psychic Survival in Troubled Times*. New York, NY, Norton.

Lechevalier, B. (1997). Expressions of annihilation anxiety and the birth of the subject. In Mitrani, T. and Mitrani, J. (eds.) *Encounters with Autistic States: A Memorial Tribute to Frances Tustin* (pp. 327–339). Northvale, NJ, Jason Aronson.

Leuzinger-Bohleber, M., Canestri, J. and Target, M. (2010). *Early Development and Its Disturbances: Clinical, Conceptual and Empirical Research on ADHD and Other Psychopathologies and Its Epistemological Reflections*. London, Karnac.

Mahler, M. (1952). On child psychosis and schizophrenia: Autistic and symbiotic infantile psychoses. *Psychoanalytic Study of the Child* 7: 286–308.

―― (1958). Autism and symbiosis: Two extreme disturbances of identity. *International Journal of Psychoanalysis* 39: 77–82.

―― (1961). On sadness and grief in infancy and childhood – Loss and restoration of the symbiotic love object. *Psychoanalytic Study of the Child* 16: 332–351.

―― (1968). *On Human Symbiosis and the Vicissitudes of Individuation. Vol. I. Infantile Psychoses*. New York, NY, International Universities Press.

―― (1974). Symbiosis and individuation – The psychological birth of the human infant. *Psychoanalytic Study Child* 29: 89–108.

Mahler, M. and McDevitt, J. B. (1982). Thoughts on the emergence of the sense of self, with particular emphasis in the body self. *Journal of the American Psychoanalytic Association* 30: 827–848.

Mahler, M., Pine, F., and Bergman, A. (1975). *The psychological birth of the human infant. Symbiosis and individuation*. New York, NY, Basic Books.

Maiello, S. (1997). Going beyond: Notes on the beginning of object relationships in the light of 'the perpetuation of an error'. In Mitrani, T. and Mitrani, J. (eds.) *Encounters with Autistic States: A Memorial Tribute to Frances Tustin* (pp. 1–22). Northvale, NJ, Jason Aronson.

Matte-Blanco, I. (1975). *The Unconscious as Infinite Sets.* London, Duckworth.
—— (1988). *Thinking, Feeling and Being.* London, Routledge.
McLuhan, M. (1964). *Understanding Media: The Extensions of Man.* London, Routledge, 2004.
Meltzer, D. (1960). Kleinian child psychiatry. In Hahn, A. (ed.) *Sincerity and Other Works: Collected Papers of Donald Meltzer* (pp. 35–89). London, Karnac, 1994.
—— (1975). Adhesive identification. *Contemporary Psychoanalysis* 11: 289–310.
—— (1983). *Dream Life: A Re-examination of the Psycho-analytical Theory and Technique.* Strath Tay, Clunie Press.
—— (1986). *Studies on Extended Metapsychology.* Strath Tay, Clunie Press.
—— (1987). On aesthetic reciprocity. *Journal of Child Psychotherapy* 13: 3–14. (Reprinted in Meltzer, D. and Harris Williams, M. *The Apprehension of Beauty* (pp. 42–58). Strath Tay, Clunie Press, 1988).
—— (1992). *The Claustrum: An Investigation of Claustrophobic Phenomena.* London, Karnac, 2008.
—— (1995). *Psychoanalytic Work with Children and Adults: Meltzer in Barcelona.* London, Karnac, 2002.
Meltzer, D. and Harris Williams, M. (1988). *The Apprehension of Beauty.* Strath Tay, Clunie Press.
Meltzer, D., Hoxter, S., Weddell, D. and Wittenberg, I. (1975). *Explorations in Autism.* Strath Tay, Clunie Press.
Milner, M. (1955). The role of illusion in symbol formation. In Klein M., Heimann P., and Money-Kyrle, R. E. (eds.) *The Suppressed Madness of Sane Men* (pp. 82–108). New York: Basic Books.
Mitrani, J. (2001). *Ordinary People and Extraordinary Protections: A Post-Kleinian Approach to the Treatment of Primitive Mental States.* London, Routledge.
Mitrani, T. and Mitrani, J. (eds.) (1997). *Encounters with Autistic States: A Memorial Tribute to Frances Tustin.* Northvale, NJ, Jason Aronson.
Money-Kyrle, R. (1968). Cognitive development. In Meltzer, D. (ed.) *The Collected Papers of Roger Money-Kyrle* (pp. 416–433). Perthshire, Clunie Press, 1978.
—— (1969). On the fear of insanity. In Meltzer, D. (ed.) *The Collected Papers of Roger Money-Kyrle* (pp. 434–441). Perthshire, Clunie Press, 1978.
Munro, L. (1955). Steps in ego integration observed in a play analysis. In Klein, M. et al. (eds.) *New Directions in Psychoanalysis* (pp. 109–139). New York, Basic Books, 1955.
Nissen, B. (2008). On the determination of autistoid organizations in non-autistic adults. *International Journal of Psychoanalysis* 89: 261–277.
Ogden, T. (1989). On the concept of an autistic-contiguous position. *International Journal of Psychoanalysis* 70: 127–149.
—— (1997). Some theoretical comments on personal isolation. In Mitrani, T. and Mitrani, J. (eds.) *Encounters with Autistic States: A Memorial Tribute to Frances Tustin* (pp. 179–207). Northvale, NJ, Jason Aronson.
—— (2008). Working analytically with autistic-contiguous aspects of experience. In Barrows, K. (ed.) *Autism in Childhood and Autistic Features in Adults* (pp. 233–242). London, Karnac.
Panksepp, J. (1999). Emotions as viewed by psychoanalysis and neuroscience: An exercise in consilience. *Neuropsychoanalysis* 1: 15–38.

Piontelli, A. (1992). *From Fetus to Child*. London, Routledge.
Postman, N. (1985). *Amusing Ourselves to Death: Public Discourse in the Age of Show Business*. New York, NY, Penguin, 1986.
Quinodoz, D. (1998). A fe/male transsexual patient in analysis. *International Journal of Psychoanalysis* 79: 95–111.
Quinodoz, J.-M. (1994). Clinical facts or psychoanalytic clinical facts. *International Journal of Psychoanalysis* 75: 963–976.
Rayner, E. (1990). *The Independent Mind in British Psychoanalysis*. London, Karnac.
Reich, W. (1933). *Character Analysis* (3rd ed.). New York, NY, Noonday, 1962.
Rescher, N. (2001). *Paradoxes: Their Roots, Range and Resolution*. Chicago, IL, Open Court.
Rhode, M. (1997). The voice as autistic object. In Mitrani, T. and Mitrani, J. (eds.) *Encounters with Autistic States: A Memorial Tribute to Frances Tustin* (pp. 41–61). Northvale, NJ, Jason Aronson.
—— (2004). Different responses to trauma in two children with autistic spectrum disorder: The mouth as crossroads for the sense of self. *Journal of Child Psychotherapy* 30: 3–30.
—— (2005). Mirroring, imitation, identification: The sense of self in relation to the mother's internal world. *Journal of Child Psychotherapy* 31: 52–71.
—— (2008). Joining the human family. In Barrows, K. (ed.) *Autism in Childhood and Autistic Features in Adults* (pp. 147–170). London, Karnac.
—— (2012). Whose memories are they and where do they go? Problems surrounding internationalization in children on the autistic spectrum. *International Journal of Psychoanalysis* 93: 355–376.
Riley, C. (1997). Between two worlds: Hope and despair in the analysis of an autistic child. In Mitrani, T. and Mitrani, J. (eds.). *Encounters with Autistic States: A Memorial Tribute to Frances Tustin* (pp. 63–82). Northvale, NJ, Jason Aronson.
Riviere, J. (1936). A contribution to the analysis of the negative therapeutic reaction. *International Journal of Psychoanalysis* 17: 304–320.
Rodrigué, E. (1955). The analysis of a three-year-old mute schizophrenic. In Klein, M., Heimann, P. and Money-Kyrle, R. E. (eds.) *New Directions in Psychoanalysis* (pp. 140–179). New York, Basic Books.
Rosenfeld, H. (1987). *Impasse and Interpretation*. London, Routledge.
Rustin, M. (1991). *The Good Society and the Inner World: Psychoanalysis, Politics and Culture*. London, Verso.
Salomonsson, B. (2007). Semiotic transformations in psychoanalysis with infants and adults. *International Journal of Psychoanalysis* 88: 1201–1221.
—— (2012). Has infantile sexuality anything to do with infants? *International Journal of Psychoanalysis* 93: 631–647.
Searles, H. F. (1965). *Collected Papers on Schizophrenia and Related Subjects*. New York, International Universities Press.
Segal, H. (1952). A psycho-analytic approach to aesthetics. *International Journal of Psychoanalysis* 33: 196–207.
Spillius, E. B. (1988). Introduction to part four: Pathological organizations. In Spillius, E. B. (ed.) *Melanie Klein Today: Developments in Theory and Practice. Vol. 1: Mainly Theory* (pp. 195–202). London, Karnac.
—— (2002). De l'alterité de l'Autre. In Botella, C. (ed.) *Penser les limites. Écrits en l'honneur d'André Green* (pp. 403–408). Paris, Delachaux et Niestlé.

—— (2007). *Encounters with Melanie Klein*. London, Routledge.
Spitz, R. (1964). The derailment of dialogue: Stimulus overload action cycles, and the completion gradient. *Journal of the American Psychoanalytic Association* 12: 752–775.
Stern, D. (2008). The clinical relevance of infancy: A progress report. *Infant Mental Health Journal* 29: 177–188.
Strachey, J. (1934). The nature of the therapeutic action of psychoanalysis. *International Journal of Psychoanalysis* 15: 127–159.
Symington, N. (1991). *Narcissism: A New Theory*. London, Karnac.
Toth, K. and King, B. H. (2008). Asperger's syndrome: Diagnosis and treatment. *American Journal of Psychiatry* 168: 953–958.
Tronick, E., Als, H., Adamson, L., Wise, S. and Brazelton, T. (1978). The infant's response to entrapment between contradictory messages in face-to-face interaction. *Journal of the American Academy of Child and Adolescent Psychiatry* 17: 1–13.
Truckle, B. (2010). Book review of autism in childhood and autistic features in adults. In K. Barrows (ed.) *International Journal of Psychoanalysis* 91: 1543–1545.
Tuckett, D. (1997). Mutual enactment in the psychoanalytic situation. In Ahumada, J. L. et al. (eds.) *The Perverse Transference and Other Matters* (pp. 203–216). Northvale, NJ & London, Jason Aronson.
Tustin, F. (1972). *Autism and Childhood Psychosis*. London, Hogarth.
—— (1981). *Autistic States in Children*. London, Routledge and Kegan Paul.
—— (1984). Autistic shapes exemplified in childhood psychopathology. In *Autistic Barriers in Neurotic Patients*. New Haven and London, Yale University Press, 1990.
—— (1986). *Autistic Barriers in Neurotic Patients*. New Haven and London, Yale University Press.
—— (1988a). The 'black hole': A significant element in autism. *Free Associations* 1: 35–50.
—— (1988b). Psychotherapy with children who cannot play. *International Review of Psychoanalysis* 15: 93–105.
—— (1990). *The Protective Shell in Children and Adults*. London, Karnac.
—— (1992). *Autistic States in Children* (Rev. ed.). London, Routledge.
—— (1993). On psychogenic autism. *Psychoanalytic Inquiry* 13: 34–41.
—— (1994a). Autistic children who are assessed as not brain-damaged. *Journal of Child Psychotherapy* 20: 103–131.
—— (1994b). The perpetuation of an error. *Journal of the American Psychoanalytic Association* 42: 1307–1308.
Valls, J. L. (1995). *Diccionario Freudiano*. Madrid, Julian Yébenes.
Winnicott, D. W. (1949). Birth memories, birth trauma, and anxiety. In *Through Pediatrics to Psychoanalysis* (pp. 174–193). New York, Basic Books, 1975.
—— (1953). Transitional objects and transitional phenomena. In *Through pediatrics to psychoanalysis* (pp. 229–242). New York, Basic Books, 1975.
—— (1960). Ego distortion in terms of true and false self. In *The Maturational Processes and the Facilitating Environment* (pp. 142–152). London, Karnac, 1990.
—— (1962a). A personal view of the Kleinian contribution. In *The Maturational Processes and the Facilitating Environment* (pp. 171–178). London, Karnac, 1990.
—— (1962b). Ego integration in child development. In *The Maturational Processes and the Facilitating Environment* (pp. 56–63). London, Karnac, 1990.

—— (1963a). Morals and education. In *The maturational processes and the facilitating environment* (pp. 93–105). London, Karnac, 1990.

—— (1963b). The mentally ill in your caseload. In *The Maturational Processes and the Facilitating Environment* (pp. 217–229). London, Karnac, 1990.

—— (1965). New light on children's thinking. In Winnicott, C., Shepherd, R. and Davies, M. (eds.) *Psychoanalytic Explorations* (pp. 152–157). London, Karnac, 1989.

—— (1967a). Mirror-role of mother and family in child development. In *Playing and Reality* (pp. 111–118). London, Routledge, 1991.

—— (1967b). The etiology of infantile schizophrenia in terms of adaptive failure. In Shepherd, R., Johns, J. and Taylor Robinson, H. (eds.) *Thinking about Children* (pp. 218–223). London, Karnac, 1996.

—— (1968). The concept of clinical regression compared with that of defense organization. In Winnicott, C., Shepherd, R. and Davies, M. (eds.) *Psychoanalytic Explorations* (pp. 193–199). London, Karnac, 1989.

—— (1969). The use of an object and relating through identifications. In *Playing and Reality* (pp. 86–94). London, Routledge, 1991.

—— (1970). The mother-infant experience of mutuality. In Winnicott, C., Shepherd, R. and Davies, M. (eds.) *Psychoanalytic Explorations* (pp. 251–260). London, Karnac, 1989.

—— (1971). *Playing and Reality*. London, Routledge, 1994.

—— (1974). Fear of breakdown. In Winnicott, C., Shepherd, R. and Davies, M. (eds.) *Psychoanalytic Explorations* (pp. 87–95). London, Karnac, 1989.

—— (1987). *The Spontaneous Gesture: Selected Letters of D. W. Winnicott*. Rodman, F. R. (ed.). London, Karnac.

—— (1989). *Psychoanalytic Explorations*. Winnicott, C., Shepherd, R. and Davies, M. (eds.). London, Karnac.

Wittenberg, I. (1975). Primary depression in autism – John. In Meltzer, D., Hoxter, S., Weddell, D. and Wittenberg, I. (eds.) *Explorations in Autism* (pp. 56–98). Strath Tay: Clunie Press.

Wright, K. (1991). *Vision and Separation*. London, Free Association Books.

Index

Abraham, Karl 47, 117–19
adhesive identification 8, 9
aesthetic conflict 9–10
affective neuroscience *xiv*
affects 3, 144–5; attention-deficit/ hyperactivity disorder (ADHD) 63; Freudian definition of 126; instincts and 126–7; psychic distance in 134; unpredictability of 163
Age of Media 63, 130, 131, 136–7, 159; humanisation of media-bred animal-child 77–85; initial interviews 63–4; sessions for Juan 64–77
Age of Neurosis 129
alpha-betisation 139–43
alpha-elements 139–41
alpha-function: notion of 37, 140–2, 148
Alvarez, Anne 15, 16, 17, 32–4, 37, 62
American Academy of Pediatrics *xiv*, 2
anal stage: dynamics of 118
anorexia nervosa 120
The Apprehension of Beauty (Meltzer and Harris Williams) 9
Aristotle 39*n*1
Asperger, Hans 2
Asperger's syndrome *xiii*, 44
at-oneness (same wavelength) 78–9, 85, 140, 142–3, 150, 159
attention: quality of 20, 31–9, 45, 160
attention-deficit disorder (ADD) *xiii*
attention-deficit/hyperactivity disorder (ADHD) *xiii*, 63
autism 21, 48; conceptual language for 152–3; etiology of *xiv–xv*; mimetic-type 15, 18–19, 57–62, 77, 123–4, 129, 131, 135–7, 139, 141, 146, 152–4, 158–9; outset of 18; psychogenic 57, 151–2, 154–5; schizophrenic-like 10–11, 14, 59; segmented children 15; shell-type 7, 10–11, 13–15, 18, 34, 36, 59, 148; treating encapsulated, after trauma 41–5; types of 14–20
Autism and Childhood Psychoses (Tustin) 13, 16
autism cases: encapsulated autism after trauma (Axel) 41–5; high-functioning (Tom) 131–3; mute autistic girl (Lila) 21–39; screen-bred animal-child (Juan) 63–85; "thin-skinned" narcissist (Florence) 133–6; transvestism (Jaime) 87–116; two-ness of autistic girl (Sophia) 48–62, 139–43, 145–6, 152–4, 158–60, 162–3
Autism Proper: concept of 10–11
autism spectrum disorders (ASD) *xiii–xv*, 39*n*1
autistic-contiguous position 119, 121, 147, 153, 161-3
autistic disorder 63
autistic-mimetic dynamics 139–46, 152–4, 158–9
autistic mindlessness 9
Autistic Phenomena Proper 11
autistic spectrum disorders: mimetic-autistic dynamics 123–4; psychoanalysis 118
Autistic States in Children (Tustin) 15, 148–52, 158
Autistoid Age 15, 124, 129, 131, 133, 135–7
An Autobiographical Study (Freud) 127
autotomy 47, 48, 124, 141, 156

Index

Balint, Alice 47, 120, 125
Balint, Michael 48, 120, 126
Ban Ki-moon *xiv*
Barbie 96, 99, 106, 113; and Ken 30, 52, 90, 94–5, 113
Barcelona seminars: Meltzer 32, 37
Barrows, Kate 16
beta-elements 139–41, 144
Bettelheim, Bruno 2–3, 7–8, 11, 13, 39, 45, 124, 135–6
Bick, Esther 7, 8, 12, 148–50, 161, 164
bi-dimensionality 9
Bion, Wilfred 11–12, 37, 58, 79, 82, 112, 120–1, 124; theory of thinking 139–46
bisexuality 96, 116
black holes: image and autistic children 13–14, 17–18; stage of "interplanetary journeys" 100, 102–3, 106–7, 110, 113–16
Britton, Ron 85
broken-away phenomenon 150–1

Call, Justin 35, 37, 82
Centers for Disease Control and Prevention (CDC) *xiii*
Character Analysis (Reich) 84
Civilization and its Discontents (Freud) 125
clinical process: mute autistic girl (Lila) 23–31
cognitivism *xiv*
Collingwood, Roger 129–30
container: analyst as 25, 78; skin as 8–9; term 148, 149
containment 62, 66, 78, 80, 85, 159
context of togetherness 36, 58–9
corrective symbiotic experience 6
Cottingham, John 145
countertransference 32, 34, 53, 115
crisis of two-ness 47–8, 56, 59–60, 62, 77, 79–80, 136, 139, 142–3, 148, 151, 158

Darwin, Charles: baby-mother primal dialogue 147; instincts and affects 126–7, 144
da Vinci, Leonardo 83–4
Davis, Madeleine 157
delimitation 114, 142–4
Descartes, René 126, 144–5, 158, 162
The Descent of Man (Darwin) 126, 144
Deutsch, Helene 117

Diagnostic and Statistical Manual of Mental Disorders (DSM-5) *xiii*
Diagnostic and Statistical Manual of Mental Disorders (DSM-IV) 63
dimensionality 9
discernment 79–80, 85, 114
dual unity 4, 6, 47, 125, 150–1

early mind 117–19; evolution of post-Kleinian thought on 119–21; Freudian influence on 125–8; mimetic identicity 122–3; roots of conceptual bearings 123–4; Winnicott vis-à-vis Klein 121–2
ego: notion of purified pleasure ego 4
The Ego and the Id (Freud) 125, 144
Elmshirst, Isaacs 150
The Empty Fortress (Bettelheim) 2
Encounters with Autistic States (Mitrani) 124
epidemic of autism *xiii*
Explorations in Autism (Meltzer) 8, 11, 19

Fairbairn, Ronald 117
false self: term 34, 154
Ferenczi, Sándor 3, 47–8, 58, 120, 124–5, 141, 147, 156–7
Ferro, Antonino 79, 139–46, 152, 155
Findings, Ideas, Problems (Freud) 126
Freud, Anna *xiv*, 58, 123–4
Freud, Sigmund 4, 47–8, 57, 60, 83–4, 87, 111, 114, 117, 119, 122–3, 131, 141, 144, 147, 149–50, 155, 157, 162, 166–7; early mind contributions 125–8

Gaddini, Eugenio 12, 48, 59, 133
Gaddini, Renata 48, 59
gaze 143; analyst's 60, 145, 153, 160; autistic child 21–2, 25, 41, 48–9, 51–3, 56; avoidance of 41, 159–60, 164, 167n1; dynamics of 60, 159; level of 145, 160; mother-infant 82, 158, 164
going-on-being: concept of 7
Green, André 119, 124, 157
Grotstein, James 121, 158

Haag, Geneviève 16, 148, 150, 159
Hermann, Imre 47
homosexual/homosexuality 87, 88, 125, 129
honesty of ignorance 150
humanisation: of screen-bred animal-child 77–85
humanness 25, 32, 149

hypersensitivity 33, 115, 133
hysteria: concept of 117

Id-Ego 125
Id-Ego-Superego model 125–7
identity: fusional 146; imitative 77; mimetic 77, 79, 122–3, 145; primary 59
identification: imitative 117; mimetic 118, 123; projective 8–9, 14, 32, 77–8, 115, 120, 123, 140
impingement: concept of 7
indifferentiation: self-object 118; or stupidity 140; term 4, 145
infantile autism 3, 5
infantile psychosis syndrome 6
infantile schizophrenia 7
infant scenes: everyday 163–7
Inhibitions, Symptoms and Anxiety (Freud) 83–4
instincts: affects and 122, 126–8; drives 125–8, 144; life and death 121; relationship 149, 158, 166; satisfaction 147
International Journal of Psychoanalysis (journal) 16
intimacy: at-oneness 78–9, 85, 140, 142–3, 150, 159

Johns Hopkins Hospital 1
Joseph, Betty 87, 165
Joyce, Angela 38, 147, 152–6, 158–63; infant scenes 163–7

Kanner, Leo 1–3, 6–8, 11, 14, 32, 78, 124, 137, 142, 145, 149
Klein, Melanie *xiv*, 3, 8, 12, 19, 47, 85, 87, 119–21, 123–4, 127–8, 136, 162, 166
Klein, Sydney 12, 16, 48

Langer, Susanne 127, 155
Lasch, Christopher 130, 135
Leonardo (Freud) 47, 83, 125, 131
libidinal phases 117
Lion King (film) 64, 69, 72, 74, 79–80, 83

McLuhan, Marshall 63, 130
Mahler, Margaret 2, 3–6, 8, 11–12, 14, 17, 38, 47, 58–9, 120, 124, 147, 149–50, 155
Matte-Blanco, Ignacio 60, 123, 145, 165
Meltzer, Donald 8–12, 19, 32, 37, 45, 118, 120–1, 124, 139, 141, 148–50, 161

memories in feelings: Klein 127–8, 166
Memotest 27–8, 41–3
me-ness: sense of 14, 77–8, 80, 85, 135
milieu intérieur 4
Milner, Marion 113
mimetic-fusional dynamics 159
mimetic identity 77, 79, 122–3, 145
mimetic identification 118, 123
mimetic-type autism 15, 18–19, 57–62, 77, 123–4, 129, 131, 135–7, 139, 141, 146, 152–4, 158–9
mind-blindness: maternal 17–18, 49, 57–8, 60
mindlessness: autistic 9, 132, 134–5
mind-reading 35, 148, 149
minimal self 130, 136
The Minimal Self: Psychic Survival in Troubled Times (Collingwood) 130
mirroring 7, 22, 34, 124; affective 137; concept of 7; confrontation 79; frame of reference 4; imitation and 60; kind of maintenance of identity 4; mimetic 143, 145; mimetic transference 59; notion of maternal 35
Mitrani, Judith 17, 124
Mitrani, Theodore 124
moments of contact 36, 58–9, 77, 142
moments of sharing 36
Monsters Inc. (film) 71, 72
mother: mind-blindness 17–18, 49, 57–8, 60
mutual cuing 4

narcissism 5, 48, 120, 126, 130–1, 135
narcissistic identification 47
National Health Service (NHS) 16
Nissen, Bernd 124, 132

obsessionality 9
Oedipus complex 5, 47, 83, 87–8, 111, 121
Ogden, Thomas: autistic-contiguous position 119, 121, 147, 153, 161–3
one-dimensionality: autism 9
On narcissism: an introduction (Freud) 131
oral sadism: transvestism 111–12, 114
oral violation 82
Orthogenic School in Chicago 3

Panksepp, Jaak *xiv*
pansexuality 130
paranoid-schizoid position 8
parasitic symbiotic 4

pathology: pre-Oedipal 47, 118, 121
perceptual awareness 163, 166
pervasive developmental disorder (PDD) 21
phallic dynamics 81, 83–5
phallic-genital impulses 18, 99, 112, 114, 116
phallic monism 87, 111
phallic phase: chronology of 83–4, 87
play-as-such: concept of 7
Playing and Reality (Winnicott) 156
Pokémon 68, 72, 74, 81–3
Postman, Neil 63
potential space 157
Power Rangers 66–8, 74–5, 80–3
pre-Oedipal stages 47, 118, 121
primal depression 13
primal dialogue 127, 144, 146–7, 162; baby-mother 35–8, 82, 118–19, 125, 128n1, 146, 147; mirroring and sustaining 22, 34, 45, 124; reawakening of 38, 58; rupture or deadening of 18
primal identification: concept of 60
primary identification 47–8, 58–9, 61
primary love 48
primary maternal preoccupation 39
projective identification 8–9, 14, 32, 77–8, 115, 120, 123, 140
protagonism 66, 78, 81, 131
protodiakrisis 5
pseudo-stupidity 59
psyche 15, 58–9, 125, 127, 144–5, 156–7, 162
psychoanalytic developmental theory 154–5
psychogenic aetiology 17
psychogenic autism 57, 151–2, 154–5
psychopathology 16, 63, 87, 117, 129, 131; anal-expulsive phase 117, 118; anal-retentive phase 117, 118; genital phase 117; phallic phase 117
psychotic: term 119
psychotic depression: notion of 13

quality of attention 20, 31–9, 45, 160
Quinodoz, Danielle 116

rapprochement phase 5
reclamation: Alvarez's notion of 33–4, 37
Reich, Wilhelm 84
reverie: emotional contact 78–9, 142–3; negative 139, 141; positive 140; of receptive mind 139
Rhode, Maria 16, 149

Riley, Charlotte *xv*
Rivière, Enrique Pichon 35
Riviere, Joan 124, 136
Rodrigué, Emilio 7
Rosenfeld, H. 133
Rustin, Michael 12

sadism: transvestism 111–12, 114
schizophrenia *xiv*, 3; childhood 2–3, 6–7; infantile *xiv*, 7; schizophrenic-like autism 10–11, 14, 59
Scott, Clifford 113
screen-bred animal-child: humanisation of 77–85; initial interviews 63–4; screen-world *vs* life-world 79, 81–5; sessions (Juan) 64–77
screen technology 18, 68, 75–7, 79–85, 95, 137, 142, 159
Searles, Harold F. 48, 124
Segal, Hanna 85
segmented children 15
self-differentiation 145
self-discernment 79
self-interpretive space 143
self-object affective discrimination 163
self-object differentiation 120, 124, 139, 149
self-object discrimination 118, 120–1, 145
self-object emotional distinction 166
sensation: autistic-contiguous mode 161–3; auto-sensuous 77; "hard" autistic objects 84; "me" 13–14, 32; metapsychology of mind 121; raw 158, 163; softness and hardness 148; term 84, 144, 145, 162
sensoriality: alpha-betisation of 139–43; autism 147; Bick's and Meltzer's' ideas of 161; term 144–5
sensory impressions 161–2
separateness 5, 12, 61, 124; awareness of 22, 120; bodily 13–14, 47–8, 61, 150–1; discovery of 62; evidence of 164; level of 166; non-separateness and 120, 158; otherness and 136; primary 154–5, 157–9, 166–7; tolerance of 160; trauma of 84, 131, 135
sexual identity 84, 87, 115
shell-type autism 7, 10–11, 13–15, 18, 34, 36, 59, 148
Shepherd, Ray 157
smartphone screen 137
Spillius, Elizabeth 119–20, 136
Spitz, René *xv*, 35, 39, 82, 119, 124, 129

splitting-and-idealization 8
Stern, Daniel 154–5
stupidity 59, 139–41
subjective object 153, 155, 157
symbiosis 4, 47–8, 57–8, 58, 124, 157; symbiotic infantile psychosis 3; symbiotic psychosis 3, 5–6, 14
symbol-formation 3, 47–8, 61–2, 71, 78–9, 85, 143

Tavistock Clinic 8, 12
The Thinking Heart (Alvarez) 17
Three Essays (Freud) 115, 131, 149
transitionality: concept of 7
transvestism in autistic child 87, 111; Barbie 88, 90, 94–6, 99, 106, 113; black holes 100, 102–3, 106–7, 110, 113–16; blue hole 102, 103, 107, 115; clinical material 88–9; conceptual ideas on clinical material 111–16; drawing of brain 96, 97; feminine personifications 88, 111; mouth in therapy 102, 104, 105; Oedipus complex 5, 47, 83, 87–8, 111, 121; return of the *Titanic* 108–11; role of Norma Beatriz 95–6, 98–9, 102, 104, 106–7, 110, 112–14; stage of "interplanetary journeys" 100–108, 114; stage of "little tablecloths" 91–4, 113; stage of the "cacas" 90; stage of the "Senorita" 95–8; stage of "Titanic" 98–100, 113–14
tri-dimensionality of self 9

tripartite therapeutic design 6
Tustin, Frances *xiv*, 3, 7–8, 11–19, 32–6, 38, 45, 47–8, 55, 59, 77–8, 81, 84–5, 114, 120–1, 124, 135, 144–5, 147–67
two-ness: conceptual comments 57–62; crisis of 47–8, 56, 59–60, 62, 77, 79–80, 136, 139, 142–3, 148, 151, 158; initial interviews 48–50; initial interviews of case subject (Sophia) 48–50; points on first 18 months of Sophia's treatment 50–4; psychogenic autism 57, 151–2, 154–5; scene (communal) after the holidays (Sophia) 54–6; session at 14 months of Sophia's treatment 56–7

unconscious level of mind 125, 127, 132, 136, 141–2, 144, 151, 154–5, 158, 165–7
United Nations *xiv*
United Nations General Assembly 129
US National Institutes of Mental Health *xiv*

Vision and Separation (Wright) 153
visual violation: experiment 82, 160

Winnicott, Donald *xiv*, 7, 12–13, 32, 34–5, 112, 118–21, 123–4, 127, 136, 142, 147, 152–60, 163, 165–6; early mind 121–2
Wittenberg, Isca 19, 33
World Autism Awareness Day *xiv*, 129

Yu-Gi-Oh! cards 74